PROFESSIONAL

# Does Collective Impact Work?

# Does Collective Impact Work?

## What Literacy Coalitions Tell Us

Frank Ridzi and Margaret Doughty

LEXINGTON BOOKS
*Lanham • Boulder • New York • London*

Published by Lexington Books
An imprint of The Rowman & Littlefield Publishing Group, Inc.
4501 Forbes Boulevard, Suite 200, Lanham, Maryland 20706
www.rowman.com

Unit A, Whitacre Mews, 26-34 Stannary Street, London SE11 4AB

British Library Cataloguing in Publication Information Available

**Library of Congress Cataloging-in-Publication Data Available**

ISBN 978-1-4985-0845-2 | 978-1-4985-0846-9 (electronic)

∞™ The paper used in this publication meets the minimum requirements of American National Standard for Information Sciences—Permanence of Paper for Printed Library Materials, ANSI/NISO Z39.48-1992.

Printed in the United States of America

# Contents

# Preface

This book is the culmination of the collaborative vision of the Literacy Funders Network (LFN), an affinity group of the Council on Foundations that was founded in 2009 in response to an identified interest from the funding community to develop a formal collaboration to advance the literacy funding field and, in turn, build stronger, more resilient individuals, families, and communities. In recent years, many foundations supporting literacy have been highly engaged in community literacy, coalition development, and in strategies for community change. As such, a planning group of the LFN has explored ways to share knowledge and to create a peer learning network. Since its inception, the mission of the Literacy Funders Network has been to increase the philanthropic community's knowledge and understanding of literacy as a systemic issue and to explore collaboration and collective impact as a tool for community change. This book is a concrete manifestation of the LFN's stated goals of sharing best practices, research, and lessons learned through peer dialogue and networking, learning how other foundations interact within their communities around literacy through effective grantmaking strategies, promoting and strengthening accountability and impact measurement for literacy, promoting advocacy and awareness about literacy, and coordinating interdisciplinary dialogue in key literacy sectors.

This book has been made possible by the generous support of the Central New York Community Foundation (CNYCF). The CNYCF aspires to serve as a catalyst, convener, and facilitator by stimulating and promoting collaborations among various organizations to accomplish common objectives. It is this aspiration and the visionary leadership of President and CEO Peter Dunn that has led to an interest in learning more about literacy coalitions and their best practices across the nation so as to best support the coalitions it has funded and cultivated in New York's Onondaga, Madison, and

Cortland Counties. Le Moyne College has, in complementary fashion under the inspired leadership of President Linda LeMura, made a commitment to supporting applied research that benefits the community and as such has provided the Institutional Review Board oversight for the qualitative interview and observation research that appears in the following pages as well as for the national surveys of funders and of literacy coalitions that were conducted in collaboration with the LFN and CNYCF.

We are also indebted to John Eberle, President and CEO at The Community Foundation for the Greater Capital Region (and founding member of the LFN), who initially provided the research questions that drive this work: What forms can coalitions take? How are other funders thinking about them across the country? Is there any evidence of impact from these coalitions? And what, if any, best practices are emerging for local coalition builders to emulate? These questions have been a most recent guiding force in a heritage that has included notable leaders that have helped the LFN grow to this point, including Clotilde Perez-Bode Dedecker at the Community Foundation for Greater Buffalo, Nancy Anthony and Mary Surbeck at the Oklahoma City Community Foundation, Sharon Bush at the Grand Victoria Foundation, and Kim Scott of Literacy Powerline.

While Margaret and Frank served as the primary writers, this book is the epitome of a collaborative effort. The insights of the first substantive section on the many faces and forms of literacy coalitions nationwide is made possible by the leadership of Bob Paponetti, executive director of The Literacy Cooperative of Greater Cleveland and who also serves on the LFN's leadership team as its incoming president. The work on the relationship between foundations and coalitions was made possible thanks to the work of fellow LFN executive team members Joe Welsh who leads Community Initiatives and Partnerships at the United Way of Allegheny County, PA, and Jeff Conyers Executive Director of the USA division of The Dollywood Foundation.

The section on the relationship between coalitions and community indicators was produced thanks to collaborative consultation with Dr. Monica Sylvia and the LFN's co-members of the National Results and Equity Collaborative (NREC), a project of the Center for the Study of Social Policy in Washington, D.C. The NREC was initiated by a group of national organization founding partners, joined by leaders from communities working on multiple initiatives sponsored by the founding national partners. Founding partners hope that many other national, state, and local organizations, coalitions, initiatives, policy makers, funders, and individuals working towards school success for our nation's most vulnerable children and youth will join in accelerating the rate of positive change we can best accomplish together. The NREC promises to share what it learns as it uses shared definitions and measures and aligns technical assistance, tools, and resources in a uniformed manner across the nation. In particular, this chapter was produced in collaboration with helpful insights from multiple colleagues, including Nina Sazer O'Donnell, former Vice President, Education United Way Worldwide. We have also benefited from the diligent data processing and editorial work of Narcisa Ledesma, Amy Goodall-Ayers, Lindsay Nash, Rachel Sier, and Renee Gadoua.

A special thanks to all who helped in the process (especially those who contributed their experiences and insights) who are too numerous to name here. Last, but not least, we wish to thank our families (Edith, Jody, Quinn, Kenna, and Emma) who have been the staying force behind this project of many collaborators.

—Margaret and Frank

# Introduction

For nearly 20 years, we have been told that we are in a period of social decline. A wide range of civic indicators, first brought to our attention in 2000 by Robert Putnam's book *Bowling Alone*, suggest that the United States has seen an erosion of social capital that has threatened to move us toward intensifying isolation of the individual.[1] Whether it is a decline in church attendance, parent teacher organization membership, and bowling leagues, or an increase in televisions, single-player video games, and texting instead of talking, people seem to be interacting less and becoming more passive observers than collaborative doers.

However, one area of civic engagement has grown both as an idea and as a concrete reality in communities across the nation: cross-sector community coalitions seeking to make a collective impact. This growth is part of a larger shift toward collective impact, a vision that "large-scale social change comes from better cross-sector coordination rather than from the isolated intervention of individual organizations."[2] In metaphorical terms, it is a shift away from looking for a "silver bullet" for each social problem we face and a shift toward thinking about how we can act collectively as "silver buckshot" to address intractable challenges such as poverty, homelessness, and disease.[3]

Indeed, this was the idea behind some of Putnam's follow-up work with Lewis Feldstein, such as *Better Together*, in which people collaborated across boundaries to create new forms of community rich with social capital.[4] Yet, there is something distinctive about recent conceptualizations of collective impact. Of course, collaboration and social capital are not new ideas. What sets this new wave of community collaborations for impact apart is what Kania and Kramer (2011) identify as six key features:

- A centralized infrastructure
- A dedicated staff
- A structured process that leads to a common agenda
- Shared measurement
- Continuous communication
- Mutually reinforcing activities among all participants[5]

Together, these characteristics form a constellation that helps to narrow and define the topic. It is not so much about brief instances of people banding together to rally against a proposed new trash dump site (although these are certainly concrete exercises in social capital), but more about the types of civic structures that communities create to attack persistent, long-term social challenges such as poverty, poor health, and low literacy—often issues of equity.[6]

Community coalitions—roughly defined as "multi-sector alliances of individuals and groups that promote change through citizen-based involvement"[7]—tend to embody the key elements set forth by Kania and Kramer and others such as Butterfoss[8] because they have a lasting quality to them. They are distinguishable from brief community rallies and short-lived collaborations because they are durable structural arrangements that seek to routinize or institutionalize cross-sector collaboration aimed at preventing or ameliorating clearly defined community problems. What's more, they have grown in reputation and scholarly attention over recent decades. Their rapid rise in popularity inspired one author to quip, "Coalitions are the rage. Every community has one by now or one is most certainly coming to a community near you."[9] If scholarly attention is any indication, the field has grown exponentially from approximately 80 academic articles in 1980 to over 5,000 at the turn of the millennium.[10]

Recent estimates suggest that several thousand community coalitions exist across the more than 3,000 counties in the United States.[11] Over the past few decades, interest in coalitions has emerged across a spectrum of causes, including community health,[12] environmental justice,[13] urban neighborhood development,[14] stopping gun violence, and creating affordable housing.[15] Such attempts at coalition formation have also been accompanied by academic interest across disciplines including psychology,[16] criminology,[17] sociology,[18] health sciences,[19] and communications.[20]

This growing phenomenon of community coalitions begs the question: Why? What is it about this form of civic participation that has led to such a rise in popularity at precisely the time other forms of civic engagement are in decline?

## WHY ARE COALITIONS GROWING?

Part of the appeal of community coalitions is their mixture of rugged individualism and the potential for lasting and impactful institutional change. In this sense, community coalitions seeking collective impact are a variation of the social entrepreneurship craze that is sweeping the nation and the world. At the heart of this movement is the notion that social entrepreneurs are the heroes of our day. They are the people who blend the traditional skills of entrepreneurs—resourceful, inventive, and determined—with the hearts of saints—driven by a desire to make life better for others. Indeed, while some have wondered if the mythology of the entrepreneur as a larger than life figure has been blown out of proportion in recent decades,[21] Bill Drayton, founder of ASHOKA, one of the first organizations designed to support social entrepreneurs, gives voice to the big dreams that tend to drive such innovators: "Social entrepreneurs are not content just to give a fish, or teach how to fish. They will not rest until they have revolutionized the fishing industry."[22]

In this vision lies a critical aspect of the social entrepreneurial movement: institutional change. Institutional change has been identified by Crutchfield and Grant,[23] authors of *Forces for Good*, as a hallmark of "high-impact" practice.[24] "The secret to success lies in how great organizations mobilize every sector of society—government, business, nonprofits, and the public—to be a force for good. In other words, *greatness has more to do with how nonprofits work outside the boundaries of their organizations than how they manage their own internal operations.*"[25] They go on to assert that the most effective organizations do not focus on achieving internal perfection, but outward, "spending their time and energy focused externally on catalyzing large-scale systemic change."[26] In essence, they "seed social movements and help build entire fields" or institutions, by working with and through, rather than in competition with others in the same field of interest.[27]

In the entrepreneurial sense, collective impact community coalitions are not that different from the institutional entrepreneurs that the business and organizational development literatures have celebrated for so long.[28] They are a bit like Thomas Edison or Dr. Spencer Silver (the chemist at 3M who invented Post-it® Notes) in that they involve a lot of trial and error and they eventually end up changing whole regimes of how we interact. Think of all the housing infrastructures that needed to be changed when retooling for Edison's new way of lighting. Or imagine life without Post-it® Notes? In the same way, institutional entrepreneurs aspire to restructure the basic patterns of interaction that we, as a society, take for granted and rely on in our day-to-day lives; they want to transform social institutions. While electricity and

Post-its® arguably make our lives better, social entrepreneurs are more overt in their altruistic intentions. For instance, Benjamin Franklin's purported invention of the free library, Robert Redford's creation of the Sundance Film Festival as an outlet for independent films, and Muhammad Yunus' invention of the Grameen Bank to provide microloans to poor people to start businesses—each of these revolutionized an industry in a way that offered people new opportunities for richer lives.

Indeed, it is not only individual institutional entrepreneurs who have sought to bring about such structural change through targeted contributions; a growing literature on catalytic philanthropy describes grantmakers who have sought a similar impact for their investments.[29] Philanthropic organizations and their resources have helped create a number of familiar institutions through innovation and the implementation of divergent change. Among others, these institutions include the community college system (Kellogg Foundation), the network of public libraries, children's educational programming (*Sesame Street*, Carnegie Corporation and Ford Foundation), portable retirement plans for college faculty (Carnegie Foundation), polio vaccination (Rockefeller Foundation), and the 911 emergency response system (Robert Wood Johnson Foundation).[30] In this tradition an "institutional entrepreneur" is cast as an agent, not necessarily a person, who mobilizes resources to create or transform institutions.[31] Along these lines, Carl Schramm, then president of the Ewing Marion Kauffman Foundation of Kansas City, thought to be the nation's largest foundation to focus on entrepreneurship, has outlined this sort of work as one of philanthropy's two primary foci, stating: "the foundation fulfills two functions: it serves as a mechanism for the reconstitution of wealth, and it plays the role of institutional entrepreneur, challenging other social institutions."[32]

In the same tradition of the social entrepreneur, community coalitions seek collective impact by transforming society at the level of its institutions. They are based on a belief that we need to change not just individual lives, but also the social institutions that at their worst maintain the status quo of social problems, or are simply ineffective at solving them. Coalitions by their very nature are institutionalized efforts to shift away from today's dominant paradigm of "isolated impact"—in which organizations try to stand out as being the sole solution or the silver bullet to a problem, and move toward one of "collective impact"—in which organizations see themselves as part of the silver buckshot, or part of a collaborative impact model.[33] This is at the heart of community coalitions seeking collective impact: the belief that better progress can be made in addressing society's most intractable social problems when "nonprofits, governments, businesses, and the public [are] brought together around a common agenda to create collective impact."[34] It is a paradigm shift away from searching for a single undiscovered program that will be the missing solution that we have all been waiting for and a commitment to an inclusive, multi-faceted, and collaborative approach. In essence, collective impact seems to place its faith in the value of cultivated and targeted social capital. But what do we know of how this vision has played out across the nation, and can this approach claim any successes? We can begin to answer this question by looking specifically at literacy coalitions.

## THE CASE FOR LITERACY COALITIONS

Far from being merely a convenient sample, literacy coalitions can be considered lynchpin coalitions; most, if not all, other social problems in a community can be tied to and impacted by literacy. If every individual was provided an exceptional education and was able to take advantage of the opportunity to be well prepared for life in their family, work, and civic roles, there would be no need for literacy coalitions. But that is not the case. We can also ask whether literacy is the goal or the tool to reach the goal? Whether we are discussing crime, poverty, unemployment, or lack of civic-mindedness, each of these problems can be connected to a root cause, further upstream. For instance, lack of strong literacy skills leads to lower school performance, which, in turn, leads to lower skill attainment and lower paying job opportunities. This, in turn, leads to a higher likelihood of unemployment and living in and around poverty, which is associated with higher crime. Ultimately, a key tool in advocating for solutions to any and all of these problems—civic engagement—is undercut by a lack of literacy skills. Ironically, it is these same literacy skills which could both facilitate awareness of problems via accessing traditional and social media and empower advocacy in literacy-heavy fields such as law and public policy. This lack of literacy skills prevents individuals from realizing their full potential but it also threatens our success as a nation because of its magnitude. According to the U.S. Department of Education and the National Institute of Literacy "32 million adults in the U.S. can't read. That's 14 percent of the population. 21 percent of adults in the U.S. read below a 5th grade level, and 19 percent of high school graduates can't read."[35]

While we see a logical flow from low literacy to crime and poverty, in truth, the directionality is unclear. This is not only because it can be disputed which negative outcome causes the other, but also because these social problems are often intergenerational in nature, making the initial cause difficult, if not impossible, to isolate. For instance, if we look at one child's lack of literacy skills as the initial cause of a chain of negative outcomes, we might find that this lack of literacy may be a result of family stress due to their parent's unemployment (whether due to parental illiteracy or something more macro in scope, such as the downsizing and offshoring of U.S. manufacturers). Or the child's lack of literacy may result from exposure to crime in the neighborhood, or poor dental care that distracts him or her from focusing on learning.

While determining the exact causal chains connecting low literacy to other major social ills such as poverty, crime, and unemployment are beyond the scope of this book, it is important to point out that low literacy is part of a broader, interconnected web. Furthermore, it is a key factor that, if improved, could positively impact the comorbidity of these other conditions because of their connections. It is this connection that is also a strength when it comes to coalition formation because the interests of a variety of different parts of society can be seen to be mutually reinforcing. For instance, as Bill Millett pointed out in his advocacy for early education investment, through literacy, we can see the intertwining interests of the business community, government, law enforcement, and the military, not to mention the obvious connections to schools and human services organizations.[36]

Possibly one of the most recognizable is literacy's connections to crime. In cities across the nation, police chiefs who have teamed up with the organization Fight Crime: Invest in Kids can be heard pleading with their communities to be more proactive than reactive when it comes to children. Embedded in their message is the theme that communities will have to pay for children whether they realize it or not. As their message goes, either pay for children when they are young by providing them rich opportunities to grow up as law-abiding citizens, or, if we fail to do this, we will end up paying for these same children when they become involved in crime. As local sheriffs, police chiefs, and prosecutors explain it, invest in kids now, or "I'm the guy you pay later."[37] In the words of the organization's brochures, which are customized to each individual community that participates in the campaign:

> Reducing crime is one of the key reasons why Governors and state legislators across the political spectrum, have made bold commitments to high-quality early education and care . . . . Law enforcement leaders know that one of the best ways to keep young people from dropping out of school and becoming criminals is to make sure they have a foundation for success in their earliest years. By standing up in support of high-quality early education for kids today we hope to see less crime and incarceration in years to come . . . . An independent analysis of over 20 preschool programs demonstrated that quality preschool returned an average "profit" (economic benefits minus costs) to society of $15,000 for every child served, by cutting crime and the cost of incarceration, and reducing other costs such as special education and welfare.[38]

This project is not alone. The U.S. Bureau of Justice Statistics estimates that approximately 41 percent of inmates in the nation's state and federal prisons and local jails and 31 percent of people on probation have not completed high school or its equivalent.[39] This is in contrast to 18 percent of the national population age 18 or older who did not complete the twelfth grade.[40] Academic research suggests that, "On any given day, about one in every 10 young male high school dropouts is in jail or juvenile detention, compared with one in 35 young male high school graduates."[41] Research also supports that increases in graduation rates are associated with reductions in murder and assault rates.[42] Law enforcement has estimated that, "Increasing the graduation rate in Oregon by 10 percentage points would prevent approximately 17 murders and 1,300 aggravated assaults in Oregon each year."[43]

Literacy and educational success has also caught the attention of the military. Not only does early investment in learning prevent crime, but it is also seen as providing a steady pipeline of future soldiers. In the words of Mission: Readiness, a "nonpartisan national security organization of over 550 retired admirals, generals, and other retired senior military leaders calling for smart investments in America's children,"[44]

Currently, more than 70 percent of 17- to 24-year-olds in the U.S. cannot serve in the military, primarily because they are too poorly educated, too overweight, or have a serious criminal record. Investing early in the upcoming generation is critical to securing our nation's future. Retired admirals and generals understand that whether young people join the military or not, we must increase investments so that all young people can get the right start and succeed in life—whatever career path they choose.[45]

As a result, Mission: Readiness, which functions under the auspices of the nonprofit Council for a Strong America, has become a vocal advocate of early childhood education and strengthening the traditional education system.

Perhaps less than obvious to the casual observer, literacy and the broader educational achievement it enables is critically important to employers. Over 10 percent of the working age population, ages 24–65 failed to achieve a high school diploma or GED in 2014.[46] Admittedly, this is a long-term issue and one that an individual employer might easily overlook in their quest to fill jobs and make payroll on a daily basis. But one need only look at the rising instances of unfilled positions due to a lack of qualified candidates to see how an insufficient pipeline of educated candidates can impact a business' ability to grow and ultimately increase its bottom line. In policy circles, this is discussed as spatial (geographic) and skills mismatch, which fails to align opportunities for business growth with requisite stocks of labor. The recent record-breaking economic growth of China over an unprecedented number of decades is perhaps the greatest example of how realigning workforce with opportunities can have a positive impact on the bottom line. The simple shift of potential workforce from rural to a majority urban population and the rapid explosion of education[47] (in conjunction with a revamped public safety net) has unlocked unimaginable economic prosperity that, between 1990 and 2005, amounted to more than 75 percent of global poverty reduction and propelled the world toward the United Nation's millennium goal of cutting extreme poverty in half.[48] When viewed in such broad societal and global terms, it becomes easier to see how the business community's fate is tied to the labor pipeline, and how that, in turn, is tied to ameliorating massive social problems such as poverty.

Given this broader perspective, it is no wonder that the U.S. Chamber of Commerce has advocated strongly for a robust educational system. In its PRE-K–12 Education Policy Declaration, the Chamber makes clear that a strong educational system is in its interest:

> To keep America competitive and strong, the business community must be actively engaged on issues related to our nation's educational system as a means to ensure an educated citizenry of self-sufficient, lifelong learners who have the skills needed to thrive in the global workplace, today and in the future. The coordination of community resources, school support systems, family engagement programs, and classroom teachers' efforts can diminish the barriers to learning. Employer engagement must be significant and have the ability to address some of the greatest challenges facing education in this country. These challenges include the lack of preparation of early learners who enter school for the first time, the significant learning and education gaps among groups of students, as well as the unacceptable number of students who never complete a secondary education or have the skills necessary to enter the world of work or continue on with higher education.[49]

Lack of a sufficient educational pipeline is not just a potential future problem. A 2009 survey found that "32 percent of manufacturers, a sector that supports an estimated 18.6 million jobs in the U.S. (about one in six private-sector jobs), reported moderate to serious shortages of qualified workers."[50] Speaking with similar urgency, the National Association of Workforce Boards stated:

> Workforce development is a critical component of local, state and national economic well-being. To compete globally, employers need a capable, flexible, innovative and productive workforce with:
>
> • English proficiency;
> • Literacy and comprehension ability;
> • Math proficiency;

- Soft skills—i.e., critical thinking, problem solving, communication and creativity; and
- No barriers to employment—e.g., incarceration or substance abuse.

But America doesn't have enough employees with these skills and qualities. Even with states reporting thousands of unemployed residents, jobs remain unfilled due to gaps between the attributes that employers need and those that workers possess. For example, in late 2009 and early 2010, despite 300,000 unemployed Washington state residents, more than 10,000 jobs went unfilled because of difficulties in finding qualified applicants. As of July 2011, approximately two million job openings could be found on Craigslist and five million on Monster.com (both popular job-searching websites).

Companies are struggling to fill these positions.[51]

As the Business Roundtable, an association comprised of chief executive officers from leading U.S. companies, has advocated in a tone reminiscent of law enforcement and the military, solving the problem requires investments up front, "Estimates of the return on investment of high-quality programs for low-income children range from $4 to $7 for every $1 spent. However, the research is clear: the return on investment is linked to quality; simply increasing participation without ensuring program quality will not produce positive results."[52] As of today, advocates have not seen the types of investment they feel are necessary. As the Business Roundtable stated in its January 2015 report, "Achieving America's Full Potential":

The CEO members of Business Roundtable, who lead major U.S. companies operating in every sector of the economy, believe that realizing America's full potential to create more high-wage jobs for U.S. workers and greater opportunity for middle-class families should be the nation's top priority . . . . The CEOs of Business Roundtable have identified three additional areas for action in 2015 to strengthen the U.S. economy and create more opportunity for all Americans: [including] Strengthen the Education & Skills of America's Workforce...Business leaders are all too familiar with the "skills gap" in the U.S. workforce. For example, more than 95 percent of surveyed Business Roundtable member CEOs indicated that their companies suffer from skills shortages.[53]

While many have emphasized the national payoff for educational investment, the Committee for Economic Development (CED), a business-led public policy organization suggests that this challenge is one of global proportions:

Global competition and a growing achievement gap have brought America to an economic and educational crossroads. As the need for unskilled labor falls, the demand for a more educationally prepared workforce rises. . . . Child Care and early education play a critical role in our national economy. Local spending on the care and education of young children has been shown to strengthen families, communities, and economic development. . . . In its report, CED calls for a national strategy to ensure that all children have access to high quality child care and early education from birth to third grade that promotes their learning and development while strengthening and engaging families in their children's education. "Unfinished Business" [the name of this report] challenges business leadership to do more towards ensuring opportunity for every child in America.[54]

Part of that unfinished business is reflected in the low percentage of preschool attendees. In 2012–2014, 54 percent of 3- and 4-year-olds did not attend preschool.[55]

Early childhood education is, hence, also introduced as a part of the problem. This focus on the educational pipeline can be seen to reflect sentiments that "The relatively weak math and science aptitude in the U.S. certainly contributes to the dearth of engineering graduates and partially frames the broader challenges for the manufacturing workforce. This problem casts a cloud on the outlook for future U.S. innovation strength."[56] As the Manufacturing Institute noted in its 2015 report:

A brighter economic future may lie ahead, and as a result, many U.S. manufacturers are optimistic they will regain momentum. Despite this favorable outlook, they will likely face some familiar, yet significant, challenges. Not least among these is talent. This is not new—for years, manufacturers have reported a sizeable gap between the talent they need to keep growing their businesses and the talent they can actually find. [57]

However, rather than despair, there is a new hope among executives, with "72 percent agreeing involvement with local schools and community colleges is effective. This reflects an understanding of the multidimensional nature of the skills gap as manufacturers see the need to develop the talent pipeline both in their companies and communities."[58]

The fact that national coalitions of law enforcement, military, and business exist and focus on literacy, among other things, suggests that literacy is, indeed, a core underlying issue that can cut across many areas of interest. One might wonder, if literacy is such a fundamental common denominator, why have such groups not already banded together?

## IS LITERACY A NEW ISSUE?

Concerns about low literacy are not new; they have been woven into the history of the United States for many of the reasons we are discussing. George Washington, for example, established a school for illiterate soldiers at Valley Forge during the Revolutionary War.[59] Cora Wilson Stewart adopted the concept "each one teach one" in the 1920s, and citizenship educator Septima Poinsette Clark prepared African-Americans for voting rights in the 1950s, helping pave the way for the civil rights literacy agenda at the Highlander Center in Tennessee where Rosa Parks took tutor training.[60]

Identifying illiteracy as a national issue to be supported by legislation took time. Some efforts were made during both world wars by linking literacy with the need for national defense. That was followed with efforts to address illiteracy in the black population.[61] Ambrose Caliver, a leading African-American educator, drafted the first illiteracy bill, which was introduced into the Senate by Harley M. Kilgore in 1948. Caliver served in the U.S. Department of Education under Presidents Herbert Hoover and Franklin D. Roosevelt, creating the "Freedom People's" series and addressing topics of social justice and educational equity. Caliver was the director of the Project for Adult Education and was one of the first to measure adult literacy levels and train literacy teachers.[62] The first version of the Adult Basic Education Act was introduced by Carl Perkins in 1962 after President John F. Kennedy's powerful education message that there were "twin tragedies of illiteracy and dependence" passed "from generation to generation."[63]

In the 1980s, the nation once again faced recession and high unemployment rates.[64] The unemployed with low literacy skills were among the people hardest hit. The growing numbers of immigrants entering the country added to a functionally illiterate underclass that could not meet the increasing skills demands and growing technology needs of the workplace. What emerged was a new dialogue about adult education and the formation of the first literacy coalitions. Many of the early coalitions of the 1980s had a strong social justice mission and literacy marches under the banner of "With Literacy and Justice for All" and a logo showing a fist grasping a pencil. The messages of the educators and social activists Paulo Freire and Miles Horton came together in the 1990 book *We Make the Road By Walking*, and, indeed, the coalition leaders did not have a designated road to follow; they surely made the road by walking.

## IS COLLECTIVE IMPACT A
## NEW THEORETICAL PARADIGM?

While this book is about literacy coalitions, to some extent literacy is simply a backdrop context within which we are exploring an emergent social phenomenon of collective impact community coalitions. In order to better articulate the uniqueness of this social phenomenon we turn to social theory in the area of social movements. In the realm of theory, the content area that social

movements focus on is less important. It is in the way in which these movements develop that we can see similarities across movements and identify
new innovations as they emerge. In the following pages we first compare and
contrast collective impact community collations with the existing literature
on social movements to highlight that there are indeed areas of divergence in
which existing theory does not adequately explain collective impact coalitions.
These areas of divergence help us to see that this is indeed a distinct phenomenon. By elucidating these areas of difference we can also come to see that
there is much that can be learned by collective impact efforts who study social
movements. Ultimately, though we can see both social movements and collective impact community coalitions as complementary efforts directed at solving
some of the same persistent social problems (e.g., poverty, illiteracy). In the
following pages we first explore some of the ways in which social movement
theory fails to fully explain collective impact. We then turn to ways in which
the two distinctive approaches can be seen as complementary.

## Collective Impact Divergence from Social Movements

Collaboration is not new. We need only look to the long national history of
labor unions and social movements to see a rich heritage of community organizing around issues of pressing concern to individuals. However, there is a
distinctive shift in nuance that distinguishes the rise of the collective impact
approach from previous eras of civic mobilization. In short, the collective
impact approach is much more grasstips when compared to our nation's history of grassroots efforts.

Scholarly literature abounds on social movements, or explaining why and
how social mobilization occurs. Historically, the focus of this research has
been anchored in class conflict or the tension between different social classes
of people over resources. This approach is perhaps most familiar to the general
public when they think of Marxian historical materialism and the rising up of
poor and oppressed classes against their rulers. However, the theoretical tradition is much more widely applicable and has been used to help understand a
multitude of historical transitions in government, national, and local power.
For instance, analyses that emerge through the lens of relative deprivation
have articulated how a sense of feeling deprived or of being treated unequally
can motivate people to form groups based on shared interest and to rise up
and take action.[65] In the case of collective impact literacy coalitions, there is
certainly a sense that inequality and deprivation are present. As some of our
analyses will suggest, coalitions may be more likely to arise in communities
in which poverty and failing schools are prevalent. Furthermore, in many
cases, there is a poignant sense of inequality that poor families and failing

schools exist just miles from areas of considerable affluence. However, while collective impact coalitions tend to be comprised largely of local leaders who see a community problem that they are compelled to solve, relative deprivation approaches tend to concentrate on understanding how the downtrodden themselves are driven to action. For instance, such theories are more likely to emphasize how psychological experiences of frustration and aggression with their lot in life, sufficiently prolonged and acutely felt, lead people to engage in political violence such as riots, rebellion, and coups. Lest we write this off as inapplicable to today's context of social safety nets that prevent destitution, this approach holds that such social movements are also likely to arise from frustration over the discrepancy between what people think they deserve in life and what they believe they will actually attain.[66]

Rational choice theory, another approach that has been applied to social movements, emphasizes the role of individuals in rationally weighing the costs and benefits of alternative courses of action. From this perspective, social movements are most likely to arise when a multitude of people come to see this course of action as in their own personal best interest. Akin to characteristics of economic theory, with which it shares many similarities and overlap, much of this approach is based on, and thus vulnerable to, the weaknesses of assumptions. For instance, as with economic theory, we must often assume perfect knowledge of an overall economic situation and one's place within it. In this day and age, political, economic, and even power dynamics are diffuse, obscured in complexity and opaque, to say the least. If people are angry that their neighborhood is poor, their schools are failing, and their children are exposed to chronic violence, it is not necessarily clear who deserves blame and what types of political action are in their own personal interest. There is not exactly a local despot to rebel against, nor, due to frequent turnover in political elections, is there a monolithic government that can be seen as responsible for the cumulative social and economic distress that has evolved over years or decades. In the coalition approach, this issue is somewhat circumvented by de-emphasizing blame and emphasizing the view that everyone, all social institutions, share responsibility for moving forward.

Since there are implicit, albeit under-theorized, connections between macro- and micro-level social movement standpoints, rational choice can be applied on a social institutional level, as well as an individual level.[67] For this reason, challenges such as that of the "free rider problem" can be seen to exist on the organizational level, just as they are seen on the individual level. In the case of collective impact approaches, this dilemma spurs us to ask what leads coalition members to move off the sidelines and into the fray, to roll up their sleeves and take action in solving a community problem? Rational reasoning, after all, suggests they will benefit just as much if they stay back and let others tackle shared social problems such as low community literacy and poverty. Furthermore, rational choice has a difficult time explaining why any organization would step into action since, as a free rider, it would actually be conserving limited resources for other uses. Indeed, participating in a collective impact community coalition has an opportunity cost that is not fully explained by social movement theory.[68]

Some social movement theorists have emphasized how changing structural situations impact willingness to join in activities. These theorists emphasize a broader conceptualization of what counts as a social movement and help to elucidate the role of government and its comportment to creating a space for movements to take form.[69] Others, such as those emphasizing claims making processes, stress not only the importance of connecting with sympathetic audiences in different social sectors, but also the role such potential allies play as audiences whom messaging and strategic use of media can help to recruit to a cause.[70]

While much of the social movement literature holds gems of insight for understanding the collective impact community coalition movement, literature using the interpretive lenses of social movement impact theory and new social movements are perhaps the most closely related to the collective impact movement.

As with collective impact, social movement impact theory sets out to devise ways to assess the impact that social movements have on society. While philanthropic literature has pointed out how collective impact coalitions can have an array of scales of impact, including individual, organizational, interorganizational, and societal levels,[71] scholars of social movement impact theory have pointed out related types of impact. For instance, they have focused more on how social movements can create society-level impact through transforming institutions, often by pulling the levers of political systems, or even changing them.

As we will see, many coalitions set institutional or policy change as a goal. This also appears to be related to more positive social indicators such as education levels. However, while coalition research tends to emphasize individual level changes, that over time can be aggregated into community level change (i.e., helping so many children develop a love of reading through distributing books that eventually the entire school district's grades increase), social movement theory tends to start with institutional change that is brought about through the overwhelming efforts of many individuals. Think, for instance, of poor people's movements or farm workers' rallies, or even of the civil rights or women's suffrage movements.[72] In all these cases, many individuals rally for change that begins with a massive institutional reform (such as awarding of suffrage or labor or affirmative action law) that trickles down to transform the lives of many individuals. Furthermore, in these paradigms, change is often brought about by massive movements of the populace to bring about disruptive turbulence needed to shake things up and lead to structural changes through the formation of new political alliances.[73]

Structural changes in this realm might include influencing policymaking, democratic rights, elections, legal rulings, political parties, and government bureaucracies.[74] This is in stark contrast to collective impact emphases on clients served by programs and making efforts toward better organized, more rational, more nimble, collaborative, and innovative bureaucracy. There is some irony that collective impact approaches that tend to arise from bureaucratic leaders focus more on transforming the lives of individual community residents, whereas social movements that tend to arise from community members historically focus on transforming the fundamentals of bureaucracies.

Perhaps this is partially due to the fact that it is often easier to gain traction and buy-in around the notion that the way "others" go about things needs to change, and there is a tendency to not want to change one's own patterns of action. Along these lines, some social movement theorists are dubious that lasting accomplishments can be achieved by the formal organizations of working class and other affected peoples, also worrying that bureaucratic organizations are likely to be co-opted by elites. While these approaches may seem miles apart, both can be integrated theoretically.

## Social Movements and Collective Impact as Complementary

Both the collective impact and social movement impact traditions find complementarity when viewed within a loose interpretation of the ecological systems theory.[75] Pioneered by Urie Bronfenbrenner in 1979, ecological systems theory (also known as development in context or human ecology theory) has been a major proponent of interpreting individual behavior within the broader context of the community and larger society where we spend our daily lives. From this perspective, we come to see our day-to-day lives and the broader society around us as interconnected such that a change in one can be seen to ripple through to effect change in the other. This understanding helps to place collective impact coalitions and social movements in a complementary context since one could conceivably bring about the same changes by starting at the individual or larger structural end.

The ecological systems approach describes communities using five concentric environmental systems with which an individual interacts. At the center of the concentric circles, the microsystem is the most grassroots in that it consists of the individual's day-to-day acquaintances such as family members, people they see at school or church, at work, or in their neighborhood.

At the next level (i.e., the second inner concentric circle), the mesosystem is conceived as the interconnections between the things that comprise the microsystem. It is at this level that coalitions and other social programs often work to effect change. By working to have families and teachers and social service agencies work together in a more coordinated and holistic manner, collective impact efforts hope to catalyze better outcomes for the individual community members at the center of this model. The coalitions themselves might be conceived of as occupying the next concentric layer out, that of the exosystem, which consists of larger institutional actors that may never directly interact with the individual but that nevertheless have an impact on their life. For instance, by providing professional development for human services workers or building mechanisms for communication between teachers and afterschool providers, actors within the exosystem may effect true positive change in the lives of children without ever meeting the children themselves.[76] The exosystem is the realm of governmental policy, and it is at this level of laws and community governance that many members of collective impact coalitions ply their trade. As the executive directors of organizations, directors of programs, and officials in the school system, mayor's office, or local government administration, these are people who set policies for their organizations and who have the power to tweak such policies to better coordinate with the policies of the others around the table for the benefit of clients that they mutually serve. This is the realm of community collective impact coalitions, but it is also the target area of many social movements that seek to bring about similar changes by rallying for such changes as new laws, government reform, environmental regulation, or business and industry changes. In a sense, social movements seek to bring about changes in the exosystem by applying pressure from the outside, while collective impact coalitions seek to transform exosystems by working from within. In both cases it is hoped that changes will take place that will improve the lives of individuals.

To some extent, the contrasting forces that we elucidate here have already been identified separately in terms of the ecological systems model and social work as well as in reflections on building coalitions within the field of social work. As some have pointed out, ecological systems theory can be used both to help maintain the status quo and, by more radical adherents, to effect system change. As such, ecological systems theory is applicable to both the dual functions of social work: "to serve as an instrument of both social stability and social change."[77] Similarly, in the opening preface to the guide published by Sage entitled, "Building Coalitions in the Human Services," the author identifies political advocacy as "one of the most frequently ignored skills of practice in social work and the human services professions."[78] The guide goes on to argue that "the successful use of coalitions is only one of the many skills needed by practitioners in social work and the human services as they strive to become successful political advocates for the disadvantaged, but it is a skill that is essential in today's political and economic environment."[79] However, in this guide, much as with the previous focus on ecological systems, coalitions can be seen to serve both functions of social work:

> Even though the primary emphasis in coalitions is on achieving the political goal of having a successful impact on the public policy process, coalitions also engage in a wide variety of activities that are aimed at such nonpolitical goals as educating the community about critical social issues, generating nongovernment resources, improving service coordination and service delivery through cooperative efforts, sharing resources among organizations, and facilitating agency and program mergers.[80]

While ecological systems theory is helpful in explaining the efforts of social movements and collective impact movements, it is also useful in elucidating the rising trend in collective impact approaches. As we will discuss in chapter 2, the many purveyors of coalitions and national attention can be considered a phenomenon of the wider macrosystem. Conceived as the broader culture of a nation that permeates local communities, many national initiatives, such as the Campaign for Grade-Level Reading (CGLR), can be seen as offering direction and structure that leads many local efforts to develop with a certain degree of isomorphism, or striking parallels. In this sense, local institutional entrepreneurs are developing their initiatives and reforms not in isolation, but within a textual and interpersonal milieu that leads to many striking similarities. It is the many similarities on this level that help to define the phenomenon that is the subject of this book. Without them, we might not recognize the local activities happening in communities across the country as coalitions and we would have a hard time considering them a national phenomenon. Finally, since the topic of this book and the ways in which such collective impact approaches develop is a moving and evolving target, Bronfenbrenner's concept of the chronosystem is also an important concept that reminds us that there is a sociohistorical context to how these phenomena occur. As a result, future chapters will seek to offer the perspective of how collective impact approaches (much like social movements) have evolved over time and how distinctive and meaningful differences characterize coalitions embarked upon at different periods in our national history.

Hence, both collective impact coalition and social movement approaches seek to bring about change within the ecological systems, or ecosystems in which individuals live. They simply apply their tools and approaches to different pressure points. Social movements are more likely to mobilize the individuals in the microsystems to create organizing bodies within the mesosystem. Collective impact and coalition approaches, by contrast, devote their energies to improving the relationship between organizations and institutions at the mesosystem. In both cases, the goal is to improve the lives of individuals at the center of the model, and both approaches can try to achieve this goal through the transformation of legislation and other major macrosystem institutions that shape day-to-day life.

While both social movement impact theory (or outcome theory) and collective impact coalition theory can be thought of as different approaches to shifting institutional relationships within an ecological systems model, they are also very similar in that their progress has been largely stalled when it comes to measuring impact due to methodological issues. Impact on a community level is very difficult to prove, and when change does happen, determining the causal factors can be daunting, if not impossible. Both outcome theory in the area of social movements and collective impact coalition literatures tend to be comprised mostly of case studies.[81] While these can be elucidating and have the descriptive qualities needed for theory building, they are notoriously less useful for theory testing and they tend to leave unanswered the looming questions of the effectiveness of such movements.[82]

While both traditions have devoted attention to key issues of resource mobilization and organizational forms or "mobilizing structures," framing strategies, and political opportunities and contexts, there is also agreement that success is easiest to measure when one important political goal, such as gaining suffrage, banning alcohol, or improving school graduation rates, can be identified as a rallying point.[83] Notably, however, social movement goals tend to be stated more in terms of rights and long-term improvements in political representation and leverage, while collective impact goals tend to be stated in more bureaucratically compliant or standardly defined and measured terms, such as children vaccinated or educational outcomes. In this distinction of defined success, we also see a contrast in locus of control. Social movements tend to define the problematic as an oppressive power arrangement that leads to disempowerment of certain parts of a population who see a benefit in rallying together out of their shared interest. For collective impact coalitions, the locus of control is seen to be much more individually situated; it is poor or uneducated individuals or victims of gang violence that must be helped to overcome these situations.

Although defining success reveals fundamental differences between social movement and collective impact coalition approaches, this does not mean that they are not both applicable to a wide diversity of settings. Just as collective impact coalitions can be found in neighborhood violence, education, and environmental and health concerns, social movement literature has found ample case studies in areas as varied as labor, civil rights, race, gender and sexuality equality, environmentalist and anti-war movements on the left and nativist/supremacist, and Christian identity movements on the right.[84]

Despite the wide applicability of social movement theory, defining success has often been plagued by disagreement over what exactly such movements are designed to accomplish. Furthermore, many positive impacts may be more latent and unforeseen, or at least unanticipated. Collective impact theories tend to focus more on defining success and its measures from the outset but, due to the complex nature of large community collaborations, it is generally conceded that it would be impossible to foresee all the positive impacts that might emerge, especially when a goal of many coalitions is building social capital and good will among community stakeholders that will lead to more opportunities for community benefit in the future. Such aspirational goals are admittedly broad and vague. In this regard, social movement theory's reliance on collective goods criterion is of use, since this approach avoids defining success narrowly according to attainment of specific goals, but regards as successful any positive motion—material or even political or discursive—that improves the well-being of the target population, either directly or indirectly.[85]

## WHAT DO WE KNOW SO FAR
## ABOUT HOW COALITIONS WORK?

Social problems are social problems precisely because there is no quick fix. While collective community coalitions may begin having impact within as short as a year's time, truly restructuring society to solve such intractable social problems as poverty, low literacy, and failing schools will take a sustained collective impact. As a result, coalition growth has corresponded with a desire for sustainable models and has been promoted by funding for coalitions from the federal government,[86] private foundations—such as the Robert Wood Johnson[87] and the Kauffman Foundations[88]—and community foundations.[89] Correlated with this massive investment, there has been a growing interest in implementation science—studying how people implement programs, projects, and initiatives so as to glean lessons for implementations elsewhere.[90]

In general, literature on the creation of coalitions, whether from the community empowerment approach,[91] the community coalition action theory model,[92] a competencies approach,[93] or the institutional entrepreneurship model[94] tends to follow three basic steps. They are: gathering members of the community around a cause, creating some form of institutional structure to carry out actions, and carrying out permanent changes that have community-wide macro-level impact. Clark et al. asserts that there are three primary aspects to the process that appeal to communities and encourage citizens to participate in coalition formation, which in some instances can take years.[95] First, in a democratic society, people have the right and obligation to participate in the transformation of their communities. Second, more inclusive participation leads to broader acceptance of and commitment to the decisions and actions established. Third, the collective wisdom of crowds is believed to be more reliable than the discernment of a few select individuals.[96]

In addition to the civic attractiveness of coalition formation, their presence is perceived to have considerable payoffs. The literature reports positive community results corresponding with coalition formation and persistence along three main dimensions: better collaboration, more resources, and measurable impact. With respect to increasing a community's capacity to collaborate (i.e., breaking down silos), the literature has noted that the organizational structure and programs of coalitions tend to create collaborative capacity.[97] In many cases they are intentionally designed to foster collaboration[98] and as a result, they build the social capital necessary among community players to successfully catalyze and carry out community and policy change.[99]

In terms of marshaling resources to address agreed upon needs, coalitions by their very nature convene a variety of organizations and thus gain access to cross-cutting or interdisciplinary pathways to grant funding. Such actions have been found to mobilize resources to address community goals.[100] The collective spirit is believed to be inspiring to donors and allows coalitions to knit together the resources of multiple donors, while avoiding the fragmentation typical to philanthropy.[101] It is notable, however, that the coalition approach is still relatively new and often requires a paradigm shift for funders.[102] Nevertheless, the assumption is that community coalitions that prosper will do so by identifying new sources of funding to maintain their community impact in the long term.[103]

Finally, if the previous two outcomes are thought of as intermediate goals, the long-term outcome of coalitions is believed to be catalyzing collective implementation of programs that have a population-wide impact. Coalitions are typically focused on implementation at the local level,[104] but they are in a better position to bring about social change,[105] whether by offering programs and services or by efforts at policy and system change, because they can include both professional and grassroots organizations.[106] It is believed that such reinforced multi-organizational working relationships enhance potential for integrating service delivery and strengthening local systems.[107]

Given these three theorized areas of community impact, we would expect strong coalitions to increase the collaborative nature of their professional community, increase the material resources of the nonprofit members of the community and, ultimately, have an impact on measurable community-level indicators such as community health or, in the case of literacy coalitions, educational achievement.

In addition to the growing literature on the creation of coalitions across a broad spectrum of fields, there are three main types of evaluation that have emerged to examine the impact of coalitions: program level evaluation, coalition level evaluation, and community level evaluation. Thought of in conjunction with the three coalition impacts theorized above (social capital, resources, and community impact), these three levels of evaluation form a matrix.

To date, the literature tends to center on two areas—the social capital building outcomes of coalition work and the community outcomes of programs that are run by coalitions. The coalition-level evaluation work has tended to focus on plotting the processes and actions that building a community coalition entails.[108] In essence, the "tracking of coalition actions"[109] has ranged from system changes to policy changes and has emphasized the end goal of "institutionalizing" coalitions such that they become an embedded and active part of the community's culture.[110] A variety of evaluation tools have been used to do such things as measure the "level of institutionalization,"[111] chart the types of activities that comprise the phases or steps needed to institutionalize,[112] document the changing dynamics of inter-organizational relationships,[113] and assess the characteristics of effective coalition work.[114] While diverse in approach and type of coalition examined, these studies are united by the fact that they tell us more about the social capital building role of coalitions than about their community impact or marshaling of resources.

When it comes to community impact, the literature is guided by the assumption that, "when coalition initiatives are well organized and delivered effectively, they should produce community-wide results that remain durable."[115] Insofar as measuring these efforts, researchers have relied on three key sources of data: surveys of key leaders, community surveys, and trend analysis of archival data. Surveys of key leaders can be a means to assessing the levels of awareness, concern, and action among community leaders with respect to the issue at hand.[116] They can also measure the perceived effectiveness of a coalition[117] across a battery of areas such as vision, efficient practice, relationships, and activities.[118] Such studies take the pulse of public perception of a coalition's impact but fail to measure actual change among community members. Seeking to move beyond perceptions of leaders, some have utilized community surveys (i.e., paper or phone) of residents in parts of the community targeted by initiatives[119] and participants in programming sponsored by initiatives.[120] While these certainly can measure changes in behavior of citizens such as drug use,[121] they tend to reflect the programming a coalition runs rather than reflect the impact of the coalition itself. In other words, measuring the effectiveness of a book distribution program at getting parents to read to their children more frequently might prove that the program works, but it does not necessarily elucidate the value of having a coalition run that program rather than some branch of government or a solitary nonprofit.

## THE CONTRIBUTIONS OF THE PRESENT PROJECT

While the literature on coalitions is indeed growing, to date, nearly all the research is in the form of case studies, so we are forced to rely on anecdotal evidence to estimate patterns in both coalition formation and impact. As Kania and Kramer admit, "evidence of the effectiveness of this approach [collective impact] is still limited . . ." mainly to examples that suggest promising results.[122] While these case studies are indeed promising and rich with detail, they are hard to generalize to other situations and communities.[123] Similarly, in the literature on coalitions, an entire symposium bemoaned the fact that evidence beyond case studies is both problematic and absent.[124] As a result, one leading scholar in the field of community health coalitions has concluded:

> In searching the community-organizing literature for the foundation of the modern coalition, one is struck by the lack of recent historic perspective on the subject. Because we are currently in the midst of writing the history of coalitions, perhaps we are waiting for the verdict as to whether these organizations are effective, sustainable, and durable before we consign them to the history books.[125]

This book sets out to address this lack of information by taking a deep look at literacy coalitions as they have grown in popularity across the United States since the 1970s. We use the first-ever national database of coalitions to assess not only what patterns exist in their launch, sustainability, and interaction with funders, but also whether coalition communities are indeed better off. In this endeavor, this project builds on the suggestions of experts in the field of coalition building. Seeking to capture the overall gestalt of a coalition, some have turned to trend analysis of archival data.[126] For instance, Harry Hatry and Elaine Morley, in their "Guide to Performance Management for Community Literacy Coalitions" point to data found in the U.S. Census and, specifically, the annually conducted American Community Survey as one of the best means to "examining overall community literacy" that by extension "provides a way to track the success of the community's literacy efforts."[127] More precisely, they suggest that years of schooling completed is a reasonable proxy for literacy. While this approach has been used in individual communities to track progress, it has yet to be used as a national basis of comparison among coalition and non-coalition communities.

The present research builds on this holistic approach to measuring the overall level of literacy in a community by using number of years of schooling as a proxy. It also builds on the work of others who have suggested the need for comparison groups when examining community changes. Perhaps the most ambitious to date is the work of Clark et al., who linked coalition work in the areas of community health outreach, civic engagement, and policy changes to changes in asthma symptoms.[128] They used a community survey approach by recruiting participants in community programming from both targeted areas and non-targeted areas (to serve as a comparison group). The present research differs from their work because they compared subpopulations within several communities while our research compares communities across the nation. In so doing, we also respond to the noted lack of a national study in a literature dominated by single community case studies.[129]

## WHY FOCUS ON LITERACY COALITIONS?

As Berkowitz points out, historically, a major barrier to national research is that no coalition registry has existed from which to draw a sample.[130] We address this problem by relying on the recent rise of a professional affiliation organization for literacy funders (the Council on Foundations' Literacy Funders Network) and an affiliated group of coalitions from across the nation that have been meeting and holding annual conferences since 2007 (Literacy Powerline—now a service of the National Center for Families Learning—has served as the primary conference organizer) (see figure 0.1). In addition, finding appropriate dependent variables (or outcome data) that are relevant across coalitions has been a problem.[131] Since literacy coalitions all focus on literacy,

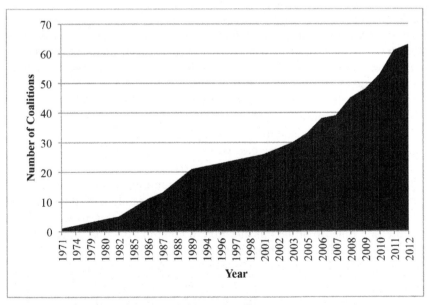

**Figure 0.1.  The rise of literacy coalitions nationally.**
*Source:* Data collected by the authors in collaboration with the Literacy Funders Network, 2012.

it makes sense to use educational outcome as a uniform measure of success.[132] Finally, with recent changes in the U.S. Census that threaten to discontinue the annual American Community Survey, now seems like an appropriate time to do a study, given future data availability is questionable.

In short, focusing on the impact of literacy coalitions across the nation as a way to learn about the impact potential of coalitions in general is a matter of both feasibility and the urgency of an uncertain future for national data collection. But focusing on literacy alone is also a strategic choice. It makes sense to focus on only one field at a time (i.e., literacy alone as opposed to mixing it with community health or gun violence coalitions) so as to rule out variations in structure and impact that are more due to differences in goals than the attempts to reach them. Some goals may just be easier to reach, and if we are to discern patterns of success for coalitions and seek best practices, we need to ensure that we are comparing coalitions that have the same ultimate goals and we need to use standardized measures that all communities will recognize as representing desirable outcomes. The data used in the following pages comes close to this goal and are drawn from a variety of reputable sources: the U.S. Decennial Census, the American Community Survey, the Internal Revenue Service, the Department of Education, the Robert Wood Johnson Foundation, and two national studies conducted by the authors in collaboration with the Literacy Funders Network—one of all known literacy coalitions nationally and the other of known literacy funders nationally.

Although these data are far from perfect, they do allow us to do things that we have never done before. First (chapter 1), they provide us with our first look at the variation and normative patterns of coalition formation, structure, and sustainability—i.e., what does a normal coalition look like? Here it is advantageous to be looking at only one type of coalition—those focused on literacy—since we can rule out that these variations and patterns are due to differences in substantive areas of focus. Second (chapter 2), these data allow us to examine national patterns in the relationship between grantmakers in a given area (we narrow our focus to literacy for consistency) and the variety of investments they make through such vehicles as venture, capacity building, and catalytic philanthropy. Here we are able to probe why funders invest in coalitions through catalytic approaches and what they hope to gain in terms of impact. Third (chapter 3), we are able, for the first time, to probe this question of community impact on a national level. Specifically, we do this by using the main indicators identified in the literature of higher community resources (Internal Revenue Service and Department of Education data), higher community social capital (in terms of participation in national initiatives), and superior educational attainment (U.S. Census and American Community Survey data and the Robert Wood Johnson Foundation). These data are, to date, the best we have, and they do reveal some interesting and robust patterns. Finally (chapter 4), we are able to use these data to put to the test existing theories about what makes coalitions more effective. The intent is not to issue a final verdict (other than that more research and better national measures of success are needed), but to begin to discern, for the sake of our national history, what sorts of community successes are attributable to collective impact community coalitions. Perhaps most transformative is that, for the first time, we are able to ferret out promising practices for future examination and replication based on what is done in the communities that are succeeding the most, as opposed to arbitrarily highlighting "best practices" based on convenience or anecdotal evidence from single case studies. In a sense, our guesses about what works become much more precise and evidence based.

## MAJOR FINDINGS AND THE OUTLINE OF FUTURE PAGES

Coalitions, this research confirms, are not destinations or end goals, but implementation vehicles for getting where communities want to go; many don't even provide direct services to community residents. It may be helpful to think of coalitions through the metaphor of a bicycle. As with bikes, communities that have coalitions get where they want to be faster than without them. There is a fairly substantial caveat to this: We can't prove that it is by riding bikes (i.e., having a coalition) that communities get there faster. We know only that they get there faster. Coalition counties lead other communities on average with respect to high school graduates and nonprofit revenues and assets. In addition, we notice bumps in high school graduate populations when comparing pre- and post-coalition data. Furthermore, zip codes with literacy coalitions are more successful in competing for U.S. Department of Education grants. Finally, communities with coalitions seem to be improving their high school graduation rates faster than other communities.

As with bicycle riders, it takes continuous conditioning and practice to make coalitions run well. Those that do more things together have better results. Gaining balance with a coalition (as on a bicycle) is cumulative; you don't tend to lose it, but you can lose your conditioning if you are out of practice. So, too, do relationships across organizational silos change the community ethos once you begin collaborating; nevertheless, they demand ongoing time and attention to work best.

Just having a bike does not guarantee you will travel faster than pedestrians, but communities with coalitions tend to outpace the average community in this country with respect to resources and outcomes. Both bikes and coalitions have a learning curve; there is a life course to coalitions. They develop over time. However, once you have a coalition, as with a bike, it becomes a resource or a tool ready when you need it. You can use it effectively to travel toward new goals and opportunities such as newly identified community problems or new collaborative grant opportunities. As Butterfoss notes, the existence of a coalition builds capacity to address future community issues.[133] Aldrich et al. similarly explained, when it comes to coalition building, collaboration is an end in itself: "although interventions come and go, sustaining the capacity to collaborate means the community will always have a durable resource with which to address common concerns."[134]

Finally, like bikes, coalitions have a wide diversity—instead of colors and makes and models and bike frames, we have different forms of backbone organizations or engine agencies. Older coalitions tend to be of one type and younger another but, interestingly, which you choose doesn't seem to matter that much—a bike is a bike. You will still tend to outperform non-coalition communities. Coalitions tend to have training wheels—community foundations and private foundations, which fund much of their operations during the early phases of life (first five years), then begin to taper off and let them fly on their own. In sum, coalitions are a form of "civic muscle" that takes considerable effort to build, but, in the end, are highly correlated with a higher standard of living.[135]

## NOTES

1. Putnam, 2000.
2. Kania & Kramer, 2011, 3.
3. Kania, Hanleybrown, & Splansky Juster, 2014. Silver buckshot metaphor was first seen in John Kania's 2012 presentation at the All America Cities / Campaign for Grade-Level Reading conference in Denver, Colorado.
4. 2003.
5. Kania & Kramer, 2011, 3.
6. Kania & Kramer, 2015.
7. Watson-Thompson et.al. 2008, 25.
8. 2007:71.
9. Kaye, 2001, 269.
10. Berkowitz, 2001.
11. Kegler et al. 2010, 1.
12. Office of Health Policy, ASPE, 2010.
13. Mix, 2011.
14. Watson-Thompson et al., 2008.
15. Berkowitz, 2001.
16. McMillan et al., 1995, Cox, 2009.
17. Fagan et al., 2009.
18. Mix, 2011.
19. Office of Health Policy, ASPE, 2010.

20. Broom & Avanzino, 2010.

21. The result has been an enduring visage of the entrepreneur as a heroic loner (Zilber, 2007, 1037) and the perpetuation what Lawrence, Suddaby, & Leca rightly point out as a mythos of "hypermuscular institutional entrepreneurs" (Lawrence et al., 2009, 1).

22. Amenta, E., Caren, N., Chiarello, E., & Su, Y. (2010). "The Political Consequences of Social Movements." Annual. Retrieved April 3, 2017, from http://www.socsci.uci.edu/~ea3/Amentaetal.ars.2010.pdf.

23. 2007.

24. Crutchfield & McLeod, 2007.

25. 2007, 19 emphasis in original.

26. 19.

27. 19–20.

28. Pacheco, York, Dean, & Sarasvathy, 2010.

29. Kramer, 2009.

30. Schramm, 2006; Philanthropy Magazine, 2011; Philanthropy New York, 2011.

31. Pacheco, York, Dean, & Sarasvathy, 2010.

32. Schramm, 2006.

33. Silver buckshot metaphor was first seen in John Kania's 2012 presentation at the All America Cities / Campaign for Grade-Level Reading conference in Denver, Colorado.

34. Kania & Kramer, 2011, 3.

35. Illiteracy Rate. Huffington Post. (2006, September 13). Retrieved April 2, 2017, from http://www.huffingtonpost.com/2013/09/06/illiteracy-rate_n_3880355.html.

36. A special thanks to Bill Millett, President of Scope View Strategic Advantage, whose work and public presentations have helped to inform the following pages by pointing out many of these organizations. In the following pages we work to represent Millett's argument using many of the same sources he has used in his national presentations.

37. Fight Crime: Invest in Kids. Executive summary. (n.d.). Retrieved from http://cdn.fightcrime.org/wp-content/uploads/I'm_The_Guy_Report.pdf.

38. Fight Crime: Invest in Kids. Executive summary. (n.d.). Retrieved from http://cdn.fightcrime.org/wp-content/uploads/I'm_The_Guy_Report.pdf.

39. Special Report: Education and Correctional Populations. (2003, April 15). Retrieved April 2, 2017, from http://www.bjs.gov/content/pub/pdf/ecp.pdf.

40. Special Report: Education and Correctional Populations. (2003, April 15). Retrieved April 2, 2017, from http://www.bjs.gov/content/pub/pdf/ecp.pdf.

41. (2009, October 12). Retrieved April 2, 2017, from http://www.nytimes.com/2009/10/09/education/09dropout.html?_r=3.

42. Lochner & Moretti, 2004.

43. (2012, February 13). Retrieved April 2, 2017, from http://www.politifact.com/oregon/statements/2012/feb/13/ben-cannon/canon-gets-connection-between-reading-and-crime-ri/.

44. (2006, September 6). Retrieved April 2, 2017, from http://www.huffingtonpost.com/2013/09/06/illiteracy-rate_n_3880355.html.

45. Mission: Readiness, Military Leaders for Kids. (n.d.). Retrieved April 2, 2017, from http://www.missionreadiness.org/.

46. (n.d.). Retrieved April 2, 2017 from http://datacenter.kidscount.org/data# USA/1/8/10,11,12,13,15,14,2719/char/0.

47. Angang, H., Linlin, H., & Zhixiao, C. (2003). China's economic growth and poverty reduction. Retrieved April 2, 2017, from https://www.imf.org/external/np/ apd/seminars/2003/newdelhi/angang.pdf.

48. Stuart, E. (2015). "China has almost wiped out urban poverty. Now it must tackle inequality." Retrieved April 2, 2017, from http://www.theguardian.com/business/ economics-blog/2015/aug/19/china-poverty-inequality-development-goals.

49. PRE-K–12EDUCATION Policy Declaration.. (n.d.). Retrieved April 2, 2017, from https://www.uschamber.com/sites/default/files/legacy/issues/education/files/us chamberprek12policydeclaration.pdf www.uschamber.com.

50. "Investing in America's Future Workforce." (n.d.). Retrieved April 2, 2017, from http://www.nawb.org/documents/PEW-NAWB%20Brief%20Early%20Child hood.pdf.

51. "Investing in America's Future Workforce." (n.d.). Retrieved April 2, 2017, from http://www.nawb.org/documents/PEW-NAWB%20Brief%20Early%20Child hood.pdf.

52. "ACHIEVING AMERICA'S FULL POTENTIAL: More Work, Greater Investment, Unlimited Opportunity." (2015, January). Retrieved April 2, 2017, from http://businessroundtable.org/Growth.

53. "ACHIEVING AMERICA'S FULL POTENTIAL: More Work, Greater Investment, Unlimited Opportunity." (2015, January). Retrieved April 2, 2017, from http://businessroundtable.org/Growth.

54. Business Leaders Outline Critical Need for Early Childhood Education at CED Report Event in Detroit PNC and Kelly Services CEOs Voice Commitment. (n.d.). Retrieved April 2, 2017, from https://www.ced.org/pdf/CEDUnfinishedBusinessPP DetroitFinal6–26–12.pdf.

55. (n.d.). Retrieved April 2, 2017, from http://datacenter.kidscount.org/data# USA/1/8/10,11,12,13,15,14,2719/char/0.

56. "Average High School Math and Science Scores by Selected Country." (n.d.). Retrieved April 3, 2017, from http://www.themanufacturinginstitute.org/Research/ Facts-About-Manufacturing/Workforce-and-Compensation/Math-and-Science/Math -and-Science.aspx.

57. "The skills gap in U.S. manufacturing 2015 and beyond." (2015). Retrieved April 3, 2017, from http://www.themanufacturinginstitute.org/~/media/827DBC7653 3942679A15EF7067A704CD.ashx.

58. "The skills gap in U.S. manufacturing 2015 and beyond." (2015). Retrieved April 3, 2017, from http://www.themanufacturinginstitute.org/~/media/827DBC7653 3942679A15EF7067A704CD.ashx.

59. Wildes, 1938, 257.

60. Baldwin, 2006. Note that while Stewart adopted the "Each one Teach one" motto, its origin is also thought by some to be from and African American proverb.

61. Rose, A. D. (n.d.). Ends or Means: An Overview of the History of the Adult Education Act. Retrieved April 2, 2017, from (http://www2.ed.gov/about/offices/list/ovae/pi/AdultEd/anniv40/end-mean.pdf.

62. (n.d.). Retrieved April 2, 2017, from http://www.blackpast.org/aah/caliver-ambrose-1894-1962#sthash.LgPSGgMx.dpuf.

63. John F. Kennedy: Special Message to the Congress on Education.—February 6, 1962. (n.d.). Retrieved April 07, 2017, from http://www.presidency.ucsb.edu/ws/?pid=8858.

64. Auxier, Richard C. 2010. "Reagan's Recession," Pew Research Center December 14, 2010. Retrieved June 26, 2017, from http://www.pewresearch.org/2010/12/14/reagans-recession/.

65. Gurr, 1970.

66. Gurr, 1970.

67. Opp, 2009.

68. Opp, 2009.

69. Meyer & Minkoff, 2004.

70. Best, 1990.

71. Ridzi, 2012.

72. Piven & Cloward, 1977.

73. See for instance Piven & Cloward (1977, 91 of 1979 edition) talks of "pushing turbulence to its outer limits."

74. Amenta, E., Caren, N., Chiarello, E., & Su, Y. (2010). "The Political Consequences of Social Movements." Annual. Retrieved April 3, 2017, from http://www.socsci.uci.edu/~ea3/Amentaetal.ars.2010.pdf.

75. Bronfenbrenner 1979, 1986, 1995.

76. See for instance Ridzi, Sylvia and Sigh (2014).

77. Siporin, M. (1980). "Ecological Systems Theory in Social Work." Retrieved April 3, 2017, from http://scholarworks.wmich.edu/jssw/vol7/iss4/4.

78. Dluhy & Kravitz, 1990, 7.

79. Dluhy & Kravitz, 1990, 7.

80. Dluhy & Kravitz, 1990, 93.

81. Amenta, Caren, Chiarello, & Su, 2010.

82. Amenta, Caren, Chiarello, & Su, 2010.

83. Amenta, Caren, Chiarello, & Su, 2010.

84. Amenta, Caren, Chiarello, & Su, 2010.

85. Amenta, & Young, 1999, 22.

86. Office of Health Policy, ASPE, 2010.

87. Clark et al., 2010.

88. Watson-Thompson et al., 2008.

89. Ridzi, Carmody, & Byrnes, 2011.

90. Fixsen et al., 2005.

91. Fawcett et al., 1995.

92. Butterfoss, 2007; Kegler et al., 2010.

93. Foster-Fishman et al., 2001.

94. Ridzi, Carmody, & Byrnes, 2011.

95. 2010, 904.

96. Surowiecki, 2004; see also Ridzi, Carmody & Byrnes, 2011.

97. Foster-Fishman et al., 2001.

98. Butterfoss, 2007.

99. Fawcett et al., 1995.

100. Butterfoss, Goodman, & Wandersman, 1993.

101. Kramer, 2009.

102. Kania & Kramer, 2011.

103. Office of Health Policy, ASPE, 2010, 3.

104. Butterfoss, 2007.

105. Wolff, 2001.

106. Butterfoss, 2007.

107. Vicary et al., 1996.

108. Goodman et al., 1996; Watson-Thompson, 2008; Ridzi, Carmody, & Byrnes, 2011.

109. Goodman et al., 1996.

110. Goodman et al., 1996; Ridzi, Carmody, & Byrnes, 2011.

111. Goodman et al., 1993, 56 in Goodman et al., 1996.

112. Ridzi, Carmody, & Byrnes, 2011.

113. Clarke-McMullen, 2010; Frey et al., 2006.

114. Cramer et al., 2006.

115. Goodman et al. 1996, 53.

116. Goodman et al. 1996, 53.

117. Feinberg et al., 2004 in Kegler et al., 2010, 2.

118. Cramer et al., 2006.

119. Clark et al., 2010.

120. Ridzi, Sylvia, & Singh, 2011.

121. Goodman et al., 1996.

122. 2011, 3.

123. Butterfoss, 2007, 89.

124. See the 2001 symposium in the Journal of Community Psychology American Journal of Community Psychology.

125. Butterfoss, 2007, 12.

126. Goodman et al., 1996, 55.

127. Hatry & Morley, 2008, 9.

128. 2010.

129. Berkowitz, 2001, 218.

130. 2001, 215.

131. Berkowitz, 2001, 216, 221.

132. as outlined in Hatry & Morley, 2008.

133. 2007, 62.

134. 2009, 147.

135. David M. Laird of the Central Carolina Community Foundation coined this term in a personal communication.

*Chapter One*

# The Many Faces of Collective Impact Community Literacy Coalitions

In the first chapter we examined the flourishing of community literacy coalitions in recent years as a case study in the growth of social capital directed at collective impact. In this chapter we look deeper into this recent phenomenon by scrutinizing the homogeneity of coalitions. This is important for understanding just what it means when we say coalitions are on the rise. It is also critical when it comes to evaluating the impact of coalitions on communities. As we will see in future chapters, there is some variation in the degree to which having a coalition in a community corresponds with desirable community outcomes. In this context, it is very helpful to know the extent to which coalitions are uniform and the degrees to which each is unique as opposed to comparable with others. In the following pages we first explore the visions that have guided communities and their institutional entrepreneurs in establishing coalitions. We then further examine national data from a survey of literacy coalitions to gain a sense for who joins them and what they do. Given the centrality of local actors and the variety of mechanisms by which they have been propagated, we find that coalitions are highly unique in many ways that seem to be rooted in their community's needs. Nevertheless, despite this diversity, coalitions have certain core features that enable us to think of them and research them as a singular phenomenon. Finally, we add the dimension of time by introducing a series of specific coalitions from across the nation and discussing how coalition formation has evolved over the decades.

## ORIGINS OF COALITIONS—THE VISION
## OF INSTITUTIONAL ENTREPRENEURS

The diversity, despite similarity among literacy coalitions, is perhaps best understood by examining who is creating them and how. To get a sense of this, we surveyed 120 known literacy coalitions that were part of the Literacy Funders Network in 2012. Of those surveyed 78 responded. We then followed up with a series of interviews and group discussions as well as ongoing conversations at conferences and other professional events with coalitions and funders (approximately 46 participants in all). (In subsequent examples in this chapter, the location of the program or coalition follows the quotation to offer a sense of geographic diversity.) We found that while the impetus for creating coalitions varied, it typically has an individual or group of individuals that served the role of entrepreneur in creating a new community institution. In some communities, it is an individual person who provides the spark. For instance, in one community it began when a new leader came to town:

> It began as a new community leader moved into the city and realized there was no one addressing literacy problems here. She attempted to get the library to start something but finally began a grassroots organization to address the problem. (Indiana)[1]

In another community, a coalition was formed through the vision of a local pediatrician:

> The Literacy Coalition was formed from a vision of a local pediatrician, who sought to bring literacy focused individuals together to address early literacy. The grassroots effort resulted in a coalition being organized to address literacy across the lifespan. (Indiana, a different community than the one noted above)

While having an individual hero to point to conforms to the stereotypical narrative our culture has built up around entrepreneurs as rugged individualists, coalitions are more often than not born out of the vision of a group that found working together useful and wanted to continue doing so, as voiced in the following comment:

> A group of literacy partners gathered together to plan an event, "Celebrating Volunteers." After the event was over, we decided to form a coalition so that our literacy efforts would be united in the community. (Illinois)

Far from making a grand entrance, coalitions are frequently born of a small group of people interacting, such as the following group of literacy teachers:

Our coalition was started by two teachers who wanted to teach a few adults to read who had never learned to read. They tutored these adult learners in the library. Other teachers and learners joined, and an agency gradually grew from this concept. (Texas)

Whether they be teachers, or as in the following case, medical librarians, the recurring theme is that, over time interest began to snowball until the ranks swelled to create what we might today consider a coalition.

It grew out of discussions at meetings of local medical librarians who had started a small network. Then interest in Health Literacy Month helped to increase interest in engaging more people and the organization emerged. (Arizona)

While narratives such as the above tend to hint at a bottom-up approach to the spread of coalitions, plenty of other communities attribute their coalition's inception to a top-down approach taken by organizations of major community clout that urged action along these lines as a good way to address local needs. For instance, a number of coalitions began at the urging of foundations, as in the following case:

We were started by a couple of very active philanthropists on the Education Committee of the local chamber of commerce. Everything was trending up except for public education. Organizations were doing good things and reporting back success to the funders, but when they looked at the whole they saw 54 percent graduation rates. That was not good enough. We needed a board of directors with high-level and influential stakeholders like the mayor and director of schools, but those people are more than a few levels removed from what is happening on the ground. We had some work groups that would have some influence, but be more in touch with what is happening on the ground—we call that our operating board (the co-chairs of all of our different alignment groups). They meet monthly and provide accountability for our alignment teams. They coordinate our teams doing the work on the ground. Alignment teams focus on issues including such things as supporting pre-K through eighth grade literacy, high school, and behavioral health. The teams are co-chaired by a decision maker on behalf of the school district and an influential community leader. Early on there was a lot of pushback to creating a new organization. But if it is not someone's job to work on this every day, then it is not going to happen. (Tennessee)

Other literacy coalitions similarly have their origins in foundation work. Here is how some coalitions describe their roots:

• A foundation initiative to identify systemic changes in how literacy services are integrated into community initiatives and to act as an advocate for quality literacy services. (Ohio)

- Foundation's initiative for adult literacy, which evolved into a countywide literacy coalition supporting literacy development for all ages. (California)
- The Literacy Initiative was formed as an outgrowth of the [local private] Foundation Literacy Initiative. (South Carolina)
- A local foundation convened the Literacy Coalition as one of the community initiatives. (California)

In other communities, coalitions found their roots in civic groups such as the Junior League or the Rotary, or even the United Way:

> United Way conducted a needs assessment and came to realize that low literacy levels were impacting so many other areas that were being served by United Way. After a great deal of discussion, task groups, etc., the decision was made to form a coalition to improve the quality of adult literacy instruction, increase the quantity of services available, and to improve community awareness of the issue of adult literacy. (Texas)

In quite a few instances, not civic groups, but arms of government took the lead in forming coalitions. Whether it was the county board of commissioners, the county supervisor, the town hall, a congressional representative, or a mayor, government is well represented as a convener and resource for coalitions.

> Our coalition was founded by the mayor to serve as the adult literacy convener and resource for the metropolitan area. The coalition's executive director held a seat on the Mayor's Cabinet (until 2011). The coalition received city funding and redistributed those funds through grantmaking to support literacy programming. (Maryland)

While in these cases it is clear that government or civic groups, rather than individuals, have taken the lead, this does not mean that community members felt forced. On the contrary, as in the following example, community organizations can only provide the forum and conduct an initial convening of stakeholders. It is up to the community members themselves to decide to continue to meet and to move forward toward the creation of a vibrant coalition.

> The coalition is the extension of a series of community planning meetings that were hosted by the Junior League. Following the community planning, the participants demonstrated a desire to continue meeting in an organized fashion to share best practices, promote and organize collaboration, and celebrate community. (Texas)

In fact, from this perspective, the role of grantmakers and others can be seen as less of a force, and more of a resource or chain of resources that take turns helping the community as its collaboration evolves:

Seven cross-sector community leaders, convened by the Community Foundation, created a literacy-community concept to build on and leverage the lessons learned from [another initiative]. The group's planning and implementation was encouraged and accelerated by a community transformation grant from the W. K. Kellogg Foundation. (Michigan)

We see civic organizations serving as institutional entrepreneurs in the sense Pacheco et al. described, "as [agents who mobilize] resources to transform or create institutions."[2] Although individuals and organizations engaged in institutional entrepreneurship around building coalitions are most often seen at the local level, there is also considerable evidence that they can also serve on the national level. For instance, some coalitions noted that they were started as part of a national campaign such as that of the National League of Cities, or, in the following case, of television broadcasters:

In 1986, as part of a national outreach campaign spearheaded by PBS and ABC television networks, literacy agencies in our community formed a local task force. The task force created public awareness of the alarming number of adults in need of basic literacy services in our community. The Literacy Coalition grew out of this task force in 1989. Three years later, it received status as an independent nonprofit organization. In 2009, the name was changed to a coalition to better reflect the scope of their membership. (Wisconsin)[3]

Regardless of who receives credit for actually starting the coalition, the life course of coalition development appears strikingly similar across communities. For instance, reviewing the following three narratives of an individual champion, a grassroots scenario, and a government-led effort, we find that the story turns out quite the same and that it tends to have a similar host of characters in terms of literacy providers, advocates, and public officials. Furthermore, there is a clear pattern of growth that mirrors what is found in the literature on institution building, in which people are brought together to consider a problem, realize it will take some time so they organize themselves, and then they set out to take actions such as running events, programs, or services that will help the community reach that goal.[4]

## Individual Champion

Our literacy coalition is a non-profit 501(c)(3) organization organized in 2008 with the vision that every child and adult in our community is a lifelong learner skilled with the highest levels of literacy. In the fall of 2007, our congressional representative convened a group of community leaders for a meeting concerning literacy needs. This meeting created an effort that involved the participation of over a dozen community agencies including universities, community colleges, and grassroots agencies. The purpose of the coalition is to lead an active collaboration of literacy programs, learners, and supporters, toward coordinated and integrated resources promoting literacy services, present a unified voice on the goals of literacy, and help create economically sustainable communities. Since that time the coalition has been making an impact in communities by advocating for literacy services and providers, by implementing family literacy events, and by distributing books to children, youth, and adults. (Texas)

## Grassroots

Our coalition was formed in 1982 as a grassroots movement to provide a unifying voice for adult basic literacy providers. The organization obtained 501(c)(3) status in 1985 and, thanks to a grant from a foundation in 1986, was able to hire its first staff member. The coalition focuses on recruiting volunteers, training professionals, raising awareness of literacy needs among adults, and on creating a forum for public and private literacy providers who share the same client populations. It continues to harness community advocates and public officials to inform and offer an opportunity to share best practices. Today, in addition to the valuable resources provided, the coalition is organizing statewide conferences, creating an online tutor training program, and offering a cash award to the agency that responds to the needs of the adult learner in a significant and effective manner. (Tennessee)

## Local Government

The coalition's history rests in the dramatic evolution of the county from a homogenous suburb to a diverse metropolis that is today home to [much] of the state's immigrant population. In 2002, responding to the county's rapidly changing demographics (including a limited English-proficient population that had doubled in the last decade), the County Council members and other community leaders mobilized around the critical need to improve capacity, coordination, and collaboration among adult English language literacy service providers. A 2003 study determined that while many community-based adult English language and literacy providers were highly effective in attracting and building relationships of trust among a diverse immigrant client base, the majority of programs identified a lack of resources, coordination, and expertise in delivering adult education programming. This movement and study led to the founding of the coalition, which was created as the countywide coordinating entity. (Maryland)

Each of these cases remind us that the value added by and the commonality between coalitions is not the programming that they run, since this is quite varied, but rather in the "convening" and "coordinating" of stakeholders in an ongoing and institutionalized manner. As in the following example, what sets coalitions apart is that they aspire to a "coordinated" communitywide approach to addressing community problems.

A county supervisor and local newspaper publisher recognized the need for a countywide literacy effort that would raise literacy to a higher level of prominence and urgency in the community and generate resources to support local literacy programs. (California)

As Aldrich et al. (2009, 147) explained, with respect to coalition building, collaboration can be seen as an end in itself: "although interventions come and go, sustaining the capacity to collaborate means the community will always have a durable resource with which to address common concerns." The result of such efforts can be a coalition of people who are collaborating and ready to collaborate when the next problem or opportunity comes along.[5]

As seen in the case of the following coalition, even grassroots efforts can grow into durable community institutions over time.

We started as an all-volunteer grassroots coalition in 2000. Citizens from the library, service groups, health care, human services, parents, educators, and early childhood providers began meeting monthly in a conference room at the Medical Center. They adopted the theme "Read to Succeed" and wrote a one-page document outlining how they could connect readers with young children.

The coalition learned about a nonprofit organization in Illinois that was reporting positive results working with families. A local Rotary provided funds for a two-day training in 2001. Participants from many local groups learned about the non-profit model.

While researching effective strategies, coalition members discovered the national Reach Out and Read program, an evidence-based model using well-child checkups to encourage parents to help their children love books, learn, and eventually succeed in school.

The Rotary Club helped launch several components of the Reach Out and Read program. Rotarians created a public reading corner in the pediatric clinic's waiting room. It included a comfortable chair and a bookcase displaying a collection of high-quality children's books.

The Rotarians donated 500 *Baby Faces* board books and several pediatricians began giving them to children at six-month checkups. This modest start blossomed into a countywide program in just a few years.

After a few years, coalition leaders felt a need to formalize their structure. They wrote articles and bylaws with the help of a local attorney and received a Certificate of Incorporation from the Iowa Secretary of State in 2004. In 2005, the organization received federal income tax exemption under Section 501(c)(3) of the Internal Revenue Code. (Iowa)

Through such a maturation process, even the most grassroots of efforts can bring community members together in the long run, often snowballing as it goes.

## WHO JOINS COALITIONS?

Given the importance of collaboration then, it is quite instructive to examine a key component: coalition membership. The literature to date suggests that coalitions range from a few individuals or organizations to a few hundred.[6] Among the literacy coalitions in our sample, the number of members ranged from four to five hundred, with a national average of fifty-nine member organizations. Asked about the types of organizations that comprise their coalitions, on average nonprofits that primarily focus on literacy (i.e. GED and tutoring) made up approximately 39 percent of membership, followed by nonprofit organizations that do not have literacy as a primary focus (18 percent), schools (11 percent), libraries (10 percent), institutions of higher education (7 percent), churches/faith communities (5 percent), for-profit businesses (4 percent), government agencies (4 percent), and foundations (2 percent) (see figure 1.1).

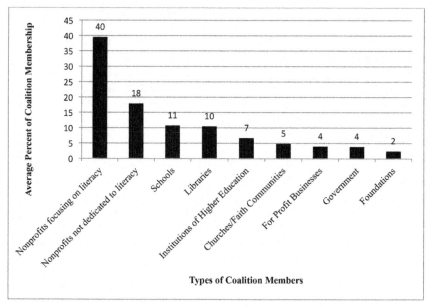

**Figure 1.1. Average percent of coalition members.**
*Source:* Data collected by the authors in collaboration with the Literacy Funders Network, 2012.

The membership of literacy coalitions nationally reinforces our understanding of coalitions from other fields as an apparatus of cross-sector collaboration. Coalitions have traditionally been defined as groups "of individuals representing diverse organizations, factions or constituencies who agree to work together to achieve a common goal."[7]

While we can say with certainty that coalitions are characterized by cross-organization collaboration, there is considerable variation among them. For instance, while on average of approximately 40 percent of coalitions are comprised of nonprofits that focus primarily on literacy, some coalitions were completely made up of this type of organization and others, perhaps surprisingly, had none. This same pattern can be seen for each of the categories, with libraries ranging from 0 to 100 percent, non-literacy nonprofits ranging from 0 to 92 percent, faith communities ranging from 0 to 75 percent, and the rest ranging from 0 to 40 percent of a coalition's members.

Regardless of the actual membership composition, literature tells us that what sets community coalitions apart is their inclusion of both professional and grassroots members who seek to work together to better their community.[8] Drawing from the U.S. Department of Health and Human Services (DHHS), we find that literacy coalitions, as seen here, fit squarely within their description of coalitions used to address community health issues:

> Community coalitions bring together community groups, grassroots organizations, faith-based groups, universities, government agencies, and other organizations. The activities of community coalitions are as diverse as their memberships, including advocacy, outreach, education, assistance, prevention, service delivery, capacity building, empowerment, community action, and systems change.[9]

## THE INVISIBLE HAND:
## WHAT DO COALITIONS ACTUALLY DO?

As the DHHS noted, previous literature has identified coalitions as largely program agnostic. They are more about the mode of collaboration than the specific project. Emphasizing this aspect, nearly half of the coalitions that participated in this research saw this as their only function, with only 51 percent actually providing direct services to learners. As one coalition explained:

> It is important to know what we can expect to accomplish as a coalition since often we are not direct service providers. Advocacy is one priority. What has helped us get funders on board is understanding that someone doesn't learn to read in a vacuum. It takes a village and it is a community responsibility. That is something that has resonated very well. (California)

As another coalition explained, not providing direct services to clients can be a critical function of a coalition since it allows the coalition to create a neutral space that fosters collaborative activities. If the coalition did begin providing services, it might be seen as competing with other community organizations for funding, a clear impediment to a collaborative environment.

> We have spent a lot of time learning from other models like Strive and Say Yes to Education. One thing we do is stay in our lane as a neutral convener; we do not run any programs. We try not to compete for funding with any of the organizations that we are working to align with. (Tennessee)

Some communities have learned the hard way that competing for funding is like throwing oil on a fire; funding competition incentivizes local providers to root for the failure of the coalition rather than collaborate toward its success. Others have entered into service provision only cautiously, after ensuring that no other nonprofit in the community is interested in offering such services.

While it is certainly true, as the DHHS states that "the activities of community coalitions are as diverse as their membership,"[10] when we examine the prevalence of activities more closely, we find that certain types of activities are more prominent than others (see figure 1.2).

For instance, the most common activity of coalitions (seen in approximately 86 percent of coalitions) was carrying out community convening and

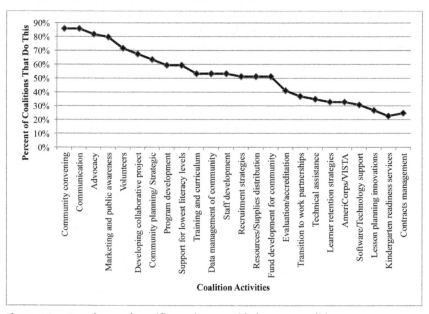

**Figure 1.2. Prevalence of specific services provided among coalitions.**

*Source:* Data collected by the authors in collaboration with the Literacy Funders Network, 2012.

communication functions. These were followed closely by such community building and collaborative undertakings as advocacy, raising public awareness, and developing collaborative projects and community strategic planning. In contrast, activities associated with direct service provision, such as kindergarten readiness services, contract management, and lesson planning, were seen in less than a third of all coalitions. As the following example illustrates, communication is often a goal in itself:

> Once our literacy coalition was able to establish itself as a nonprofit, it took over the role of organizing the coalition. The coalition meets quarterly and maintains monthly communication with participants. (Texas)

As another coalition noted, sharing ideas is a central value added:

> Our coalition was formed to share resources and ideas, and address literacy issues. (California)

Among coalitions that did serve people directly, adult learners were the most likely target of such services. As we will explore later, this decision is very much related to the time period in which a coalition was formed and will have a variety of implications when it comes to measuring coalition impact. Overall, 91 percent of coalitions served adults, 66 percent served seniors and 64 percent each served Early Childhood and K–12. When deciding who to serve, resources were a major theme:

> The coalition was formed as part of a three-year grant from the Community Foundation to strengthen adult literacy efforts in the county. The coalition is a group of twenty adult education, workforce development, and literacy agencies that meet monthly to determine adult literacy priorities, identify and expand resources, and align services and programs in the county. (Michigan)

Furthermore, more often than not, this expansion of resources was articulated as a goal of coalition collaboration. The following case illustrates how planning leads to seeking greater resources, which is theorized to lead to increased literacy within the community:

> Our coalition formed as a result of a comprehensive community planning process. Our mission is to increase adult literacy by supporting existing adult literacy programs and advocating for increased resources and support for adult literacy initiatives in the region. (Louisiana)

As another coalition member and literacy professional explained:

> Adult education is where the funding stream for coalitions originally came from. Larger cities tend to be more adult education focused, and smaller and middle-

sized communities tend to focus across the lifespan. A coalition is something that fits you where you are and takes you to the next level. They don't all have to be the same.

In the pages ahead we will explore some of these historical patterns of coalition proliferation and how the year of a coalition's birth, and the prevalent funding streams at the time, helped to shape the populations they chose to serve.

In future sections, we will also explore the relationships between the presence of coalitions and outcomes for these communities. Before we do that, it is helpful to examine how communities see themselves achieving these goals over time. Literacy coalitions, like other coalitions, focus on a variety of regions or communities that they tend to define on the state, regional, or even national level.[11] While some defined the communities they served as cities (7 percent), states (24 percent), or regions (21 percent), the largest proportion (48 percent) defined their community on the county level. This is critical, because by and large coalitions expressed their goals as seeking community-level change. Whether aiming for more people graduating from high school or more people going on to higher education, most coalitions articulated a need for broader change than an individual program or agency can accomplish on its own. This type of institutional change within a community does not come quickly, or easily. Rather, as coalitions shared, it requires a long-term approach that may best be delivered through a lasting institution of a coalition. The geography of focus has also changed over time:

> The National Alliance of Urban Literacy Coalitions (which later became Literacy USA) was the first convener of a coalition of coalitions. The Houston coalition started citywide, but over time spread to include the whole multi-city metropolis. More recently it has also embraced the rural communities around it. Being rural is a challenge. People who live outside of the big urban areas are really hampered by the focus on the urban. Those who live in rural areas across the country want equal opportunity. (Texas)

We further explore the changes in patterns over time in the next section.


## THE EVOLUTION OF COALITIONS OVER THE DECADES

While coalitions are diverse, they also follow many patterns. Perhaps not surprisingly, these patterns often coincide with the era in which they were launched. In the following pages we offer examples of coalitions formed in each decade from the 1980s through today to help elucidate how time period has influenced the nuances of coalition functioning.

## Coalition Development in the 1980s: Five Examples

As the United States shed jobs in the 1970s and suffered from recession and massive bankruptcies in the 1980s, the unemployed with low literacy skills, especially immigrants, were among those hardest hit.[12] What emerged from this was a new dialogue about adult education and the formation of the first literacy coalitions. Amendments to the Adult Education Act (AEA) were introduced as connections between literacy and economic development were identified. These amendments, however, did not involve a large infusion of federal funding to address the issue, but instead focused on the value of the nonprofit sector, the use of volunteers, cutting of federal programs, and a new dialogue with private and corporate funders. The 1984 amendments to the AEA expanded the act's basic goals: to improve reading and writing instruction, by including the new national priority to "enable all adults to acquire basic literacy skills necessary to function in society."[13] The 1980s saw a significant increase in national attention to adult illiteracy, yet funding for adult education didn't expand during the Reagan administration's early years.[14] With no infusion of funding, but a growing concern and awareness of the low literacy skills crisis, several large cities took the initiative to fill the gap that the federal government was addressing by creating the country's first literacy coalitions.

The AEA required state plans to describe how volunteers were to be deployed, insisting that these volunteers "should 'supplement' and not 'supplant' salaried employees."[15] These changes were accompanied by new planning and evaluation requirements. The language alienated some of the nonprofit service delivery sector, and a two-tier service delivery provider model emerged. The vast majority of federal funds flowed to school districts and colleges with little, if any, funding assigned to community-based organizations that were addressing the needs of adults with the lowest literacy levels. No funding was assigned to the new literacy coalitions.

### San Diego Council on Literacy

In the late 1970s and early 1980s, San Diego, a beautiful coastal port and tourist destination, suffered severely as the military reduced its presence and major industries left. There were also a series of scandals playing out in the media. During this time, the city's population grew as more Latino immigrants moved across the border from Mexico and, as a result of the 1965 Immigration Act, immigrants from Hong Kong, Taiwan, and China arrived, joining the hundreds of functionally illiterate San Diegans. A diversified population with limited literacy skills severely impacted the possibilities of sustained economic development for the city. Growing numbers of high school dropouts and limited job opportunities for the unskilled increased concern about low literacy and the need for increased English language services.[16] Literacy providers, mainly small nonprofit organizations, were underresourced to deal with the growing literacy problems. To address the issue, in 1986 the *San Diego Union-Tribune* publisher and former U.S. Congressman Brian Bilbray founded the San Diego Council on Literacy.[17]

The council's original goals were increasing public awareness of literacy services and gaps in them where there was a need for cooperation among the county's literacy programs. The providers in the coalition did not receive federal adult education funding and were challenged to raise the resources to address the problem. Providers also took on advocacy and fund development.

## San Antonio Commission on Literacy

San Antonio, known as "the place where the sunshine spends the winter," was growing its financial services, health care institutions, and military bases in the 1980s. However, poverty, homelessness, and low literacy plagued the city. Low-wage and low-skilled jobs predominated in the fast-growing Latino-majority community, and new leadership was needed to address housing, poor services, and educational inequity in the city's west side.

Henry Cisneros was a significant figure in the city's approach to low literacy. His public service began in 1974, when at age 27, he became the youngest council member ever elected to office in San Antonio. Cisneros developed a partnership to explore resources and support for the Latino population, many of whom had limited English literacy skills. Cisneros, who went on to become secretary of Housing and Urban Development under President Bill Clinton, was highly popular as San Antonio's mayor from 1981 to 1989.[18]

Despite his popularity, in the 1980s Cisneros was facing a crisis. Much of the population had limited literacy skills. A review of the flow of federal adult education funds to San Antonio revealed that the city was returning unexpended funds. Adult education was offered through several of the over a dozen school districts in San Antonio but the demand was greater than the supply of services. Rather than arrange for funds to flow to the nonprofit providers, though, the excess funds were returned. In August 1987, San Antonio's City Council appointed an advisory commission to address the issue. Mayor Cisneros appointed to the commission both ex-officio members and a representative from each of the ten council districts. These members provided input and suggestions on ways to improve literacy levels. They worked with a team of literacy providers that represented adults, out of school youth, the library, the numerous San Antonio school districts, and local businesses.

The commission worked closely with the city council and believed that the issue of literacy belonged to the community at large and that the solution lay in the ability of the community to work together in each council district. The commission created a plan that required city funding to support an increase in literacy training locations, a citywide referral service, a volunteer center for literacy, and a central hotline for community information and referral.

The most creative element of the plan was the idea to build a Learning and Leadership Development Center in each council district. The first was completed through a bond as a demonstration in 1998. The bond issue of $5.8 million for the construction of eight learning and leadership development centers was approved unanimously. (Seven more were built, each offering up to thirty adult education classes per week.) This initiative has not been replicated anywhere in the United States.

## The Literacy Coalition of Palm Beach County

Florida's Palm Beach is known for its coastal tourism and residential areas that boast enormous wealth and elegant homes. Inland, sugar cane farms and vegetable nurseries employ thousands of low-paid, low-skilled workers. Each year the workforce expands with migrant workers from Mexico and Central America. Haitian, Cuban, and Mexican immigrants who have settled in the area.

Increasingly high levels of low literacy and limited English proficiency raised a red flag for county leaders and in 1988 stakeholders initiated a community dialogue to address the problem. As a result, a variety of community members, including schools, the media and business, as well as literacy providers, created the Literacy Coalition of Palm Beach County in 1989.

A former marketing executive and community relations director at *The Palm Beach Post*, was the first board chair. She spent many hours in the early weeks of the coalition making calls to rally the community. A publisher provided the backing of the paper to help the effort. An early win was the creation of a countywide literacy hotline, providing a single number for Palm Beach County to call for information about literacy services.

For the first two years of the coalition there was no paid staff. "I just feel it's so important to read," a member of the board said. After the first two years, two $20,000 grants from the James M. Cox Foundation and the Knight Foundation allowed the chair to hire the first employee and president of the Literacy Coalition.

## Philadelphia

In the 1980s, the City of Brotherly Love faced serious crime and the threat of bankruptcy. Parts of the city were infested with crack houses, and gangs and the Mafia was thought to rule South Philadelphia. The murder rate was high and violent race-related tensions were commonplace. Some of these tensions emerged from adult education and job-training-related politics. Anne Fadiman, author of *The Spirit Catches You and You Fall Down*, a 1998 book about Hmong immigrants (a considerable number of which settled in the city after the Laotian Civil War), said that "lower-class residents resented the Hmong receiving federal grants for employment assistance when they were also out of work; they believed that American citizens should be getting assistance first."[19] They believed other neighborhoods and communities also needed literacy as a stepping stone out of poverty.[20]

Then around 1984, Mayor W. Wilson Goode, who in 1984 became Philadelphia's first African-American mayor, created the Commission on Literacy in Philadelphia as a highly visible City Hall initiative. The goal was to build a large-scale literacy coalition that would significantly increase the number of individuals receiving services through volunteer tutor involvement. A carefully constructed strategic plan for a citywide, largely volunteer literacy effort was developed, coordinating activities with existing organizations and agencies in providing cost-effective services. The services included marketing, tutor training, data collection, and development of a resource directory. Staff support was provided through the hiring of an executive director and an administrative assistant located at City Hall in a suite adjoining the mayor's office. The city invested funding that flowed through the Philadelphia Free Library.

The first executive director started her literacy career as a GED teacher and moved on to instructional technology and curriculum development. When the commission was formed, she became its first executive director. Reflecting on her experiences in 2012, she shared: "My varied experience gives me a broad understanding of the field and of agencies of all types and sizes," she said. "I have responded to and advocated for the broad range of providers, moving the field forward, not just the agenda of any one agency or group."[21]

### Houston

In the early 1980s, Houston, nicknamed Space City, was regarded as one of the fastest growing of America's big cities. The economic boom of the 1970s made the city a world leader in the energy business. Hundreds of companies, primarily oil and gas, located their headquarters there. People flocked to the city; a popular car bumper sticker read, "Will the last one out of Michigan please turn out the lights." Houston also began absorbing refugees after the 1975 fall of Saigon and became a magnet for refugee resettlement. High employment, an entrepreneurial spirit, and plenty of entry-level jobs made it an ideal place for relocation. It was a powerful, energetic city and a buzzing, shapeless, sprawling unzoned metropolis. After years of growth, the oil industry went bust in the mid-1980s. NASA's space industry suffered with the loss of the Challenger in 1986. Nearly a dozen banks closed their doors in 1987. Unemployment, a low-skilled workforce, a growing limited English proficient population, and rising poverty highlighted the city's low literacy crisis.

Houston's first female mayor, Kathy Whitmire, asked a council member to head a task force to assess the issue. The council member convened a six-month series of meetings with representatives of the school district, the community college, literacy providers, the director of Houston Public Library, the business community, the *Houston Chronicle*, and key volunteers. The task force published a report recommending the creation of a mayoral commission to address the literacy needs of the city. It primarily focused on adult education through the early learning needs of children and families. The commission was the Mayor's Coalition for Literacy and represented all the sectors involved in the crisis.

The city voted on an initial annual $200,000 grant per year for the development and maintenance of centralized services (tracking learners, recruitment, training and placement of volunteers, and an annual challenge grant for provider support). The remaining funds were to be raised from community businesses and from a fund development committee headed by a *Houston Chronicle* executive. The newspaper raised $1 million in seed funding. In addition, a workforce development Job Training Partnership Act grant (a federal program) was made by the Workforce Investment Board to support a demonstration learning center at the commission's Latino Learning Center site. Office space was provided at no cost high in the Texas Commerce Tower overlooking the city. The superintendent of the Houston Independent School District provided a computer analyst and literacy curriculum specialist as executive director for one year. (That loan was eventually extended for twelve years.) Within six months, the executive director relocated the commission from its prestigious downtown location to a second community learning center in the heart of Houston's Third Ward, an area of high literacy needs and poverty.

## What Connected Early Coalitions?

Goals of the early coalitions included:

- connecting the service providers, especially the nonprofits not funded with federal dollars, whose centers were overflowing with students
- coordinating volunteer recruitment and training

- assisting learners to locate programs by setting up awareness networks and literacy hotlines

The early coalitions worked because of local leadership, especially mayoral support. Coalitions formed as mayoral commissions—for instance in Philadelphia, San Antonio, Houston, and Canton, Ohio—have lasted. One exception is Columbus, Ohio. In Columbus, the coalition took for granted that they would receive city funding each year for operations and did not diversify their funding base. When the annual request for proposals came from the city, the staff did not respond, and the coalition was not funded. It closed within four months. It was a lesson for other coalitions.

Newspaper underwriting was a kingpin of corporate support and both Gannett and Hearst corporate foundations assisted coalitions across the country. The *Houston Chronicle, Los Angeles Times, San Diego Tribune* and *Palm Beach Post* all invested heavily in literacy, and their highly visible support leveraged the support of other corporations. This was, of course appreciated and it reflected an ulterior motive for this investment by news media; it was linked with the paper's bottom line. With a non-literate populace, business could not thrive or even survive over the long haul. It was the perfect partnership for newspapers. The partnerships started as a philanthropic community investment with a long-term vision of improved readership. Initially, as circulation declined, investment increased, but over time the papers created more self-interested proposals that included the distribution of papers to literacy classrooms and grants that included the purchase of papers. The *Houston Chronicle* (Hearst) reduced its funding and then stopped altogether and the *Los Angeles Times* reduced the Literacy Network of Los Angeles suite of offices to a small area as newspaper profits declined and the digital era advanced.

Volunteer leadership and corporate investment is apparent in each of the five examples above. High-powered, well-respected community leaders volunteered hundreds of hours to connect the dots and bring educational, financial, and corporate partners to the table to invest in the success of these pioneering coalitions.

## Coalition Development in the 1990s: 100 Percent Literacy through 100 Percent Community Engagement

The 1990s heralded a period of peace and prosperity in the United States. In addition to the end of the Cold War, this period saw new technology and economic development. Looking back on this era, *New York Times* columnist David Brooks suggested that the United States was experiencing "moral self-repair," as "many of the indicators of social breakdown, which shot upward in the late 1960s and 1970s, and which plateaued at high levels in the 1980s," were now on the decline.[22] The "moral self-repair" was seen in the civil society initiatives of the literacy coalitions, expanding in scale, scope, and number with passionate social justice and civil rights agendas. The movement harkened back to two sayings. The first, some have attributed to Thomas Jefferson, "A nation that expects to be ignorant and free never was and never will be."[23] The second saying is from Frederick Douglass, the escaped slave who became a social reformer and writer, who said, "Once you learn to read you will be forever free."[24]

President George H.W. Bush, First Lady Barbara Bush and President Bill Clinton strongly supported improved literacy. As Clinton noted, "Literacy is not a luxury, it is a right and a responsibility. If our world is to meet the challenges of the 21st century we must harness the creativity and energy of all our citizens."[25] And Barbara Bush reminded us, "Learning never ends, and as we enter the next century, it will be more and more important for all Americans to be lifelong learners. . . . every one of us can contribute in some way to a better-educated America.[26]

The National Literacy Act (NLA) of 1991 (Public Law 102–73) broadened literacy definitions; "for the purposes of this Act the term 'literacy' means an individual's ability to read, write, and speak in English, and to compute and solve problems at levels of proficiency necessary to function on the job and in society, to achieve one's goals and develop one's knowledge and potential."[27] The NLA created pathways for interagency engagement and the involvement of service providers and the workforce development sector. Family, health, and financial literacy were included in the definition, and an amendment to the AEA created the National Institute for Literacy (NIFL), which strongly supported the ever-expanding number of literacy coalitions.

The 1992 National Adult Literacy Survey (NALS) for the first time provided a snapshot of literacy levels in the United States. The results were alarming, confirming concerns and yielding concrete data for the literacy coalitions that reinforced their advocacy for and work toward improved and expanded services. Leaders from local governments, philanthropic foundations, chambers of commerce, United Ways, corporations, and school districts all took note. The data defined the problem and helped drive coalitions toward solutions.

The federal government in 1994 created AmeriCorps, the domestic Peace Corps program, to provide intensive community service work with the goal of providing support for social and educational community needs. The National Institute for Literacy convened the early coalitions to manage Literacy AmeriCorps as a network that included Houston, Palm Beach, Pittsburgh, Los

Angeles, New Orleans, and Seattle. AmeriCorps members committed to full-time service in community outreach, tutoring adults and children, mentoring, and a full range of service learning. Each coalition managed a team of up to eighty AmeriCorps members assigned to provider locations.

Additionally, the America Reads Challenge Act of 1997 focused on children's and family literacy with the proposal to recruit "one million volunteer tutors ready and able to give children the personal attention they need to catch up and get ahead."[28] This opened the door for existing adult education-focused coalitions to engage in the effort and embrace the growing issues of family literacy. Houston and Palm Beach coalitions were among the first to take up the challenge. The Houston READ Commission experience is described in Tutoring Programs for Struggling Readers: The America Reads Challenge.[29]

To support the new literacy dialogue, in 1990 the U.S. Department of Education partnered with the Departments of Labor and Health and Human Services to create the National Center on Adult Literacy (NCAL). Its mission "addresses three primary challenges: (a) to enhance the knowledge base about adult literacy; (b) to improve the quality of research and development in the field; and (c) to ensure a strong, two-way relationship between research and practice."[30] Further, through "applied research and development and dissemination of the results to researchers, policymakers, and practitioners," NCAL provided the research base to support the developing coalitions.[31]

Growing numbers of immigrants who needed English-language classes continued to drive coalition expansion. The 1996 welfare reform threatened to reduce rights that immigrants had traditionally retained, including access to food stamps and other federally funded social services. That spurred immigrants to seek citizenship. Despite subsequent amendments to the law, citizenship has retained an elevated profile as a goal for many adult learners from abroad. Among its many benefits are easier access to privileges such as a passport, the right to vote, and access to public benefits such as full Social Security benefits when they retire and Supplemental Security Income (SSI).[32] Additionally, it helps to reduce the risk of being deported for committing a crime and enables them to sponsor family members for immigration.[33] Coalitions supported service providers offering English-language classes and helped advocate for increased services. Houston Mayor Lee P. Brown first used the phrase "100 percent literacy through 100 percent community engagement" in 1991, and the message was picked up by coalitions all over the country, amplified by thousands of 100 percent lapel pins and marketing slogans.

The literacy coalition movement took off in the 1990s and, as it did, the need for coordination and collaboration among the coalitions became apparent. The coalition leaders in Palm Beach, Seattle, Cincinnati, Houston, San Diego, and Washington, D.C., began talking; the seeds for the National

Alliance of Urban Literacy Coalitions (NAULC) were sown in 1995 after an initial national convening by the United Way of America. NAULC's mission was "to promote and strengthen urban literacy coalitions in their efforts to create literate communities, thereby enhancing the quality of life and vitality of our cities.[34] They sought to accomplish this by "sharing best practices and resources, gathering and disseminating critical information, building awareness of the literacy issue, and advocating for literacy services."[35] The corporate advisory board was formed, including such big names as Dollar General, Verizon, Time Warner and Half Price Books. NAULC brought the coalitions together for annual meetings for the next twelve years and represented the coalitions in national forums including the National Coalition for Literacy, National Institute for Literacy, U.S. Department of Education, and the National Center for Adult Literacy and Learning.

*Literacy Mid-South (Memphis)*

In the 1990s, Memphis was the biggest urban area in Tennessee and the biggest city on the Mississippi. The city, the Birthplace of Rock and Roll, had a strong musical heritage and a growing tourism industry. FedEx Corporation (originally Federal Express) had moved its operations to Memphis in 1973 because of its advanced airport facilities. FedEx, like Verizon and Dollar General, embraced literacy as its corporate cause and started an era of substantial corporate contributions to support literacy coalitions.

The low literacy rates of the city's majority black population echoed the inequality Dr. Martin Luther King highlighted decades earlier. In 1968 when Dr. King travelled to Memphis, his goal was to address the conditions of African-American public works employees. Black street repairmen, for example, received lower pay than whites on days when weather forced cancellations.[36] The racial inequality continued well into the 1990s, underscoring the need for literacy services.

Mid-South Reads was inspired by the America Reads Challenge initiative and was started by a former executive director, the PBS station, and a local order of nuns. Housed in the University of Memphis, it had the support of the academic community and access to student volunteers. "As an organization that encourages reading and lifelong learning, Mid-South Reads recognizes the important role corporate sponsors play in our community. Our successful partnerships and book serials have proven effective in promoting the benefits of reading. We help young people become better students and lifetime readers," a staff member said.

The organization's name is now Literacy Mid-South (LMS), but the mission continues. The organization aims to create a community actively engaged in continuous learning to address the issues and inequities in Memphis by working with and through service provider partners.

## Project READ Coalition, Dayton, Ohio

Despite its storied past as the home of the Wright brothers and later in the 1990s the Wright-Patterson Air Force Base, Dayton's reputation as a hub of aeronautical innovation did not insulate it from the challenges of illiteracy. Much like the rest of the state of Ohio, where 16 to 18 percent of adults scored at the lowest levels of literacy,[37] Dayton had some work to do. Corporations needed a skilled workforce as the city grew and thrived, but low literacy levels stifled recruitment.

Ohio was unique in the strategies it adopted to implement the Adult Education Act. Enlightened leadership recognized that community collaboration and coordination would increase service delivery and provide more impactful results. The Ohio Department of Education encouraged the development of a literacy coalition in each of the state's major cities, including Cleveland, Canton, Columbus, Cincinnati, and Dayton. The state adult education department provided coordinated trainings, professional development, and intense tracking of students.

Since July 1990, Sinclair Community College has housed Project READ, Dayton's literacy coalition. The partnership was unique. Struggling college students could join adult learners in the program. Research was beginning to identify that students enrolled in community colleges seldom moved from remedial to credit-bearing classes. Project READ operated a Helpline to match adult learners and volunteers with local literacy programs. It served youth through its Miami Valley READS children's tutoring program, part of America Reads. The Literacy AmeriCorps Dayton program increased the capacity of local literacy programs by placing full-time, well-trained members to serve as instructors at a fraction of the cost of paid instructors. Finally, Project READ developed an outreach and media approach that informed the public about literacy through a multi-media campaign and involvement in local community events.

## First Literacy, Boston

With a high density of colleges and a major financial center, Boston has a diverse economic base and a high cost of living, and housing prices rocketed during the 1990s. Boston boasts the nation's first public school and first subway system. Due largely to the high density of technology companies, the economic think tank Milken rates Boston as one of the country's top cities for biotechnology.[38] This has repercussions not only for bragging rights but also because the biotech industry has a reputation for generating high-paying jobs and underwriting local prosperity. This industry has been helped along by National Institutes of Health grants that have been higher in Boston than all other cities in the United States.[39]

Dramatic population changes helped to create the literacy challenges that the city began to address in the 1990s. Between the 1950s and the new millennium, the population shifted from nearly all white to mostly not white.[40] The change was driven by immigration from Puerto Rico, Dominican Republic, El Salvador, and Guatemala as immigrants moved to the city and took low-paying jobs.

By the early 1990s, the Boston Adult Literacy Fund (now First Literacy), which had started to raise resources for literacy, began to look more like a literacy coalition than a foundation. Mayor Raymond Flynn and the *Boston Globe* publisher were part of the community leadership team that created the fund. The first executive director envisioned participatory community engagement that would set the fund apart from similar entities. Working for the Boston Adult Literacy Fund (BALF) combined staff commitment to improving the community and their passion for literacy as the tool for change. The concept of catalytic philanthropy was not popularized until after the turn of the century, but the idea was nevertheless the driving force for the work of the Fund.

## Literacy Coalition of Central Texas (Austin)

While much of the country was experiencing economic depression in the 1980s, Austin was growing as a university town and center for developing technology. By the 1990s, its reputation as a hub of government employees, high tech experts, blue-collar workers, and business leaders was flying high. The city's growing literacy problem was scarcely evident.

In the late 1990s, Austin's department heads began to meet about the low skill levels of city workers and helped to raise awareness about the issue. The Central Texas Literacy Coalition got off to a slow start. It lacked the visibility of a literacy mayor, had little funding, and relied on volunteer leadership. However, the *Austin Statesman*, like so many newspapers across the country, stepped in to help. The Central Texas Literacy Coalition marketed its goal to increase literacy levels by means of a coalition of partner organizations that aspired to a vision of 100 percent literacy that includes literacy as a universal civil right. The coalition's goal was to create effective collaborative mechanisms for people with limited literacy skills and English as a Second Language (ESL) needs to gain the skills necessary to succeed in the workforce, assist families to self-sufficiency, and improve quality of life through a lifelong learning network.

In the late 1990s Chambers of Commerce across the country joined the thriving coalition movement in significant leadership roles. Baton Rouge and Austin are great examples. The Austin Chamber of Commerce was fully engaged in projects supporting activities to ensure strong economic growth in the area. The partnership's relationship with the business community made it an ideal organization to convene discussion around the serious issue of workforce literacy, championing the work of the coalition and the providers it represented. Numerous stakeholders in the Austin area are invested in the workforce of the future, but they did not work as a cohesive unit. As the labor market changed and the need for skilled workers increased, the Chamber and the Central Texas Literacy Coalition framed their work as helping to build a stronger workforce. Austin also benefitted in those days, like many of the early coalitions, from the local newspaper. The *Austin Statesman* stepped up to provide both financial support and a tool for public awareness of low literacy.

## The Literacy Council of Central Alabama

Since its founding in 1871, all the way to the end of the 1960s, Birmingham has built a reputation as one of south's great industrial centers. The city was a hub for railroad-related industry; workers needed more brawn than brain to succeed in the big industrial plants. But while the railroad was a uniting force, there were also considerable divisions. By 1963, Birmingham was known as one of the South's most segregated cities.[41] The city was in the spotlight during the civil rights movement, a legacy President John F. Kennedy noted by saying, "The events in Birmingham . . . have so increased the cries for equality that no city or state or legislative body can prudently choose to ignore them."[42] The bombing of the Sixteenth Street Baptist Church that killed four girls in 1963 focused attention on civil rights and the role that equal education opportunity plays in the dialogue.

By the 1970s, urban-renewal efforts emerged. As the economy flourished, banking developed, and new construction marked the new found growing prosperity. In 1979, Birmingham elected Dr. Richard Arrington Jr. as its first African-American mayor, pledging to make Birmingham a city "of which all her people could be proud" and promoting educational opportunity for all.[43] However, by the 1990s, the city population was falling as "white flight" took substantial numbers to growing suburbs and many Black students attended schools that looked as if Brown vs. the Board of Education never happened.

In 2007 the Community Foundation of Greater Birmingham's president, noted that, "If we can find something to get our arms around and work together, the trust will come . . . . . by action, we're going to build this trust."[44] One thing that the city rallied behind was the developing literacy coalition. The Literacy Council of Central Alabama formed with a vision to address functional illiteracy and strengthen and support organizations teaching people to read in Jefferson and the surrounding counties. The Junior League of Birmingham and the United Way of Central Alabama formed The Literacy Council in 1991.

What were the links among coalitions founded in the 1990s? These coalitions achieved major milestones for the coalition movement including, making "With Literacy and Justice for All" a national slogan and then spreading the motto "100 percent Literacy Through 100 percent Community Engagement." Goals of the 1990s coalitions included:

- connecting service providers, especially the nonprofits not funded with federal dollars, whose doors were overflowing with students
- coordinating volunteer recruitment and training
- assisting learners to locate programs by setting up marketing networks and literacy hotlines
- advocating for change
- broadening collaborations to include children's and family literacy

## COALITIONS IN THE NEW MILLENNIUM: THE 2000s TO 2010s—FIVE COALITION EXAMPLES

With the global financial crisis in 2008 and downturn in the oil industry, the economy tried to rebound robustly from a major recession, but the return of jobs in the sluggish labor market was slow. The diversity of the United States is an enormous strength and the destiny of the labor market depends on it. The phrase "demography is destiny" is attributed to the nineteenth-century French mathematician and philosopher August Comte, the "father of sociology."[45] Immigration plays a major role in the growth and racial and ethnic diversity of the population. During this decade, population changes heralded more challenges for the growing coalition movement while also creating new opportunities.

All racial groups are projected to grow over the 2010–2020 period.[46] As the proportion of White non-Latino in the total population decreased, non- and limited English speakers, some of whom are not literate in their own language, placed an additional burden on the adult and children's education systems. That, combined with the falling birth rate, impacted the ability to maintain the size and skills of the workforce. Additionally, as the population grays, it must be replaced by a new and more skilled workforce to meet the more sophisticated and technological needs driving the economy. The developing mid-level skills gap heralded an equally significant entry-level skill deficit as coalitions promoted programs to support vocational training and skills development along with competency-based outcomes. As these changes occurred, so did the approaches to collaboration and the need for an even broader-based network of partners and the creation of more coordinated approaches to ensure a skilled workforce. It is worth noting that rural communities have lagged far behind their urban counterparts. The trend to growing urban and less rural populations continues with 80 percent of the population living in cities and only 20 percent in rural areas.[47]

This is the decade of new and improved coalitions, a mixture of "twinkle to wrinkle," child focused and adult focused, but all increasing the push toward skills and competencies. Policies such as the Workforce Innovation and Opportunity Act (WIOA), which would replace WIA from 2015–2020, sought to address this need. As the National Association of Workforce Boards asserted: "We believe that WIOA can help assure that U.S. companies will remain competitive and grow jobs, that our domestic workforce has the guidance and pathways needed to obtain required skills, and that our communities have the workforce development system to remain strong."[48] In addition, three critical changes influenced this development: collective impact; cross-sector partnerships; and the impact of new and innovative national initiatives.

An article on collective impact (written by consulting firm FSG for the Winter 2011 volume of *Stanford Social Innovation Review)* heralded a change that was embraced by the coalition movement and altered the way leadership addressed their operating systems and coalition performance. Collective impact proponents assert, "Large-scale social change requires broad cross-sector coordination, yet the social sector remains focused on the isolated interventions of individual organizations."[49] Coalition leaders adopted a new way of "seeing, learning, and doing that marries emergent solutions with intentional outcomes."[50] The collective impact model provided a framework that coalitions could easily embrace. It included the following five criteria for success: common agenda, mutually reinforcing activities, backbone support, shared measurement, and continuous communication.[51] A follow-up report in 2013, *Embracing Emergence: How Collective Impact Addresses Complexity*, by Kania and Kramer, describes collective impact as challenging conventional thinking on how to achieve social change and organizational effectiveness. Organizations, they claim "have grasped the difference our past articles emphasized between the isolated impact of working for change through a single organization versus a highly structured cross-sector coalition."[52] This decade has focused on the change from a literacy coalition struggling alone to a multi-faceted partnership of broad community collaboration. This change was partly, but significantly, driven by the emerging success of the StriveTogether Cradle to Career Network and the Campaign for Grade-Level Reading.

The Literacy Powerline network, which originally brought together more than one hundred coalitions with the help of Literacy USA, saw the Strive and CGLR collaborations more than double the number of coalitions across the country. Many embraced both new models, looking to incorporate the best and most results-based strategies of all systems. The StriveTogether Cradle to Career Network promoted collective impact with both new and re-tooling coalitions in a national network of "64 community partnerships in 32 states and Washington, D.C., working to improve education success for every child by bringing together cross-sector partners around a common vision."[53] It is based on the goal of seeking effective structure and data-driven results. Being a member of the StriveTogether Cradle to Career Network includes making a commitment to the following:

- "Improving and reporting on a core set of academic outcomes: kindergarten readiness, early grade reading, middle grade math, high school graduation, postsecondary enrollment, and postsecondary degree completion
- Building cross-sector partnerships with early childhood, K–12, higher education, community-based organizations, business, government, and philanthropy
- Developing and sustaining cradle-to-career civic infrastructure by implementing a data-driven, quality approach to collective impact"[54]

The GLR Campaign is a "collaborative effort led by foundations, nonprofit partners, business leaders, government agencies, states, and communities across the nation to ensure that more children in low-income families succeed in school and graduate prepared for college, a career, and active citizenship."[55] The campaign takes a different approach by selecting a change goal based on a point in time. It focuses on reading on grade level by the end of third grade, which is an important predictor of school success and high school graduation.

This approach is based on the belief that students who read proficiently by the end of third grade are more likely able to make the transition from learning to read to reading to learn. Poverty, poor education, limited reading modeling in the home, lack of books, and other indicators this approach highlights, can specifically predict which children will not succeed. Furthermore it holds that students who do not meet the third-grade challenge continue to struggle and are the most at risk of dropping out and feeding the ranks of the adult education programs.

Although it is the job of schools to teach reading, success is more assured with support from the community. Taking a perspective resonant with Bronfenbrenner's ecological systems model, communities began to embrace the perspective that schools cannot do it alone; in this decade, the growing numbers of coalitions took on the promotion of this community-wide message.[56] Coalitions mobilized to remove barriers to help students succeed. The CGLR focused on resolving the gaps in kindergarten readiness, attendance, and summer learning loss slide, and many coalitions joined the movement. Marketing and messaging ramped up as television and radio picked up the challenge. Coalitions operated on the truism that "When no one knows about an issue, no one cares." Marketing was seen as key to the success of a coalition.

In some communities where the CGLR and StriveTogether overlap, groups are using collective impact principles to improve grade-level reading proficiency. "Many of the Network's partnerships have taken advantage of what the Campaign offers to improve outcomes in school readiness, school attendance and summer learning and ultimately, grade-level reading," said one StriveTogether staff member.[57] She continued: "Grade-level reading is one of our six focus areas because reading proficiency by the end of third grade is the most important predictor of high school graduation and career success. More than 80 percent of low-income children miss this milestone so we are fortunate to partner with the Campaign."[58]

Concurrently, "The Campaign for Grade-Level Reading (GLR Campaign) communities across the country are finding value in incorporating tools and support from StriveTogether and other collective impact efforts into their work," said Ron Fairchild, director of the GLR Support Center, which provides assistance to over 300 local GLR Campaign initiatives in 42 states, plus the District of Columbia, Puerto Rico, and the U.S. Virgin Islands.

"One way for GLR Campaign communities to best achieve lasting results is to connect and align with broader community-change efforts that offer organizational strength and know-how to support grade-level reading work long term," Fairchild noted. "We see particular strength in communities that have used the GLR Campaign's focus on results and its framework for community solutions as an integrated component in their overall collective impact approach."[59]

On June 13, 2009, the coalitions attending the National Community Literacy Convention in Buffalo, New York, passed the Right to Literacy Declaration, another messaging tool to bring community together around the issue. The declaration spells out five "pillars" that explain the importance of literacy: "building the community; strengthening the family; ensuring people's self-determination; improving the workforce; and transforming the education system."[60] The Declaration was printed on a scroll, which convention delegates signed and sent on a journey across the United States to communities large and small.

By 2012, the declaration had collected 50,000 signatures, including those of mayors, community leaders, educators, employers, adult learners, and funders. The campaign chairs presented the Right to Literacy Scroll to UNESCO's Education Sector, at a ceremony at UNESCO Headquarters in Paris presided over by Svein Osttveit, director of the Education Sector's Executive Office. Then-Secretary of State Hillary Clinton was the final signatory prior to its presentation. Unfurled, the declaration measures 424-feet long, taller that the U.S. Capitol building and taller than the Eiffel Tower. The scroll traveled more than 485,000 miles through hundreds of postal workers' hands, supported by national organizations including the U.S. Conference of Mayors, the Literacy Funders Network, ProLiteracy, the National Center for Family Literacy, CGLR, StriveTogether, the Council on Foundations, and many others. Coalitions used the marketing event to bring together new partners, announce key goals and targets, and share successes with their communities.

But as so often happens in the literacy coalition field, as a new impetus was created an old one passed away. On September 30, 2010, the National Institute for Literacy (NIFL) closed and merged with the Office of Vocational and Adult Education (OVAE). Since its creation in 1991, the NILC had: "served as a catalyst for improving opportunities for adults, youth, and children to develop literacy as a national asset, using knowledge, research, and practice."[61] It worked with the secretaries of Education, Labor, and Health and Human Services. As "a national literacy resource, the Institute's program officers contributed to improving literacy across the lifespan."[62]

The initial focus had been to shine a spotlight on adult education as well as children's literacy. The institute had been formed by a bipartisan effort that responded to the urging of the literacy field after the growing awareness of the 1991 National Literacy Act. With an independent board, albeit one appointed by the president, it did not always align with the views of the Department of Education (DOE) and was the one federal agency that provided a voice for the coalition and the nonprofit literacy field. At NIFL, the first national plans for evaluating literacy coalitions emerged as coalition leaders and evaluation experts served on NIFL's Coalition Evaluation Committee. However, with the growing strength of early childhood education and third-grade reading, as well as the strengthening of OVAE with a workforce and vocational training mandate, change was coming. Part of the issue was that NIFL reported to three agencies: the Departments of Education (DOE), Labor (DOL), and Health and Human Services (HHS) that were also mandated to meet literacy outcomes. As one veteran of the field shares, having multiple masters meant it was hard to measure success and was an easy target in larger power struggles:

As I recall, NIFL became a political football and the administration was looking
for an example of wasteful funding and this was one area of poorly spent funds.
They cut the funds but didn't eliminate NIFL and then merged the function with
DOE. Some saw this as a move by OVAE to consolidate power. NIFL had been
criticized for focusing too much on children's literacy. (Washington, D.C.)

While collective impact was growing, federal agencies took a while to catch
up with the community-based momentum. But one of the last efforts at NIFL
before it closed was the Great Cities Summit. Adult literacy learners seeking
services in larger urban metropoles of Los Angeles, Miami, New York, Chicago, and Houston are a significant percent of all students served in federally
funded adult education programs. The challenges and opportunities that coalitions face in these large urban areas are often quite unique when compared
with those in other areas of the country.[63]

By participating, these five cities gained access to resources for increasing evidence-based teacher instruction and technical assistance in building
capacity to coordinate key partners. The 2012 NIFL white paper, "Coalition
Building: A Tool for Improved Community Literacy," developed the following thesis for coalition collective impact and in many ways foreshadowed and
reinforced the popularity of Kania and Kramer's approach:

> Common agenda: In a coalition, those gathered around the table share a com-
> mon understanding of the problem and a vision for the best way to solving it
> through collective actions.[64]
>
> Mutually reinforcing activity: A diverse group of community stakeholders
> work together, not by requiring that all participants do the same thing, but by
> encouraging each participant to undertake the specific set of activities at which
> it excels in a way that supports and is coordinated with the actions of others.
>
> Backbone support organizations: A separate organization and staff with a very
> specific set of skills serve as the backbone for the entire initiative.
>
> Shared measurement systems: A shared measurement system is in place to
> collect, analyze, and learn from data for a continuous improvement process.
>
> Continuous communications: Development of trust among businesses, school
> districts, nonprofits, corporations, and government agencies is a monumental
> challenge. It takes time and trust to build up enough experience with partners
> to recognize and appreciate the common motivation behind different efforts.[65]

Although NIFL closed, the dialogue and collaboration among the great cities
has continued. The closing of NIFL was not the only change in the landscape.
In 2015, Literacy Powerline merged into and became a service arm of the
National Center for Families Learning.

Place-based intervention was also a theme of the decade, and the Federal
Government's Promise Neighborhoods, established by the Fund for the

Improvement of Education Program (FIE), provided funding to support a vision that all children in Promise Neighborhoods would have the ability to learn at excellent schools with the kind of support that leads to academic and workplace success. The goal is to improve the education system and the educational results in the most challenged zip codes across the country. The concept was to create community transformation by:

- "Identifying and increasing the capacity of eligible entities focusing on achieving results for children and youth throughout an entire neighborhood;
- Building a complete continuum of cradle-to-career solutions of both educational programs and family and community supports, with great schools at the center;
- Integrating programs and breaking down agency "silos" so that solutions are implemented effectively and efficiently across agencies;
- Developing the local infrastructure of systems and resources needed to sustain and scale up proven, effective solutions across the broader region beyond the initial neighborhood; and
- Learning about the overall impact of the Promise Neighborhoods program and about the relationship between particular strategies in Promise Neighborhoods and student outcomes, including through a rigorous evaluation of the program."[66]

One-year grants were won in 2010 by over twenty communities. By 2012, Promise Neighborhoods were in twenty states and the District of Columbia.[67]

The common themes of each of the above collaborative initiatives further strengthened the coalition movement and added systems, structure for data collection, accountability, and a collective voice. The following coalitions serve as examples.

## Literacy Coalition of Onondaga County

Syracuse, nicknamed the salt city due to salt mining that attracted early settlers, has leveraged its location at the center of New York State. It flourished as the home of the Iroquois confederacy, and later as a crossroads of the historic Erie Canal corridor and a key player in the underground railroad. After World War II the city saw a decline in manufacturing and an increase in unemployment. Today, Syracuse has many small employers which provide a certain amount of stability, and the unemployment rate remains level.

A shift to education and service industry created a need for a more highly skilled workforce and from this foundation grew the city's reputation as a literacy leader. The region's literacy roots run deep. Syracuse has long been known as a literacy capital of the United States due to the birth of two major adult literacy organizations that eventually spread nationwide and even internationally. The Laubach Literacy method of teaching adult education was developed in Syracuse in the 1930s, and Ruth Colvin began Literacy Volunteers of America in the 1960s. The national organizations merged in 2002 with headquarters in Syracuse, becoming the largest literacy volunteer organization in the country: ProLiteracy International.

In the early 2000s the community began to address the issues of low literacy in Onondaga County that have been linked with high levels of concentrated poverty, low graduation rates, and a continuous influx of refugees. An inclusive community planning process and needs assessment led to the adoption of the motto "100 percent literacy through 100 percent community engagement" and the coalition was off and running with its lifelong learning plans. Community partners soon joined in, including colleges, child care, libraries, schools, foundations, and media. The coalition determined, "It's time for a collective approach to literacy solutions and, ultimately, measurable systemic change."[68]

The community action plan was based on seven strategic goals, each with its own action steps and impact indicators: advocate for literacy; build partnerships; grow capacity; inform the community; provide resources; evaluate and report progress; and strengthen the coalition.[69] The coalition was one of the first to join the Campaign for Grade-Level Reading and develop a Community Solutions Action Plan for early learning. The campaign recognized the coalition as a national pacesetter three times. As part of that effort, the coalition embraced the Dolly Parton Imagination Library. It has become a model site for the book distribution program and has been invited to present its ongoing research on the program's impact both nationally and internationally. As part of its approach, Syracuse also was the first city in the nation to launch Say Yes to Education citywide. This program was fully endowed in 2016 and provides to graduates of city schools last dollar grants to guarantee students will receive full college funding at a long list of participating public and private colleges.

## The Learning Network of Greater Kalamazoo

As the forests of West Michigan were logged out, paper mills closed and the city looked as if it would follow other Rust Belt cities into depression. Kalamazoo was also home to Kalamazoo College, Kalamazoo Valley Community College, and Western Michigan University, as well as major pharmaceutical and medical science companies. In the last decade, the city has also become known for its approach to "community capitalism," a concept that invests in the success and well-being of the whole community.

Kalamazoo has seen a rise in high school students living in low-income households in recent years. Approximately 66 percent of those entering ninth grade in 2010 qualified for the free and reduced lunch programs, compared to just 43 percent in 2004.[70] Despite lagging behind the state with higher poverty levels, graduation rates for the city increased over the same period. "What Kalamazoo has accomplished by pulling itself up by its own bootstraps during the past decade is truly extraordinary," said Ron Kitchens, author of *Community Capitalism*, a 2008 book about Kalamazoo. "The city has simply refused to become another dying town and its initiatives can inspire other communities to dig deep and mobilize their own resources. We believe that the principles of *Community Capitalism* can be replicated globally."[71] These principles include support for students graduating from high school to attend college through the Kalamazoo Promise. Thanks to anonymous donations, this program is able to cover up to full tuition and fees for any public post-secondary institution in Michigan.[72]

The principles of community capitalism were at work in the formation of the coalition, the Learning Network, which works with nonprofits in Kalamazoo County to increase literacy levels. The Learning Network is more than a coordinating collective impact organization and a funding network; it is also the focal point for educational dialogue and change. It creates Action Networks around the issues it addresses, looking at what works and why and replicates best practices and programs, including Parents as Teachers, CGLR, and Strive Together.

With a goal of building a lifelong learning culture the Learning Network is an example of a community adopting and adapting the best of successful collective impact and integrating it through a coalition supporting lifelong learning. The goals of the Network focus on research-based community level outcomes, driving with data and ensuring that accountability and metrics are available to measure success.

## Literacy Campaign for Monterey County, California

The county of Monterey, with an old Spanish influence and glorious coast-line, is loved by tourists and is the heart of one of the nation's most popular vacation destinations. However, outside the wealth of the city lies an agricultural farming county that struggles with issues of poverty and poor educational success. To address the county's low literacy, the Monterey Community Foundation and the Literacy Campaign Steering Committee studied the status of literacy, including both a review of published literature and reaching out to community members and local experts.[73] They discovered that a considerable number of people, especially those between the ages of 18 and 35 years, had low literacy skills. This is the only coalition that has focused on an age-based action target in this way, and they did so because these are critical years where youth make the transition to the workforce as well as often to parenting the next generation.

A literacy plan was designed to represent the broad community stakeholders and the following goals guide the daily work of the campaign:

• Raise awareness regarding literacy needs and advocate for literacy in Monterey County.
• Build partnerships with and among businesses, literacy service providers, the community, and other stakeholders.
• Provide leadership around countywide literacy efforts and promote best practices.
• Provide and support ongoing skills development of service providers.
• Evaluate the effectiveness of the county's literacy efforts.
• Identify and pursue funding sources in support of literacy initiatives.[74]

The Literacy Campaign was born as a collaborative effort to increase literacy levels and was incubated in the Community Foundation as it grew into a new nonprofit. Partners included parents, program participants, community agencies, law enforcement, churches, civic groups, schools, and businesses committed to working together to address this vital issue. Every coalition is as different as the community it serves, but the goals each sets reflect the same movement toward outcomes and community improvement.

## Community Literacy Initiative of Western Michigan (Grand Rapids)

Grand Rapids, home of Amway health and beauty products, was also renowned for its skilled woodworkers before the end of the nineteenth century. As lumber became more scarce, steel furniture production replaced many of the woodworking factories and eventually technology, advanced manufacturing, and the health care sectors grew, lessening the need for a skilled blue collar workforce.

The Community Literacy Initiative (CLI) followed a familiar coalition development pattern of support for lifelong learning in West Michigan. CLI was initially called Greater Grand Rapids Reads and is a sponsored activity of the Literacy Center of West Michigan.[75] Under the leadership of the president of the Grand Rapids Community College, the mayor and the United Way, the community initiated a planning process called Grand Rapids Reads. The group created task forces and undertook research to explore the depth and breadth of the issues of low literacy. The Community Literacy Initiative of Western Michigan took shape and began to impact the growth and development of the programs it supported. It maintained direct services, as many coalitions do, to fill gaps identified in planning. These services included tutoring programs for children and adults as well as services to employers for vocational and workforce education. Coalitions have been conflicted over the years with the question of whether it is appropriate to provide direct services or to offer indirect services that do not impact students directly but focus more on support for the partner organizations in the coalition. As in the case with Grand Rapids, many coalitions have used a guiding principle: If services conflict with a partner's program they are avoided, and if they support partner services or fill a gap, they are offered.

CLI received funding from the W.K. Kellogg Foundation and the Doug & Maria DeVos Foundation. Its goals include strategically stepping up place-based initiatives determined by specific community needs and partnering with community organizations to ensure coordination of efforts through its creation of several Hope Zones. They initially began in central and west neighborhoods before eventually expanding to eastern and southern neighborhoods.[76]

## Portland ConnectED, Maine

Portland is the economic capital of Maine, with both the state's largest port and the largest city. As a tourist destination, Portland is known for its many restaurants. It is a city that has renewed itself many times; the city seal depicts a phoenix rising from ashes to show its spirit of regrowth. Epitomizing this phoenix-like quality is the recent reinvention seen by its embracing of two key coalition development initiatives: it is both a StriveTogether community and a CGLR partner. The city took on the projects in part to address the growing education disparity in which only two fifths of Portland's low income and minority students are on grade level as compared to 63 percent of students overall.[77] After reviewing educational statistics in 2013, the Mayor of Portland, Michal Brennan, determined to explore community solutions and created Portland ConnectED. This has developed into a collaborative effort linking the Campaign for Grade-Level Reading with the Strive Together Network. "We'd heard good things about both models and knew we needed partners locally, regionally, and nationally to optimize our impact," said a representative of Portland ConnectED.[78] "We credit a lot of our growth to our involvement with both [Starting Strong and the CGLR effort]."[79] Despite a thriving economy, Portland suffers from many of the troubles that plague other cities, including an achievement gap. "The mayor and other partners immediately recognized that education was going to be the key to sustaining Portland's civic and economic growth," a staff member said.[80] "Portland ConnectED's twelve founding partners pledged to increase third-grade reading proficiency from 63 to 85 percent, especially among minority and low-income children; high school graduation from 79 to 91 percent; and postsecondary degree completion from 43 to 50 percent by 2017."[81]

The campaign helped bring together the initiative's many partners, starting in March 2013 when the CGLR's Ron Fairchild keynoted the Starting Strong conference. With a communication structure intended to keep all engaged, the partners are committed to success. With the StriveTogether support and data driven framework, tools, and sustainability plans are in place. From the beginning, Portland emphasized partnerships, "We encourage our partnerships to connect with the Campaign's network because it offers some of the most proven and promising solutions to the challenges and barriers to reaching reading proficiency, which is at the front end of StriveTogether's cradle-to-career continuum," a Strive representative said.[82]

## Themes of the New Millennium

What themes characterize the new millennium? Perhaps most striking when compared with the earlier cohorts is that these coalitions have been placing greater emphasis on young and school-aged children as well as the pipeline to college. Some have even set up full college scholarships for all their community's youth. Furthermore, efforts have relied heavily on national frameworks and champions or "purveyors" of certain coalition approaches and practices (such as StriveTogether and CGLR), an important development in the coalition movement that we will explore further in future chapters. Finally, with the continuation of coalition formation in the new millennium we see the coalition movement developing into a sustained field that has not withered away as have so many social intervention fads. Rather, it appears to be a field with staying power that continues to reinvent itself by embracing newcomers and assimilating their ideas into an evolving set of best practices. In a sense, the coalition movement has emulated the nation's immigration policy as a whole by taking pages from both its history of the great American melting pot and the salad bowl metaphor for celebrating cultural diversity (see figure 1.3).

## CONCLUSION

As seen in the preceding pages, the decades of the new millennium are characterized by creating new programs, new results, and inspiring new part-

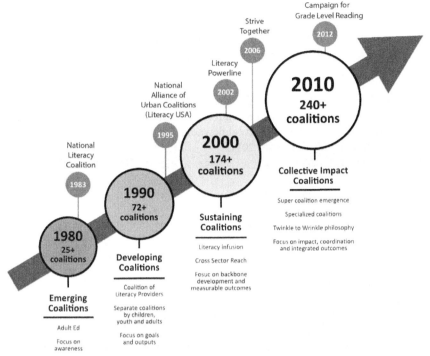

**Figure 1.3.   Dominant coalition themes over time.**
Graphic courtesy of the authors.

nerships. The three critical change agents—collective impact, cross sector partnerships, and the impact of new and innovative national initiatives—are showing promise. While space does not permit us to introduce all the national coalitions in detail, we hope these exemplars provide a feel for the local color of different coalitions across the nation and a sense of how their place in specific periods of national history influenced coalition development. Noticeable among the influential factors of the previous pages have been funder led and supported initiatives. In the following chapter, we explore the critical relationship between funders and the catalytic philanthropy strategies they use to support the coalition movement.

In this chapter, we have learned that coalitions can start from any number of individual sparks of interest and that there is no one "right" way. Coalition backbone organizations can be many sizes and shapes; no one size fits all. The lynchpin has been the dedication of the founding individual(s), the creation of powerful impactful missions, and measurable accountability, all driven by hard work and persistence.

# NOTES

1. Note: In this and subsequent chapters we identify each quote by the state they come from to demonstrate the diversity of locations involved but we do not share the specific location to maintain confidentiality. We have edited some quotations for brevity and clarity.

2. Pacheco, York, Dean, & Sarasvathy, 2010.

3. We also confirmed some of this information from the following web site (n.d.) Retrieved March 3, 2017, from www.gmlcwi.org.

4. Ridzi, Carmody & Byrnes, 2011.

5. Aldrich et al., 2009.

6. Butterfoss, 2007, 33.

7. Feighery & Rogers, 1990.

8. Butterfoss, 2007.

9. (n.d.) Retrieved April 3, 2017, from http://aspe.dhhs.gov/health/reports/2010/ sustainlit/report.shtml.

10. DHHS, Office of Health Policy, ASPE 2010, 7 http://aspe.dhhs.gov/health/ reports/2010/sustainlit/report.shtml (n.d.) Retrieved April 3, 2017, from http://aspe .dhhs.gov/health/reports/2010/sustainlit/report.shtml.

11. Butterfoss, 2007, 34.

12. (n.d.). Retrieved from http://www.amistadresource.org/the_future_in_the_ present/social_and_economic_issues.html.

13. U.S. House of Representatives 1987, 308). (Ends or Means: An Overview of the History of the Adult Education Act by Amy D. Rose Information Series No. 346—ERIC Clearinghouse.

14. Beder, 1991.

15. U.S. House of Representatives, 1991.

16. (n.d.) Retrieved April 3, 2017, from http://literacysandiego.org/about-the -council.

17. (n.d.) Retrieved April 3, 2017, from http://literacysandiego.org/about-the -council.

18. (n.d.). Retrieved April 3, 2017, from http://www.absoluteastronomy.com/top ics/Henry_Cisneros.

19. (n.d.). Retrieved April 3, 2017, from http://www.gradesaver.com/the-spirit -catches-you-and-you-fall-down.

20. http://www.gradesaver.com/the-spirit-catches-you-and-you-fall-down. (n.d.). Retrieved April 3, 2017, from http://www.gradesaver.com/the-spirit-catches -you-and-you-fall-down.

21. (n.d.). Retrieved April 3, 2017, from https://philaliteracyalliance.files.word press.com/2012/03/rose-brandt.pdf.

22. Brooks, D. (2005, August 7). The Virtues of Virtue. Retrieved April 3, 2017, from http://www.nytimes.com/2005/08/07/opinion/the-virtues-of-virtue.html?_r=0.

23. (n.d.). Retrieved April 3, 2017, from https://www.monticello.org/site/jefferson/ if-we-are-guard-against-ignorance-spurious-quotation. Note there is some discussion about the origins of this quote.

24. (n.d.). Retrieved April 3, 2017, from http://frederickdouglassiv.org/.

25. (n.d.). Retrieved April 3, 2017, from http://sbchildrenslibrary.org/wp-content/uploads/2014/07/SBCL_CampaignBroch_11–13.pdf.

26. (2009, December 28). Retrieved April 3, 2017, from http://www.bblf.org/read ers%20voice.htm.

27. US Department of Education National Literacy Act (NLA) of 1991 (Public Law 102–73), 1991, 1.

28. (n.d.). Retrieved April 3, 2017, from https://americareads.as.ucsb.edu/about-us/.

29. Morrow, L. (2001). Tutoring Programs for Struggling Readers: The America Reads Challenge. Rutgers Invitational Symposia on Education. Retrieved April 8, 2017, from https://eric.ed.gov/?id=ED480246.

30. Technology Planning for Adult Literacy. NCAL Practice Guide. (n.d.). Retrieved April 3, 2017, from http://literacynet.org/aztech/pg9502.pdf.

31. Technology Planning for Adult Literacy. NCAL Practice Guide. (n.d.). Retrieved April 3, 2017, from http://literacynet.org/aztech/pg9502.pdf.

32. Mitchell, E. (1998). Citizenship: A guide to good teaching. Retrieved April 3, 2017, from www.cal.org/caela/esl_resources/digests/civics.html.

33. Becker. (2000). Retrieved April 3, 2017, from www.cal.org/caela/esl_re sources/digests/civics.html.

34. (n.d.). Retrieved April 3, 2017, from www.prnewswire.com/news-releases/national-alliance-of-urban-literacy-coal see also (n.d.). Retrieved April 3, 2017, from http://www.prnewswire.com/news-releases/national-alliance-of-urban-literacy-coali tions-receives-100000-grant-from-verizon-foundation-71632077.html.

35. (n.d.). Retrieved April 3, 2017, from http://www.prnewswire.com/news -releases/national-alliance-of-urban-literacy-coalitions-receives-100000-grant-from -verizon-foundation-71632077.html.

36. (2016, April 4). Retrieved April 3, 2017, from http://www.racismreview.com/blog/2016/04/04/dr-martin-luther-king-jr/ and also see (n.d.). Retrieved April 3, 2017, from http://nhdexample1.weebly.com/assassination.html.

37. (n.d.). Retrieved April 3, 2017, from https://nces.ed.gov/naal/pdf/state_sum maries/Ohio.pdf.

38. (n.d.). Retrieved April 3, 2017, from http://www.milkeninstitute.org/publica tions/view/231.

39. (n.d.). Retrieved April 3, 2017, from http://www.ssti.org/Digest/Tables/022006t .htm.

40. Edward Mason. 2011. "The Face of Boston: A Majority-Minority City, But Not where its Workforce is Concerned." Boston Business Journal. September 9, 2011. Retrieved August 18, 2017 from https://www.bizjournals.com/boston/print -edition/2011/09/09/the-face-of-boston-a.html.

41. Charles E. Connerly. 2005. "The Most Segregated City in America" City Planning and Civil Rights in Birmingham, 1920–1980. The University of Virginia Press.

42. (n.d.). Retrieved April 3, 2017, from www.pbs.org/black-culture/explore/civil -rights-movement-birmingham-campaign.

43. (n.d.). Retrieved April 3, 2017, from http://www.encyclopediaofalabama.org/article/h-3244 and Our Common Ground by Graham C. Boettcher. Birmingham Mu-

seum of Art. February 6, 2017/. Recent Acquisitions. Accessed June 23, 2017, http://artsbma.org/our-common-ground/.

44. (n.d.). Retrieved April 3, 2017, from http://www.wvwnews.net/story.php?id=1064.

45. (n.d.). Retrieved April 3, 2017, from http://www.wvwnews.net/story.php?id=1064.

46. (n.d.). Retrieved April 3, 2017, from https://www.bls.gov/opub/mlr/2012/01/art3full.pdf.

47. (n.d.). Retrieved April 3, 2017, from http://www.bls.gov/opub/mlr/2012/01/art3full.pdf.

48. (n.d.). Retrieved April 3, 2017, from http://www.nawb.org/documents/Publications/WIOA_Overview.pdf.

49. Kania & Kramer, 2013.

50. Kania & Kramer, 2013.

51. Kania & Kramer, 2013.

52. Kania & Kramer, 2013.

53. (n.d.). Retrieved April 3, 2017, from /www.strivetogether.org/cradle-career-network.

54. (n.d.). Retrieved April 3, 2017, from /www.strivetogether.org/cradle-career-network.

55. (n.d.). Retrieved April 3, 2017, from www.campaignforgradelevelreading.org.

56. Bronfenbrenner, 1986.

57. Rubiner, B. (2015, November 9). "Innovation Brief: Partnering with StriveTogether." Retrieved April 3, 2017, from /glrhuddle.org/blog/innovation-brief-partnering-with-strivetogether.

58. Rubiner, B. (2015, November 9). "Innovation Brief: Partnering with StriveTogether." Retrieved April 3, 2017, from /glrhuddle.org/blog/innovation-brief-partnering-with-strivetogether.

59. Rubiner, B. (2015, November 9). "Innovation Brief: Partnering with StriveTogether." Retrieved April 3, 2017, from /glrhuddle.org/blog/innovation-brief-partnering-with-strivetogether.

60. (n.d.). Retrieved April 3, 2017, from http://righttoliteracy.org/Right_to_Literacy_Evaluation.pdf.

61. (n.d.). Retrieved April 3, 2017, from http://www.nifl.gov/about/aboutus.html.

62. (n.d.). Retrieved April 3, 2017, from http://www.nifl.gov/about/aboutus.html.

63. (n.d.). Retrieved from https://direct.ed.gov/rschstat/eval/sectech/factsheet/adult-education-great-cities-summit.html.

64. (n.d.). Retrieved April 3, 2017, from http://www.chicagocitywideliteracy.com/.

65. (n.d.). Retrieved April 3, 2017, from https://lincs.ed.gov/publications/pdf/EDVAE09C0042CoalitionBuilding.pdf.

66. (n.d.). Retrieved April 3, 2017, from www2.ed.gov/programs/promiseneighborhoods/index.html.

67. Promise Neighborhood Awards. (n.d.). Retrieved April 3, 2017, from www2.ed.gov/programs/promiseneighborhoods/index.html.

68. (n.d.). Retrieved April 3, 2017, from http://onliteracy.org/.

69. (n.d.). Retrieved April 3, 2017, from http://onliteracy.org/.

70. Mack, J. (2015, March 12). Retrieved April 3, 2017, from www.mlive.com/news/kalamazoo/index.ssf/2015/03/kalamazoo.

71. Kitchens, 2008.

72. Kitchens, 2008.

73. (n.d.). Retrieved April 3, 2017, from http://www.cfmco.org/otherGrants.php.

74. (n.d.). Retrieved April 3, 2017, from http://literacycampaignmc.org/about-us.

75. (n.d.). Retrieved April 3, 2017, from https://literacycenterwm.org/.

76. (n.d.). Retrieved April 3, 2017, from https://literacycenterwm.org/.

77. (n.d.). Retrieved April 3, 2017, from glrhuddle.org/blog/innovation-brief
-partnering-with-strivetogether.

78. (n.d.). Retrieved April 3, 2017, from glrhuddle.org/blog/innovation-brief
-partnering-with-strivetogether.

79. (n.d.). Retrieved April 3, 2017, from glrhuddle.org/blog/innovation-brief
-partnering-with-strivetogether.

80. (n.d.). Retrieved April 3, 2017, from glrhuddle.org/blog/innovation-brief
-partnering-with-strivetogether.

81. (n.d.). Retrieved April 3, 2017, from glrhuddle.org/blog/innovation-brief
-partnering-with-strivetogether.

82. (n.d.). Retrieved April 3, 2017, from glrhuddle.org/blog/innovation-brief
-partnering-with-strivetogether.

*Chapter Two*

# Catalytic Philanthropy and Community Coalitions

Philanthropic organizations have long been associated with the launch and maintenance of collective impact community coalitions. In fact, the very idea of catalytic philanthropy involves funders taking an active role in pulling together community resources to launch a campaign aimed at solving persistent social problems in a collective rather than a siloed or fragmented way (Kramer 2009). Investment in coalitions is only part of a broad portfolio of catalytic grantmaking efforts to affect positive change in the world, but it is one that seems to be growing in popularity. In this chapter we examine the wide variety of funder interactions with coalitions and reflect on why funders are so important to the collective impact community coalition movement. Seeking to explore this phenomenon also from the funder perspective, we then examine what it is about coalitions that attract some funders to help catalyze their creation—namely, their appeal as investments in large-scale community transformation. Finally, we explore the changing roles and interests of funders and coalitions, including that of purveyors of collective impact proliferation, as they negotiate some of the challenges that have emerged along the way. We base our insights on a national survey of 45 literacy funders associated with the Literacy Funders Network, an affinity group of the U.S. Council on Foundations. We also followed up as described in the preceding chapter with a series of interviews and group discussions as well as ongoing conversations with coalitions and funders at conferences and other professional events (approximately 46 participants in all).

## FUNDERS: A THOUSAND COINS OF LIGHT

Coalitions need funders; we might even go so far as to say, "No funding, no coalitions." A huge debt of gratitude on behalf of the coalition movement is owed to a wide variety of funders who have planned, nurtured, and provided long-term support to literacy coalitions. Much like President George H. W. Bush's 1988 speech in which he compared the nonprofit landscape to "a brilliant diversity spread like stars, like a thousand points of light in a broad and peaceful sky,"[1] the foundation world has stepped forward to meet the needs of coalitions in a diversity of ways. These funders have been advocates, allies, door openers, and thought partners—but above all, providers of much needed coin. Private and corporate funders such as Safeway and Dollar General maintain and support the work of many literacy coalitions while local foundations tend to fund only one or a small handful. In both cases, they select what they see as the best grantees, signal to other funders that they see them as good investments, provide performance accountability to grant recipients, and build the professionalism of the field. Foundations are uniquely positioned to tackle literacy as a social justice issue because they work across issue areas and can see the links between each.

The transformative power of funders is captured as the director of a Literacy Coalition recalled the very first flow-through funding the organization received:

> The check from Safeway arrived in the mail. My fingers shook as I steadied the envelope and slit the seal. It was the amount we had requested and the funds enabled the coalition, for the first time, to act as an intermediary and provide funds for a joint project with our members. They could really see how the coalition was benefiting their work and our joint efforts. There were tears of happiness on the checks I wrote to each member. By working together, we had reduced the competition for funds and increased our collaboration by coordinating around a project. And we increased the amount the funder was prepared to contribute! Thank you, Safeway! So exciting! (Washington)

This example emphasizes the gratitude one coalition felt toward one of its funders and the sense of empowerment that occurs when funding arrives. But raising the finances to keep a coalition in motion is not as simple as connecting with one foundation. Typically, coalitions raise funding from a variety of sources. As one Iowa coalition explained:

> Funding sources have included individual donors; private sector, service groups, corporate gifts, and competitive grants; government grants; and in-kind contributions. An annual appeal letter is mailed each November inviting donations to both the Annual Operating Fund and the Endowment Fund. (Iowa)

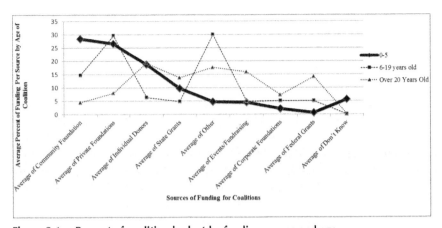

**Figure 2.1.   Percent of coalition budget by funding source and age.**
*Source:* Data collected by the authors in collaboration with the Literacy Funders Network, 2012.

While coalitions depend on private foundations for 23 percent of their income, this pattern varies considerably when looking at different age groups (see figure 2.1).

In general, the data reveal that community foundations and private foundations are major catalysts for coalitions in their early years. However, as time goes on, coalitions seem to find a more balanced portfolio of funding such that individual donors, state grants, fundraising, and other funders begin to carry a higher burden. The role of community and private foundations as an overall proportion of funding tapers off, but does not disappear.

When funding is secured, sometimes through multi-year grants, the coalition is freed from the distractions of fundraising and able to focus more on the work of the organization. The lessons learned over time are many, but ensuring a full twelve months of funding is in the bank at the beginning of the fiscal year is a critical milestone in a coalition's sustainability. And having a team working on funding at least three years into the future is not uncommon.

In this section, we explore the wide variety of funders of coalitions that include both public and private funders, local, state and national, family and community foundations, United Ways and Junior Leagues, and individual social entrepreneurs.

## Government/Public Funders

The collective impact and coalition craze has not been limited to nonprofit foundations; federal and state governments have also become involved. Continuing his metaphor of the thousand points of light, President Bush asked, "Does government have a place? Yes. Government is part of the nation of communities—not the whole, just a part."[2] And so it was that the coalition movement, which began to increase in popularity during his term, and in part due to the efforts of his wife, Barbara Bush, to promote literacy, government did play a role among the many funders of coalitions.

*Federal support.* On the federal level, the coalition approach has often been embedded into grants focusing on issues such as health and education, which use collective impact to address persistent social problems. One funding stream that has proven beneficial for coalitions and has been sustained over time is the Corporation for National and Community Service, which oversees service programs including VISTA and AmeriCorps. Through VISTA, known as the domestic peace corps, members have been instrumental in coalition start-ups across the country and AmeriCorps members have been assigned by coalitions to support provider programs and school districts for both adult and children's literacy. Washington, D.C., Pittsburgh, Palm Beach County, New Orleans, Los Angeles, Seattle, Atlanta, and many other cities have been part of the "Getting Things Done" motto of the program. Each community, within the guidelines, has developed its own programs to meet local needs and provided training and support. The Literacy AmeriCorps program was designed specifically to support coalitions and was managed initially through the National Institute for Literacy, then through the Houston READ Commission and in its final years through Literacy USA and the Pittsburgh Literacy Council.

The amnesty funding in the 1990s, which resulted from President Ronald Reagan's Immigration Reform and Control Act of 1986, was very beneficial to coalitions, as was the American Recovery and Reinvestment Act (ARRA) of 2009 stimulus funding signed into law by President Barack Obama. Certainly, over time, coalitions have specifically benefitted from substantial and valuable funding streams that have helped move a part of their agenda forward. As one coalition director expressed:

> The new Workforce Innovation and Opportunity Act (WIOA) of 2014 provides great opportunities for literacy coalitions. WIOA calls for services to "the most vulnerable" in society. WIOA also calls for greater connectivity between adult literacy providers and the workforce system. Literacy coalitions can play a pivotal role in connecting the parts of the system.
>
> There is also a growing interest in linking literacy to career pathways. Some of this interest is based on the need to fill existing jobs and projected jobs that will require some level of postsecondary education. Many people who are working or unemployed lack the postsecondary credentials and are challenged to succeed in postsecondary without literacy skills enhancement.

With the infusion of amnesty funding, coalitions were able to develop partnerships in which English language and citizenship providers dramatically increased service levels. ARRA funding enabled creative coalitions to add vocational training programs for their partner providers, but many of those programs did not continue after the grant cycle was completed. The fact that services were discontinued could be considered a failure, but hundreds of thousands of adults and youth received vocational certifications that otherwise might not have. Success does not necessarily depend on one or two steady permanent funding streams, but on the careful management of numerous grants and donations all leveraged and blended to achieve a portion of the overall mission of the coalitions.

More recently, the Health Resources and Services Administration, Maternal and Child Health Bureau established grants for fiscal year 2016 focusing on early comprehensive childhood systems impact. Specifically, they sought to use the Early Childhood Comprehensive Systems Collaborative Innovation and Improvement Network with an explicit goal of "the development of collective impact expertise, implementation and sustainability of efforts at the state, county and community levels."[3] Acknowledging the vast overlap between low literacy and other key social problems such as poverty and housing, the grant notice promised "priority points" for communities that were also participating in the Promise Zone, another coalition-friendly policy. As the grant explains, "Promise Zones are high-poverty communities where the federal government partners with local leaders to increase economic activity, improve educational opportunities, leverage private investment, reduce violent crime, enhance public health and address other priorities identified by the community. Through the Promise Zone designation, these communities work directly with federal, state and local agencies to give local leaders proven tools to improve the quality of life in some of the country's most vulnerable areas."[4]

At the state level, programs such as the New York State Department of Education's Literacy Zone program have encouraged the collective impact approach. This program competitively awarded multi-year grants to communities that sought to emulate the Harlem Children's Zone and encouraged communities to create coalitions as the organizational basis of their applications.

At the local level, Community Development Block Grants are a public funding stream that coalitions have used effectively. In such cases, the mayor has often been a major player in the coalition, but departments of education, labor, and social service funders also see the importance of increasing literacy levels. Public funders have collaborated with coalitions as intermediaries to channel funds toward a range of services including youth services, vocational training, and adult education. As with all funding streams, however, there have been times of plenty and times of famine as the economy and political environment changes.

## Private and Family Foundations

Certain private funders have aligned their mission with the work of coalitions, very much to the advantage of the field as it developed over time. The Annie E. Casey Foundation and its Campaign for Grade-Level Reading is a good example of the role funders can play, especially in building funding collaborations. Under the leadership of Ralph Smith, the foundation has spearheaded the national movement for third-grade reading success. By building local coalitions supported by coordination and national leadership from the foundation, the campaign has raised awareness, built resources, increased the profile of successful communities, and helped coalitions identify funding. The Community Coalition below is an example of an early campaign site. As a member of that group shared:

> Our public awareness effort, includes a Campaign for Grade-Level Reading website with reading tips for parents, partners, and visiting the library. This is a fantastic way that we have been able to all come together. We had billboards that ran for a whole year because of the council. Kids got to pick out their own books and were part of our book fairs. We also worked with our ten Bridges programs and as a result children were reading on average twenty-two minutes a day. We had participation from all municipalities in the County. (Florida)

The campaign brings together the components for change, with the support of the Annie E. Casey Foundation and many other funding partners, in an effort that links funding with data, community planning, innovations, and success strategies. Like other coalition efforts, the campaign preaches that no one component will create the needed change; rather, when all the parts work together, change happens.

## Community Foundations

Community foundations have been essential to literacy coalition development and have not only funded major urban literacy coalitions but staffed and incubated them until they could stand alone. There are more than 750 community foundations and more than a dozen of these have over a billion dollars in assets.[5] Because of their local focus, some speculate that community foundations are the most impactful local foundation in any community. The difference between community foundations and other private funders is that community foundations recruit living donors who provide input regarding their wishes about how funds are spent both while they are living and after their death. They teach and promote philanthropy, act as intermediary organizations, provide community leadership and support community development, increase accountability and standards for nonprofits, and often support social justice and system change. Thus, community foundations are exceptionally compatible partners for literacy coalitions.

In Tucson, the Community Foundation of Southern Arizona played the convening leadership role in funding and nurturing the emerging coalition, funding the executive director position and offering space. The Community Foundation for Greater Buffalo, with partners that included the John R. Oishei and Margaret L. Wendt Foundations, steered the coalition planning process and was instrumental in setting the stage for success. The Community Foundation of Greater Birmingham and the Junior League joined forces with the United Way as the major sponsors of the Literacy Council of Central Alabama. By providing seed funding and planning and development support, community foundations have often provided the glue that held together the major planning partners, the city, county, school district, the nonprofit providers, and other key players.

In 2014, The Cleveland Foundation celebrated its centennial; it was the first community foundation and it provided a role model for others to emulate. In 2002, it brought together community leaders to implement a planning model that was first tested in New Orleans by the organization that became Literacy Powerline. It was a "triumvirate of funders" model that collaborated to underwrite the formation and first few critical years of the coalition. The Cleveland Foundation, The George Gund Foundation and the Martha Holden Jennings Foundation created a funders collaborative to kick-start the work with a needs assessment, funding analysis, and community planning. They believed in the power of catalytic philanthropy and were fully engaged as a leadership team in the implementation of the coalition. The work was housed in The Cleveland Foundation, where new nonprofits were supported and incubated until they were ready to take off on their own. The funders have, over time, maintained their high level of engagement.

## Hospital Conversion Foundations

Hospital conversion foundations are another case in point. According to the Foundation Center, "In the past several decades, conversions of traditional nonprofit hospitals and health organizations to for-profit enterprises have had a substantial impact on the field of philanthropy."[6] These conversions promoted the formation of new foundations created from the sale of hospitals. Many emerged with new visions and missions after new foundation boards identified literacy issues as important and they selected the coalition model as the tool to address and increase literacy. Examples include the J. Marion Sims Foundation in South Carolina, the Gulf Coast Medical Foundation in Rosenberg, Texas, and the Baptist Community Ministries in New Orleans, Louisiana.

The J. Marion Sims Foundation began in 1994, when the board of trustees of a local hospital decided it was time to sell their facility. The environment was not favorable to support a small rural hospital and, by selling, two important results occurred. First, a large corporate health care system purchased the hospital and updated it with modern equipment and services. Second, the proceeds from the sale made the foundation possible. As the foundation reviewed the needs in the community, the identification of low literacy and its impact on health and poverty provided the impetus to develop the literacy coalition and support the full lifelong learning range of community literacy services.[7]

Baptist Community Ministries (BCM) traces its history to the 1920s when Southern Baptist Hospital was constructed. BCM evolved over the decades, becoming the lynchpin of healthcare support through Mercy Hospital. When, in 1995, a new and modernized medical system was needed, Mercy Hospital was sold and the BCM Foundation was created. BCM partnered with Loyola University and the Lindy Boggs National Literacy Center to help develop the Literacy Alliance of Greater New Orleans, bringing together literacy providers across the city.

As just one more example, in 1952, Gulf Coast Medical Foundation was formed for the purpose of building and operating the Gulf Coast Medical Center, in Wharton, Texas, on a not-for-profit basis. In 1980, the two hospitals that had grown out of the medical center were sold for approximately $7 million and a new, modern hospital was built. The sale proceeds flowed into the Gulf Coast Medical Foundation to support its work in the rural counties of Matagorda, Jackson, Colorado, Fort Bend, and Brazoria. Its focus on literacy education and organizational capacity building provided the basis for its partnership with the Rural Literacy Coalition and the Palacios Community Hub.

## Corporate Foundations

In addition to hospitals, community foundations and government and national funders, corporate foundations have also played a role in the spread of the literacy coalition movement. When Literacy USA, the first national literacy coalition, was building its Corporate Advisory Board, it looked to businesses that had supported literacy coalitions across the country. Those corporations included Verizon, BCI, Time Warner, Today's Vision, Wal-Mart, Dollar General, and Half Price Books. The board's business leaders shared a tremendous camaraderie. This could be due, in part, to the fact that there was only one representative from each business sector serving at the same time. As a result, members were not from competing companies, so they collaborated. They challenged each other to match grants and underwrite conferences and events.

Each of these foundations had their own reasons for supporting literacy. Some did it to honor the legacies of loved ones. For instance, the Dollar General's founder had a father who left school at age eleven to help on the family farm and never finished his education. Cal Turner Jr. created the Dollar General Literacy Foundation in honor of his father to support adults who never had the opportunity to complete their education. Others did it as part of their own evolving legacies, primarily motivated to improve corporate workforce development.

A member of a large media corporation became chair of Literacy USA's Corporate Advisory Board. As he reflected on his journey:

> I first learned of adult literacy as a feature writer working for the biggest newspaper in the South . . . During the time I was at the newspaper, I kept hearing about the Houston READ Commission. Like most folks there, I liked the idea of teaching unlettered adults to read. Sure, it was a selfish corporate motive on the part of . . . the paper's owner, but teaching folks to read was a good motive nonetheless. I bought into it heartily and swore if I was ever able, I would do what I could to help what even I realized was a growing movement, the national goal of adult literacy . . .
>
> I am a writer, a former daily newspaperman and an author. The Houston READ Commission was a natural. They, and literacy, were also an easy sell. More importantly, unlike other nonprofits, they actually did tangible good. You could really see the result as a formerly illiterate septuagenarian read a newspaper or magazine for the first time. The face actually glowed.
>
> I'm an emotional boob. When I first walked into one of the Commission's "classrooms" at a community center in a grindingly poor neighborhood and saw wonderful Black and Hispanic women and men, elderly ones, reading primary school curriculum, the tears welled, and when I got to the privacy of my car, they flowed like a river. I had to do something to help. And the problem of adult illiteracy wasn't confined to minority communities either. It was overwhelming, like a poisonous and noxious gas wafting over whole neighborhoods. As I later learned, that gas engulfed the entire nation. I had to go to work for those people. I had to make change . . .

This business leadership helped to provide ongoing support and jump-started the marketing messages for coalitions. Private foundations often do not like to be in the public eye, but corporate foundations can use their giving as a tool for business and product awareness. Perhaps for this reason, newspaper corporations had an affinity for the issue of low literacy in the 1980s. It was in their corporate best interests; if you could read, you might want to buy a newspaper. Both the Hearst and the Gannet newspaper chains were strong and visible supporters of the early coalitions. Gannet provided one of the first multi-coalition grants, funding initial development work in Philadelphia, Baltimore, Boston, and Houston.

Another newspaper, *The Los Angeles Times* not only provided funding for the Literacy Network of Greater Los Angeles, but also housed the coalition. At the birth of the coalition, one entered the very impressive LA Times building, past the huge globe in the foyer, and worked one's way down many floors into the hidden bowels of the building to a small dungeon. Eventually the paper and the coalition developed its shared message for literacy and coordinated with Reading by Six, an early learning program, and moved into a more prominent suite of offices highlighting the very visible and growing importance that the paper placed on literacy.

## United Ways

One funding stream that should not be overlooked is the United Way, which grew out of the community chest movement of federated giving. In Birmingham, Tuscaloosa, Fort Worth, and many other cities, United Ways have helped start and sustain coalition growth. They have provided structure, professional development, volunteers, and corporate engagement to many coalitions and have become even more engaged as the Campaign for Grade-Level Reading has developed and won the support of the United Way of America. In 2013, United Way Worldwide released, "Charting a Course for Change: Advancing Education, Income and Health through Collective Impact."[8] This report urges United Ways across the nation to "bring people and organizations together to create collective impact." It was a call to United Way staffs and allies to, in the words of Brian A. Gallagher, president and CEO of United Way Worldwide:

> facilitate a shared community vision and coordinated action across a diverse coalition, along with mutual accountability, sustained effort and measured results. It means working collaboratively on community wide and community-based strategies that can drive real change—not programs, or tweaks of status quo.[9]

While this sweeping change was indeed a coup to the coalition approach, it did not mean that United Ways universally endorsed coalition approaches. Rather, as a supremely decentralized organization, the choice still remained very much in the hands of local affiliates. As one local United Way representative explained:

> United Way is not McDonald's. If I go into a McDonald's in Pittsburgh and order a Big Mac and I go to one in Houston I am going to get the same product. That is not how the United Way works. To understand it, we need to understand history. In Denver, in 1887, a rabbi, two priests, a pastor, and a town person had a conversation. Denver was growing, there was a ton of need and they didn't

have enough to meet the need. It was successful raising $21,700, which was a lot of money back then. In 1918, the American Association of Community Organizations started and by 1948 there were more than 1,000 across the United States because it was also part of the war chest movement. In 2003, the United Way adopted membership standards, and, in 2009, United Way Worldwide was born. Nearly 1,800 United Ways across 41 countries and territories raised $4.27 billion in 2014.[10]

Due in part to this decentralized nature, the shift toward a collective impact coalition movement for United Ways was still very much a locally driven phenomenon. In a United Way session about coalition development at the National Center for Families Learning Summit, one participant commented on the development of the United Ways and the role they can play in coalition development:

A traditional model has emerged as we have mobilized communities, meaning we raise money, and then we do supportive services for individuals and families that improve the lives of program clients. Our accountants loved this model because, basically, we raised money and we had United Way approved partners. We just divided the money up and it went out to our partner agencies. There are plenty of United Ways that still use this model. This is a much easier method than what we are moving toward. But, for us, about ten years ago we started hearing more about return on investment (ROI). Part of this drive is from our boards, which are made up of a lot of business people. We wanted CEOs on our boards because we ran workplace campaigns. We also noted two trends: increasing needs and limited resources. (Pennsylvania)

When it comes to helping the community, the United Way is perhaps the prototypical community agent. Much like others in the field of philanthropy, they eventually tired of general responsive grantmaking that involved offering funds to whoever asked. This was seen as too random and neither concentrated nor coordinated enough to make a difference. The result was an increasing move toward collective impact approaches. One local United Way executive explained:

United Way likes to talk about "aha" moments, or epiphanies. There is a village and a river, there is a baby floating in the river. The villager saves it, then looks and sees another baby in the river, and saves it, then three or four more are floating. Villagers keep diving in to save more babies. Finally, they say, "We need to go up the river and find out why there are babies in the river." They found a troll dropping the babies in the water! This is not a true story, but there was a realization that unless we stop the troll from chucking babies in the river we will never be able to have enough impact to change enough lives.

The executive continued:

Improving lives by changing community conditions is now added to direct impact—both community impact and direct impact. We are still concerned about the individual, but we also want to see changes in the neighborhood. United Ways are still trying to figure out how they do this. It does become less about the person and more about how we change the system, so that it is different. As funders, we have a horrible problem of being fickle in our funding and thinking that once we make movement on a problem we are done with that. Then we are surprised that ten years later it is a problem again. So how do we change the way that pre-Ks and schools and hospitals all work together?

Within communities where similar shifts in thinking have taken place, United Ways have become critical allies to the coalition movement.

## Angel Investors

Last, but not least, a discussion about funding must include angel investors. The term "angel investor" might be familiar from the world of the theater. It has been used to describe affluent members of society who contributed funding to enable artistic productions that would have otherwise simply folded, perhaps because they swooped in like angels to rescue the enterprise. The term itself is thought to originate in 1978, when University of New Hampshire professor William Wetzel used it to refer to investors that helped entrepreneurs raise seed capital.[11]

Much like in the business world, angel investors for literacy coalitions could be retired entrepreneurs or business people, but they could also be retired members of the nonprofit and literacy community who seek a return in terms of community benefit rather than a financial return. For instance, the Literacy Coalition of Madison County in New York has an angel investor that started a fund to underwrite countywide programming that would otherwise not be possible in low-income neighborhoods.

Sometimes, angel investors serve on coalition boards and help inspire other board members to action. Because of their experience in the field, they often have advice to offer as well. Hershel Rich, for example, developed a love of reading and learning as a child and could not imagine anyone unable to read well. The more he researched the data about low literacy in the country, the more he knew he had to help. He was an inventor and entrepreneur constantly thinking up new ideas and designs. In 1947, he and his father built an electric fan company and part of Rich's wealth came from selling the company to Sunbeam in 1981. According to Rich's obituary, "Hershel looked at the world through the lens of an optimist, inventor, and problem solver."[12] He believed that investing in literacy initiatives provided one of the biggest returns on investment. The obituary goes on, "While reading the IRS tax code, Hershel noted that corporations were allowed to deduct only 5 percent of their income tax for charitable giving; he contacted then Vice President George Bush who helped get the law changed to 10 percent." Rich was a catalytic philanthropist; he never gave a check without first visiting the coalition's program, understanding its goals, and offering ideas to improve program productivity. He helped the coalitions he supported to develop early electronic English as a Second Language programs, helped design a prison literacy program, and helped underwrite operating costs to ensure their long-term success. Local folklore has it that Rich met with any number of wealthy local business leaders and corporations and always ended the meeting with pulling out his checkbook and challenging them to match his gift to the literacy coalition. Angels, like Rich, exist in many coalition communities, both providing support and resources according to their abilities. Without their drive, initiative, and social entrepreneurial spirit, the field would not have developed so far so fast.

While the above types of funders each have played crucial parts in the lives of coalitions, they have often done so in concert with each other. As one coalition executive director explained:

> Literacy coalitions are also tasked with bringing the funding community together. This is most successful when the funder or funders who created the literacy coalition recognize the literacy coalition as the "backbone" and function accordingly. Those funders also have a role in bringing in other funders both in terms of finance and function. (Ohio)

What entices funders to take part in coalition building in the first place? And what makes coalitions enticing so that funders can bring in other funders? We explore this in the next section.

## THE ALLURE OF COALITIONS: WHY FUNDERS ARE INTERESTED—COMMUNITY LEVEL CHANGE, COLLABORATION AND RESOURCES

Despite a considerable interest in catalytic philanthropy and institutional entrepreneurship, funder involvement in building collective impact community coalitions is far from universal. In fact, a national survey of literacy funders conducted for this research found that less than half (approximately 48 percent) funded coalitions. Hence, among those that do, it is important to examine what it is about coalitions that helps them see doing so as a positive course of action. As one coalition director with close historical ties to a community foundation explained:

> Funders who fund literacy coalitions do so to address a community need (low literacy) that is too large to accomplish by funding a single program or organization. There is an interest in breaking down silos and the usual fragmentation in the system. The literacy coalition is created to bring collaboration, alignment, and knowledge sharing. (Ohio)

In the words of one community, from a funder's perspective, building a coalition is a "strategic investment" in the long-term quality of life of the people they serve:

> We view support of our literacy council as an important strategic investment that has implications on quality/quantity of life for those served.

Fittingly, as stated above, the most prominent reason for funding is that coalitions address a community need that is too large to accomplish by funding a single program or organization. Often the realization of such a large-scale need begins with an analysis of community-level data, as in the example below:

> Our Indicators Project demonstrated the need for our foundation to take a lead and/or to support community efforts in addressing several areas of literacy. The community foundation was instrumental in creating our regional literacy coalition. (New York)

In some instances, it is a feeling that an entire community is falling behind with respect to key indicators of well-being, as in the following:

> Our entering kindergarten literacy score on average is one of the worst in the state of Ohio, so we created a coalition to work on early childhood literacy. (Ohio)

Faced with such community needs, starting a coalition is seen as a means to catalyzing and pooling local resources toward a collective impact strategy. As a national funder that works with coalitions across the country explained:

> We are stronger when we work on this together. This is a classic example of what government does, they spend 2/5 here and 1/5 here and before you know it they have spent the whole dollar and you can't tell what they spent it on. And with funders you get the same, they sprinkle it around. It is only when you get them all spending on the same thing that you will finally see impact.

Closely related to this desire to create community change for the better is a sentiment that the best way to bring about large-scale change is through collaborating across the silos, or divisions, that historically separate different organizations within a community. One funder described these silos as a "fragmentation" that leads to community vulnerability:

> We have found that the adult literacy community is extremely fragmented. This leaves it at-risk for reduced investment in programs and limited opportunities to innovate. A strong coalition could be helpful to building a strong, cohesive community; advocating more strongly for improvements in policies and practices; and identifying new resources for the community. (Illinois)

In essence, the strategy for addressing a community need is to build up and enhance the field of professionals that can best solve the problem. As the following funder explained, building up a "field" often involves community leadership and an increased awareness of the resources shared among local organizations.

> We helped start and fund our local literacy coalition because we believe that the field (adult education) needs leadership, increased awareness, and avenues for resource sharing. (California)

It is believed such sharing of knowledge and awareness will lead to collaborations. With respect to increasing a community's capacity to collaborate (i.e., breaking down silos), the literature has noted that the organizational structure and programs of coalitions tend to create collaborative capacity (Berkowitz 2001; Foster-Fishman et al. 2001). In many cases, they are purposefully structured to foster collaboration (Butterfoss 2007) and, as a result, they build the social capital necessary among community players to successfully catalyze and carry out community and policy change (Fawcett et al. 1995).

As the saying goes, "collaboration leads to collaboration." The idea is that it is only through collaborating as part of a coalition that we begin to become familiar with both the people who work in other organizations or "silos" and their priorities. Once we do this, we can begin to see how our own priorities overlap and collective solutions to community problems begin to become visible. This dynamic is borne out in the data collected by one of the authors in one community literacy coalition that asked members of one of its committees representing nonprofit organizations to list both the number of professional relationships they had with other members of the committee and describe their relationship with the people representing each of these organizations on this committee using a rating scale designed by Frey et al.[13] This

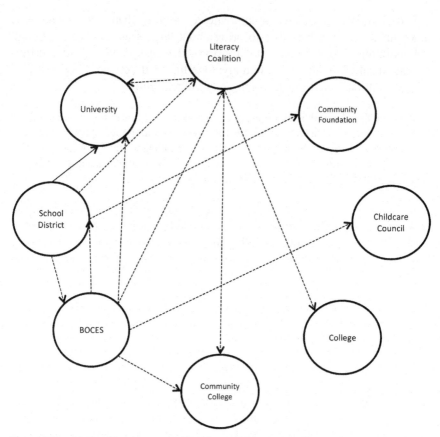

**Figure 2.2.   Networking pre-committee formation retrospective scores.**
*Source:* Data collected and compiled by author.

scale offered definitions ranging from 0 to 5: (0) No Interaction at All, to (1) Networking, (2) Cooperation, (3) Coordination, (4) Coalition, and (5) Collaboration. As seen below in the images of a group of nonprofits only, there was a noticeable change in the connections among these organizations when comparing scores from pre-committee formation to post-committee work (see figures 2.2 and 2.3).

From the pre-committee to post-committee period, the average number of links committee members reported having between organizations increased from 5.5 to 8.25. In addition, the average level of relationship inched up from closer to networking to closer to cooperation. These findings are consistent with the hopes funders espouse for coalitions. As seen in the following example, the hope is to foster collaboration that will lead to collective solutions to community challenges.

Our family foundation funds a literacy coalition to foster collaboration among literacy service providers serving local children, develop collective solutions to the community's challenges around literacy, and engage and align funders in providing resources to support these solutions. (California)

Interestingly, as noted above, the goal is not only to align providers, but also fellow funders that can provide resources to implement collective solutions that coalitions devise.

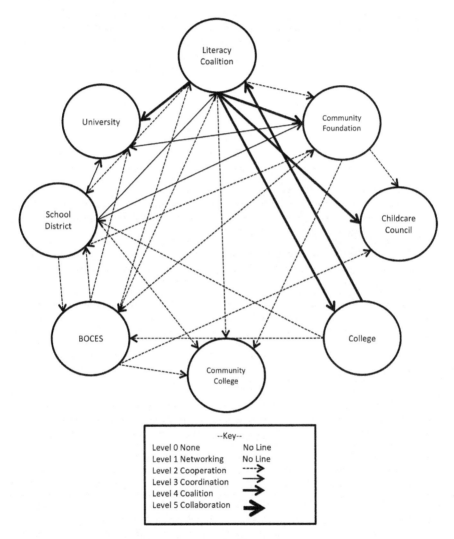

**Figure 2.3.   Networking post-committee work scores.**
*Source:* Data collected by the authors in 2011.

Funding and resource sharing was a third theme that weighed prominently in the minds of funders when discerning why they support coalitions. As one coalition explained, it is as simple as, "Improved funding, better relations with elected officials and funders, [and] more informed members." (New York) This sentiment, that collaboration among community partners will be more attractive to funders and will increase local resources, is echoed in the words of foundations, such as the following:

> Our foundation will fund operating costs in 2013 and 2014 in the amount of $22,500 for our local Coalition for Literacy. The coalition strengthens the delivery of literacy, shares resources and best practices, attracts more grant funds because of collaboration, provides training and outcome data for the entire coalition, and is the best hope for children and families in our rural area! (Texas)

Such emphasis on attracting more funding to the community helps to further explain the trends noted earlier in which funding diversifies over the life course of the coalition. While local community foundations and private foundations offer the largest proportion of funding during the start-up years, over time funding sources tend to diversify, with federal and state government grants playing an increasingly important role.[14]

Investment from funders begins slowly during community convening and rises to a peak as the convened groups begin to formalize their structure as an institution within the community. Ultimately, however, over time, and consistent with national trends, the role of a foundation's catalytic philanthropy declines but doesn't disappear. This is consistent with national data discussed earlier in which foundation funding declines over time from over 50 percent of funding during the initial start-up years to closer to 10 percent in the most mature coalitions, with additional sources providing the other 90 percent of funding needed. Importantly, this decline in overall proportion of the coalition budget that foundations comprise doesn't mean the foundation gives less. More often, other sources grew, so a steady funding amount from funders became a smaller proportion of a pie that gradually increased over time.

In many ways, this rise and fall bell curve of funding is quite consistent with the catalytic philanthropy model. The goal is to create a spark that creates a new change in the institutions of society and then let those changes lead to the betterment of community life as the funders seek new problems for which they can catalyze collective impact. This mentality is captured in the comments of the vice president of a Midwestern community foundation who explained, after a long period of extolling the virtues of his very successful community literacy initiative that, "We have been wondering about an exit strategy."

This mention of exit, however, underlies a key point of tension between coalitions and the funders that underwrite them. As one coalition director explained, funders sometimes lack the long-term attention span that intractable social problems require.

> Funders when they enter often talk about exit plans, but it is more appropriate to wait to do this until once the community problem is solved. (Illinois)

Within the context of catalytic philanthropy however, collective impact community coalitions can be seen as an "exit strategy" that is an "investment" in a community's "quality of life" that is created through institutional entrepreneurship. Some see coalitions as a way to shift their own literacy efforts toward greater community ownership.[15]

Given the high aspirations funders have for coalitions, it is no surprise that some larger funders with national scopes have sought to sow the seeds of coalitions far and wide. These "purveyors" of the coalition approach may take the form of national funders, networks of funders, or even the government.

## FUNDERS AS PURVEYORS

Given the growing popularity of coalitions and their proliferation across the country, it is not surprising that concepts from the burgeoning field of implementation science would find fertile ground in this analysis. One concept that holds purchase here is that of the purveyor, a person or organization that fosters the growth of a program or approach in multiple places over time. As Oosthuizen and Louw shared, the role of purveyors should not be overlooked because they can help communities maximize the chances that their intervention will be successful:

> Frequently, social interventions produce less for the intended beneficiaries than was initially planned. One possible reason is that ideas embodied in interventions are not self-executing and require careful and systematic translation to put into practice. The capacity of implementers to deliver interventions is thus paramount. Purveyor organizations provide external support to implementers to develop that capacity and to encourage high-fidelity implementation behavior.[16]

Funders have emerged as purveyors in two waves, first championing adult literacy and more recently emphasizing literacy across the lifespan, with an emphasis on early childhood.

### From First-Wave Adult Literacy to Second-Wave Early Childhood

As one literacy veteran recalled, the first wave of coalition purveyors focused on adult literacy:

Back in 1982 no one knew what adult literacy was. Laubach Literacy was a small organization with about twenty-four staff. Then the Ad Council based in New York decided to do a national campaign. The American Library Association had pitched to them the idea of something about reading and the Ad Council thought adult literacy made more sense. They asked Bob Wedgeworth, the president of the American Library Association, to form the National Coalition for Literacy. Barbara Bush, then wife of the vice president of the United States, was coming on the scene and she was interested in literacy. ABC took this on as the network's singular cause and partnered with PBS to form the PLUS (Project Literacy US) campaign. It was the heyday and the heaven of literacy initiatives. One of the important outgrowths of PBS and ABC TV was they tried to establish a PLUS task force in every community in the nation. These were the predecessors, progenitors of literacy coalitions.[17]

As he went on to explain:

Philadelphia, New York City, Chicago, Atlanta, LA all had mayors involved in their coalitions. There were dozens more where the mayors sanctioned these groups. Philadelphia had a mayor's Commission. New York's Mayor Ed Koch had a commission and put $23 million into it. As with any national initiative like this, there were some successes and some failures. Some brought people together without the components needed, some providers did not want to collaborate, and others had great success raising money, reaching more people, raising awareness, and coordinating people.

As with coalitions themselves, purveyors too sometimes begin with a dedicated individual. He continues:

Why did it happen? There was an alignment of stars, there was no crisis, or a big report (that came out afterward) saying this was an issue. Some credit Barbara Bush because she was so driven and so electric. Her son, Neil, had dyslexia and had trouble learning how to read. She realized if she had not gotten help for him, he would not be reading as an adult. And once you got critical mass it started to roll.

Over the next ten years, this wave continued. Most of the coalitions were coming together to solve what was observed to be a lack of coordination at the local level, that, if solved would achieve four goals: raising money, reaching more people, raising awareness, and coordinating people.

Over time, coalitions of coalitions formed, he continues:

National Alliance of Urban Literacy Coalitions (NAULC) was founded and the idea was that this would represent coalitions like Florida, Literacy Assistance Center, Cleveland, and dozens of literacy coalitions across the country. That group was trying to serve the interests of the coalitions.

At the national level, NAULC changed its name to Literacy USA since they were broader than urban areas. They continued advocating for coalitions until they had a funding crisis and had to close their doors around 1998–2000. That was the birth of Literacy Powerline. There was still a need for training and support in the area, so Margaret Doughty formed the for-profit Literacy Powerline which did consulting for coalitions across the nation. Recently they merged into the National Center for Families Learning (NCFL).

It was at this point that a shift in focus began to emerge, with a move away from exclusive attention on adults alone. Perhaps the most prominent example of this has been the Campaign for Grade-Level Reading. Begun in 2010 under the leadership of the Annie E. Casey Foundation, this campaign set out to catalyze an increase in the number of low-income children reading on grade level by the end of third grade. Like many other pilot projects purveyors launched nationally (such as the federal government's Choice Neighborhoods, Communities Learning in Partnership, Full Service Community Schools, and Strive), CGLR intended to focus on a limited number of communities (see table 2.1).

However, the popularity of this approach soon caught fire and, by 2015, well over 100 communities across over 40 states had joined the campaign network and embraced the goals of increasing literacy. One of the reasons the campaign succeeded in attracting adherents seems to be its simplicity. By focusing on the three core tenets of increasing kindergarten readiness, decreasing summer learning loss, and reducing chronic absenteeism, communities have been able to clearly articulate both a vision and a pathway to improving grade-level reading.

While the CGLR is a national purveyor of an approach, a vision and a series of peer-to-peer resource sharing forums, the campaign has always been, at its heart, "a bottom-up approach represented by local community campaigns."[18] As a leader of the campaign has shared, this means that local funders and local coalitions continue to play a larger role:

The United Ways fund a lot of the early work, so you find the ones that are most effective are the ones that can go to their strengths, even if that role is not the number one but the number two seat. And the literacy coalitions are able to pull everyone together to focus on the big result and people say we can't get there alone. Your stake in the ground is at the result level, at the early learning and attendance and summer learning, so you are able to put together some of the strongest tables. If you were to ask us this in 2010, we would not have been able to tell you any of this. Letting each community discern their own direction has been the way to go. Intelligent design may have its place, but not in this work.

**Table 2.1. Collective impact initiatives by number of sites and counties of participants**

| Collective Impact Initiatives | # of Sites | # of Counties with Initiative |
|---|---|---|
| Campaign for Grade-Level Reading | 168 | 144 |
| Cities Combating Hunger through Afterschool Programs | 13 | 13 |
| Choice Neighborhood Implementation | 11 | 11 |
| Choice Neighborhood Planning | 68 | 66 |
| Communities Learning in Partnership | 18 | 17 |
| Community Schools Leadership Network | 62 | 61 |
| EDI | 32 | 32 |
| ELEV8 | 7 | 7 |
| Full Service Community Schools | 20 | 19 |
| Let's Move! Cities, Towns, and Counties | 207 | 172 |
| Literacy Powerline Network of Literacy Coalitions | 101 | 101 |
| Middle Grades Challenge: United Way | 16 | 16 |
| Wallace Foundation-funded "Next Generation Afterschool System Building Initiative | 14 | 14 |
| National Neighborhood Indicators Partnership | 64 | 63 |
| Promise Neighborhood Implementation | 17 | 17 |
| Promise Neighborhood Planning | 58 | 50 |
| Promise Neighborhood Unfunded | 11 | 11 |
| Forum for Youth Investment | 21 | 21 |
| RB21 | 14 | 14 |
| Race to the Top District | 9 | 9 |
| STRIVE-I | 11 | 11 |
| STRIVE-M | 114 | 108 |
| Talent Dividend | 79 | 78 |
| TOTAL | 1135 | 1,055 |

*Source:* Data collected by the authors in collaboration with the Literacy Funders Network and the National Results and Equity Collaborative, 2015.

Thus, while many pre-existing literacy coalitions signed on to the campaign, many other communities that did not have coalitions were brought into the fold and exposed to the coalition approach.

Partly due to its inclination to take a "big tent coalition" approach that is more inclusive than exclusive, such as incorporating national momentum around high school graduations, the campaign has been able to "include constituencies historically averse to becoming enmeshed in public schools."[19] The star power of the campaign has also helped, enlisting the help of people like Academy Award-winning actor Morgan Freeman and other national funders, has helped to bring the goals of the campaign to local communities and to "onboard" people who have traditionally held back, often by finding a sweet spot for their involvement. As a CGLR leader shared, different officials have different "on ramps":

Every place that started with mayors the CGLR has lagged because mayors don't feel they have enough control over the schools so they have migrated to the summer and said, the summer is mine. In many places, we are finding that it is hard to get and keep the attention of superintendents unless you show up with attendance data and say, "We will now look at yours." The on ramp for superintendents is attendance and the "on ramp" for mayors is summer learning.

In addition to on ramps, the campaign offers a supportive network that helps communities engage in collective impact without reinventing the wheel. As one community partner shared:

We had Ron Fairchild from the campaign come and speak on summer slide, and Hedy Chang from the campaign came and talked about attendance and Dr. Diane Christie came in to talk about school readiness. We have tried to integrate the campaign throughout all of our programs. [In] our newest program . . . they are working thirty minutes, one-on-one, and kids' reading levels are going up, getting them ready for third grade.

The campaign offers a vision and a blueprint and resources for change, but at the same time, it takes a realistic stance, commiserating with its member communities about barriers to progress, such as gaining timely access to data and challenges that exist due to "silos" and red tape. They talk about focusing on issues that exist "outside the school door" and so take an ecological systems approach that invites all within the community to be a part of the solution. Furthermore, they appeal to collective impact sensibilities by talking about "moving the needle" in terms of seeking community indicator improvement for the better, both overall, and through closing the gaps between disadvantaged and more advantaged children.[20]

While the campaign is indeed a national purveyor, helping to create collective impact community coalitions where previously they did not exist, much of the learning is homegrown. Rather than take a highly prescriptive approach, they have chosen to set shared visions for goals and rely on local creativity to develop the actual plans to be implemented. A campaign representative explained this philosophy:

We believe in crowd sourcing, so I have been sitting in the back, listening and taking notes because this is how the campaign learns. I found out some time ago that you learn more when you are listening than when you are speaking.

Although the campaign epitomizes the shift of purveyors from adult to early childhood, this has been part of a larger trend that included a plurality of new age-specific approaches that were all competing for attention. These included family literacy, early learning, cradle to career, and lifelong learning.

*Family Literacy Focus*

As many coalitions developed, it was clear that the early learning gap needed to be addressed and the National Center for Family Literacy (Now National Center for Families Learning) and the Barbara Bush Foundation for Family Literacy both focused on parents and preschool children learning together. Many coalitions tried to walk the tightrope of tensions between adult and youth focus by addressing the need for childcare while adult learners were in class. They felt that an early learning program was vastly superior to baby-sitting. In Los Angeles, the coalition partnered closely with Reading by Six; in Houston, the coalition partnered with the Collaborative for Children; and in New Orleans, Literacy AmeriCorps members divided their time between adult learners and early childhood programs.

*Early Learning Focus*

Although providing early education as a tool to reduce poverty has long been important in our country, many point to the 1965 White House meeting when Lady Bird Johnson set the stage for the Head Start program with her tea party to announce federal funding for preschool programs as an important moment in this movement. Prior to the Campaign for Grade-Level Reading, the movement to support early learning primarily focused on the development of federally funded programs. With the campaign came the first major national focus preparing for success by third grade. With this push, coalitions in Buffalo, the Rio Grande Valley, Oakland, Sacramento, Phoenix, and other locations joined the campaign.

*Cradle to Career*

When StriveTogether coined the term "cradle to career," the focus was on the full range of education, pre-K to college, introducing the importance of the continuum of learning throughout the years of childhood and youth, but stopping at adulthood. Places such as Cincinnati, Portland, Oregon, Water-bury, Boise, and Albuquerque joined the Strive network and took on the very specific framework and outcome measures required to be a part of the system.

*Lifelong Learning (Twinkle to Wrinkle)*

The lifelong learning mantra, supported by Literacy Powerline (another pur-veyor of coalitions) and others, seeks to embrace the concept that learning is for all ages and never ends. It implies that our learning needs change over the lifespan and that even in old age the learning strategies that maintain mental acuity are as critical as the language development strategies in early learning. Palm Beach County, The Houston Blueprint for Literacy, Kalamazoo, and Memphis, for instance, have embraced these approaches.

Miami, like several communities, operated separate coalitions for each age group and they collaborated to a greater or lesser degree as projects warranted varied levels of coordination. Coalitions that have a full-blown lifelong learning plan but tackle issues in one age group, one type of literacy (financial, health, media, workforce, etc.) or even one zip code at a time may not seem to be embracing the full spectrum of lifelong learning, but no community can do it all at once. Given the choice, this wave is perhaps best characterized by communities choosing to start with, or at least emphasize, early literacy.

## Tensions between Waves

Understandably, this shift from adult toward early childhood did not occur without some tension. Not all coalitions or their members welcomed a vision of literacy service provision as a lifelong continuum. It was especially challenging for those focusing on adult education. As we have reported, many of the very earliest coalitions began with a specific focus on adult education, based on the belief that it was incumbent upon the school system to educate children. Adult educators were concerned that the appeal of supporting young children would shift their focus and reduce adult education dollars. The Ohio coalitions, for instance, were very clear that adult literacy was their focus and that any foray into children's literacy would go against the grain. Philadelphia, Boston, Pittsburgh, New York City, and Seattle all followed suit. In some cases, there was angry rhetoric and political positioning that was supported by the National Coalition for Literacy to ensure that adult education got the attention it demanded. Once coalition members or the coalition and its members sense competition, the equilibrium of collaboration is undermined. As one professional from the adult literacy field shared:

> For adult literacy providers, coalitions became less relevant as the focus on adult literacy was diluted. Anytime you are in a room along with people who are doing K–12, you are the sad sack, you are at the little kids' table because people just seem to focus on the little kids more. It's nobody's fault, it just happens that way. Adult education constituencies need to focus twice as hard to be heard. (New York)

As another shared, however, sometimes this challenge has a silver lining:

> We have a vision of 100 percent literacy through 100 percent literacy infusion. Adult education feeling threatened by focus on school readiness, is a gift to us

because we have been doing things separately for so long. Now we are working across silos. (California)

Not everyone sees it that way though. Another shared that, now that literacy attention nationally has shifted to early childhood, it has become more difficult to maintain momentum among adult focused coalition members:

There was about a five-year period when we, as adult education providers, could not spend money fast enough. From 1985 to 2000, Laubach quadrupled, as did Literacy Volunteers of America. [But this has now changed] From a coalition standpoint, there is a real loss without a national organization [like early childhood has now]. It is really difficult to maintain the excitement from initial formation to something that is ongoing. (New York)

So, despite some seeing opportunity, tensions between focusing on early childhood and older learners have become part of the changing national landscape, and funders have had a clear role in this shift. As a United Way leader explained, the shift was noticeable in, and even driven by, the changing focus of funders:

What seems to have happened is that the dollars shifted. The funders started to focus more on early childhood. The foundations shifted their focus and said, "We are going to start focusing on kids, so why don't you go ahead and form a coalition around that?" At least around here, it was the funders that drove that shift. (Pennsylvania)

Strategies of both adaptive leadership and opportunism were needed to steer sensitively through the changes. These occurred as a new crop of foundation purveyors emerged. A literacy coalition director concurred:

The old ones [coalitions] are trying to be as opportunistic as possible and are trying to either shift their focus or split their focus, still keeping their toes in the water with adult literacy and either shifting to early childhood literacy or parent engagement or family literacy. That is an easier sell. I think both nationally and locally the coalitions are going to direct their activities to what they are funded to do and if there is no funding you either have to get out or shift and the funders have driven that for us. (Ohio)

In such situations adult and early childhood constituencies within coalitions can feel pitted against one another in what feels like a zero sum game, in which a benefit for one party occurs at the expense of the other.

In one city, the coalition brought the partners together to announce a new and substantial federal funding opportunity. The providers attended a training to learn the details of how to write a winning application. Halfway through the training, someone commented that the excellent training was making the partners able to better compete with each other. A light bulb went off and someone commented that, in the efforts to be completely fair, some partners would win and some would lose. The group determined to work through the coalition to submit one application, which did, in fact, win funding for all the members.

With the growth of lifelong learning coalitions, some funders made an effort to appease both constituencies and sought applications that addressed the interdependence between the age groups and engaged the range of coalition members. However, the term "literacy" seemed to lose its luster among funders. "There is something about the word "literacy" that is so Magoo, and uninspiring," one funder said. (New York) Another respondent made the same point:

> Oh, forget it. There is something about the word "literacy." I showed funders a menu of things that they could help with and literacy did not resonate. But they liked the Campaign for Grade-Level Reading! The sponsor of this conference actually changed its name away from literacy. (Florida)

Buzzwords change from decade to decade, and many are simply new names for old concepts. But change is always difficult. However, as a foundation leader explained, there was some logic to this shift from one word to more specific definitions across the lifespan.

> The funders didn't just wake up one day and say, "Oh, kids are cute. Let's just focus on them." It has been a progression further up the line. First, they went back to look at high schools and graduations and then they looked further up the pipeline to grade level and then kindergarten and then family behaviors in the early years. I think the reason that progression has happened was because our understanding has improved. The science has improved about just how early in life these neuro pathways are laid down and if kids miss these opportunities, they don't ever get them back. I think there is something outside the funders that has happened that the funders are responding to. (Tennessee)

Another coalition executive director shared a similar perspective:

> It wasn't that the funders just changed their minds, but that the research that was coming out made them look further down the pipeline and wonder if how well a child enters kindergarten will affect how well they do in third grade and [later on in high school]. The research is getting better and that has been influencing philanthropy. (Ohio)

As this shift has occurred, purveyors such as the CGLR have helped influence discussion and discourse much like institutional entrepreneurs in other fields have done so in order to facilitate widespread change. As one local organization connected with the CGLR explains:

> It has been amazing at the state level that third-grade reading has entered the discussion and they don't even realize how the Campaign for Grade-Level Reading and others have influenced that discussion. This is happening in government discussions as they are developing governmental policies. (Tennessee)

In this sense, as with other literature on institutional entrepreneurship, discourse plays as much of a role as actors in transforming the national landscape and shaping the mold in which new coalitions are formed and to which old coalitions must adapt.[21] While there was an overall shift in popularity, this does not mean that everyone shifted. One community shared its experience:

> In these community discussions, adult literacy seemed to be totally forgotten. It was all about the kids. But my board was like, "What about the adults?"

Others have emphasized that it doesn't have to be one or the other but can be a "both/and" approach:

> Concerning the conflict between early literacy and adult literacy, I think we need to all understand that more educated and literate parents have more educated and literate children. The increased research on brain development highlights the importance of a child's first three years. Who is feeding the brain during those first three years of a child's life? The parent or adult caregiver. We need for that person or persons to be literate and value education. Adult literacy and early childhood literacy are connected. (Ohio)

To some, this approach represents a third and a fourth wave of the literacy coalition movement, focusing on family literacy and lifelong learning. While adult literacy and early learning coalitions were developing, a new type of collective impact literacy network began to emerge, one that highlighted the value of parents and children learning together. This can be seen as a third wave of coalition change. With the leadership of the Barbara Bush Foundation and the National Center for Families Learning, family literacy networks began to use the coalition model to bring partners together and engage schools, community services, local government, funders, health services, and others in a coalition process of collaboration.

One impetus for this family focus was the better understanding of the "thirty million word gap" that researchers Betty Hart and Todd R. Risley pointed out as emerging by age three.

> In this study, University of Kansas researchers Betty Hart and Todd Risley entered the homes of forty-two families from various socio-economic back-

grounds to assess the ways in which daily exchanges between a parent and child shape language and vocabulary development. Their findings showed marked disparities between the sheer number of words spoken as well as the types of messages conveyed. After four years, these differences in parent-child interactions produced significant discrepancies in not only children's knowledge, but also their skills and experiences with children from high-income families being exposed to 30 million more words than children from families on welfare. Follow-up studies showed that these differences in language and interaction experiences have lasting effects on a child's performance later in life.[22]

These networks combined the strategies of adult education with those of early learning in a dual generational approach. The term family literacy includes: (1) studying literacy within the family, (2) programs designed to help young readers learn literacy skills, and (3) interventions intended to develop literacy skills among multiple family members.[23] The Barbara Bush Foundation promoted the goal for "everyone" to achieve. "The American Dream is about equal opportunity for everyone who works hard. If we don't give everyone the ability to simply read and write, then we aren't giving everyone an equal chance to succeed."[24] The Harvard Center for the Developing Child has also spotlighted the value of dual and multi-generational learning that engages all members of the family.[25]

Even with these developments, though, many coalitions still focused primarily on "cradle to career." It was not until a fourth wave of change that the "twinkle to wrinkle" model, promoted by Literacy Powerline, developed. A continuum of lifelong learning coalitions appeared and embraced all phases of life, from birth to seniors, promoting the value of literacy and learning across the lifespan. Adults no longer stay in one field all their lives; they change careers with the changing economy. Retraining may require additional literacy skills and retooling for new sectors or occupations. Adults concerned about maintaining mental acuity in old age face issues of managing healthcare and financial systems.

For some, this development laid to rest the struggle between adult versus early learning by demonstrating that literacy is the tool for different outcomes at different stages of life and that the struggle between the need for a skilled workforce and literacy as a human right can coexist on the coalition spectrum. Some coalitions have changed to embrace the tenets of waves three and four. Others have determined that adding more could spread them too thin and have supported other efforts to fill the gaps in service ages. Not all coalitions have taken a both/and approach, though. To deal with this issue, some have focused on redefining the problem with greater clarity. One person explained:

> We do not teach anyone how to read. In our city, we are not using the word literacy anymore; we are giving people the skills they need to move their families

forward. We are calling it adult education, and when you say "adult education" they know what that is immediately. It ranges from ESL all levels and pre-GED to certificate programs. That has saved so much time, not having to explain ourselves. You should know who you are, what you do, what problem you are trying to solve and hone it, hone it, hone it. Because literacy is not understood by funders and corporations. (Texas)

While some tensions emerge between adult education and other segments of the lifespan, there are also tensions among different emphases within the adult education realm. Many of the traditional nonprofit adult literacy providers believed strongly that a learner could enter the program with any number of goals, including improving quality of life, assisting children with homework, and taking part in a learning environment with friends. As the emphasis on workforce development emerged, public funding was channeled only to programs working to accomplish specific education and workforce development levels. This created a serious tension between the mainly privately funded nonprofits and the publicly funded schools and colleges. As one adult education focused provider shared:

> I think that a lot of the job readiness discourse overshadowed the focus on literacy. At first I was not happy that employment was overshadowing adult education, but now I am kind of happy because it has given adult education a bigger platform because when we say go to this or that job training or community college program, people can't get into those programs without basic education.

As some shared, it is important to have such groups keep in communication, and national conferences have been helpful in this regard. Here's how one respondent put it:

> How do the grassroots and grasstips come together and stay in place? Someone says, "I want to do early childhood," and someone else says, "What I care about is the workforce." That is why a conference like this is important because it is top down and bottom up. If you are in a community where the funder is not connected, please get them connected.

## Money Isn't Everything: Working to Address Challenges of Catalytic Philanthropy

We have explored coalitions and foundations as largely constructive partners. However, as the debate over whether to focus on adult or childhood literacy makes evident, their relationships can also have their destructive sides. As the saying goes, "You have to crack a few eggs to make an omelet." Apparently, coalitions can be viewed the same way. As one veteran in the adult literacy field recounted:

In some cases, driving the agenda of the coalitions left behind dead bodies, such as disenchanted members of the coalitions or service providers who felt that their message was not adequately conveyed, that they wanted a bigger piece of the pie, or they had a conflict of personality. Sometimes there are clashes of leadership, such as when coalitions emerge and policy leaders go to them for advice. If you were a large literacy provider and leaders used to come to you, and now they don't, you've lost that.

Here we see that the power of agenda setting can be both constructive and destructive. The same can be said for the role that funders play in the creation of coalitions. Although coalitions and funders have a long history of alliances, the relationship is not an entirely rosy picture. At times, it can seem that funders use their clout to spur other community members to action, even when there is no consensus to act. One community member shared:

A bunch of us got together and are launching some pilot programs related to the Campaign for Grade-Level Reading. We are only doing it because a local foundation asked us to do it. You have people that come to the meetings each week and yet they don't pay attention to what is going on and so that is a pothole you have to navigate. And we are competing for limited resources.

At times, the tendency of funders to orchestrate action and control details can feel quite heavy-handed. As one coalition member explained:

To some degree, funders decide how we do business. If you are looking for evidence-based models and they come with measurement tools to be used with that model, the funder says, "No, that is early childhood, so use this measure." It is all about care, custody, and control. We all care, but the funder has custody of the data, so we lose control of the fidelity.

Balancing the will of funders with the agenda of a coalition and its constituent agencies becomes all the more complicated the more parties involved. As one coalition leader recounted, sometimes it can seem like there are too many initiatives and it can be a challenge to integrate them.

Our coalition was organized in [the late 2000s] and then [a few years later] there was all this buzz about a Strive model coming to town and a community schools model. They were bringing all these things in, but there was no grand vision for how these things fit together. There were all these organizations sitting around the table, but we never could come to consensus on how these things would fit together.

Looking back there was a lack of community vision for what it could all do and what we wanted it to do. The community schools model is now there and in place. About a dozen of us went to Nashville to learn about how it is set up and now two years later the model is there, but only about two of the original people are still there. The model is to increase graduation rates, and they had all the players that the pre-existing coalition had onboard. The distinguishing factor they made was to focus on pre-K–12, so they weren't doing early education and they weren't doing adult education. They tried to put the coalition on the bookends and say, "You can't touch anything between pre-K–12." They thought they didn't need collaboration. They didn't want to run the principals ragged with all the nonprofits involved.

The fallout from attempting to merge distinctive visions and leadership styles can seem like a mixture of too many cooks in the kitchen and the beginning of the classic children's book, *Stone Soup*, in which no one wants to take the first step to expend their resources for the good of all. The same community member explained:

We brought in the Cradle to Career Model and the coalition and community schools model all around the table and we were supposed to figure out how it all fit together. It was a toxic meeting. Everyone wanted to be the lead and offer a model, no one wanted to do the work and be boots on the ground, and no one wanted to put the funding in.

Sometimes the fallout of such processes creates a situation in which the smaller players cannot be heard over the din, as he explains:

They created a gatekeeping process: The big players with the big staffs were going to continue their relationships with the schools but the little nonprofits weren't going to get through the filter.

Given the many community players that impact social problems such as literacy, it can quickly get confusing when trying to bring appropriate players to the table. Turf issues are a reality in nonprofit life, especially when resources are scarce, as they often are. Even coalitions themselves are sometimes looked at with leery eyes as nonprofits try to assess whether helping to build one will eventually be detrimental to their own organizations since the coalition could end up competing for the same grants and other community resources. Partly for this reason, communities tend to find agreement on the importance of bringing in funding from outside their geographical borders. The hope that signing on to national pilot initiatives and programs will result in a higher likelihood of luring in new external funding, especially when they are funded by the federal government, has led some communities to seek to join any and all national initiatives that they can.

As a result, our research reveals, it is not uncommon for the same community to have signed on to multiple national initiatives. Looking just at childhood literacy and education initiatives, we see that some communities have more than a handful of programs. While only approximately 12 percent of all U.S. counties have a national initiative (for a list of initiatives refer to table 2.1), of the ones that do, approximately half have more than one. The coexistence of multiple initiatives in the same community may indeed increase the likelihood and quantity of external funding, but it also means the coalition must integrate the multiple visions, strategies, program models, and approaches. What happens when a coalition includes multiple backbone organizations, especially in a larger city? How can coalitions avoid conflict and realize collaboration? Can coalitions discard individual agendas to support a more collaborative approach? Are there scenarios in which everyone wins?

As one coalition leader explained, the difficulty that results can be more than just mere obstinacy, but can stem from more structural sources:

> These were local and regional leaders, who were wedded to their own model and there was no way they were not going to have their model. They all had their own agendas. The community college was getting pressure from its larger system to follow one model. The school services person wanted the community schools model as a way to sustain a series of programs they had started. The coalition had already started with the Campaign for Grade-Level Reading and was up and running before the other models were even being explored, so people felt it should not be just swept under the rug or cancelled because of newer fancier models coming to town. Plus, we had results. And we had many of the relationships with community leaders at our table already and had monthly meetings—but the new groups did not want to sit down at that table. They didn't see us as an equal. I think they saw us as this grassroots, hokey group of people.

In another community, a very similar thing happened, leading to frustration:

> A new coalition type structure was formed, and while it did coordinate, it basically disregarded the table that had already been meeting and had many of the same people meet at its own table.

In addition to conflicting models, the sheer number of participants can cause a problem:

> It is such a waste of people's time having people go to many different meetings, so it was contradicting what I was telling people, namely that it would save time to have a centralized coalition meeting. It ended up being the same old people on the boards and working teams of all these models. How were you expecting to get something different?

When coalitions impose new models on top of existing models without the cooperation of multiple partners, it often creates greater challenges. Coalitions that embrace existing goals and refine them with respect to multiple players and allow all partners to maintain ownership of the expanded model have a better chance of success. In some cases, despite the best of intentions, people simply must accept a coalition just doesn't work. In one city, for example, the Literacy Coalition invited all the partners to the table, including the small adult literacy coalition. The new coalition focused on lifelong learning and respected the role of the existing coalition. Amidst a long and involved negotiation a collaborative relationship was offered, but the old coalition did not accept the partnership. It continued alone, closing down eventually as resources became more scarce and the funders worked with the new coalition.

While having many initiatives in one community can seem like "too many cooks in the kitchen," over time, such confusion, despite its frustrating aspects, can help to build the civic muscle needed to move forward. This brings to bear two other axioms: "No pain no gain" and "A community moves forward at the speed of trust."

> While there was tension and angst between initiative models, going to all these different meetings reinforced relationships with a lot of other people. I feel it was definitely a family atmosphere, a very trusting atmosphere where people could bring up issues. After five years they started feeling comfortable, saying things like, "What is up with this program? We need to look into that." Some organizations started to see how their own programs could be improved. They could see how kids were being frustrated when you are giving them this test and we are giving them this other one, so they would try to be a bit more considerate.

Increased social capital and collaboration can certainly come from coalition work, but this work of gathering and coordinating people is often invisible. As one coalition executive director explained:

> In many cases literacy coalitions play that role of backbone and broker and that needs to be done every day. And the challenge is the funding. In an orchestra, who pays for the conductor? And that is where funders often won't see the value. In more cases than not, it is not something that is funded. Those struggles exist all the time. (Ohio)

Because this work is hard to define, measure, and thus get funding for, some coalitions have sought to diversify their funding streams. Often, older coalitions can be seen to do so by providing direct services that come with funding for administrative overhead.

The funding strategy is very different for coalitions that provide direct services compared to those that focus primarily on the backbone only. Those that provide direct services can add sources of funding from programs. No funder seems to want to fund the long, hard work of getting people on the same page and working together. They all seem to want to fund the programs. Running programs is a way to bring in other funding, but there is a danger to this. I know of a coalition that did focus on a program to get money but, as you know, programs come and go. Eventually those programs went away, and so did the coalition. It lost sight of its main purpose and lost its way. (Ohio)

This highlights a major Achilles heel common to nearly all relationships between funders and coalitions: dependency. While the relationship is symbiotic to the extent that coalitions help to accomplish many of the collaborative aspirations of funders, coalitions must often plan for when this dynamic of mutual benefit becomes disrupted, oftentimes through changing funder interests, strategies, and focus areas.

While these examples illustrate the close ties coalitions have had with their funders, they belie the difficulty of establishing and maintaining such relationships. Despite all the funding described in the preceding pages, coalitions are often challenged annually to raise the funds to do the work needed to achieve their missions. Frequently the funding environment changes or funders go on to support other priorities.

## The Downside of Over-Dependence on Funders

Coalitions and funders can be great partners, and, as we have explored, oftentimes these relationships can persist for long periods of time. However, this is not an equal relationship to the extent that coalitions need funders more than funders need coalitions. If a funder chooses a new focus area, ending the relationship can be done with minimal stress. However, loss of a key funder can cause a coalition to go out of existence if they are not able to compensate. As one coalition director explains:

> Some funders worry about an exit strategy. Funders don't want to be stuck funding the literacy coalition in perpetuity. Foundation funding declines over time and government funding increases. However, government funding is available only if the literacy coalition is a program provider. To my knowledge, the government does not fund the services provided by a "backbone" agency. I believe the funder or funders who created the literacy coalition needs to treat the literacy coalition as a partner in addressing this community need (low literacy) in a systematic manner. If I lose one big funder, it could take me five smaller funders to make up what I lost.[26] (Ohio)

As a result of these anticipated challenges, coalitions often try to diversify their portfolios and do things such as braid their funding (more on this later). As it turns out, this is often a wise choice. A local funder who collaborates on collective impact efforts in his community reflectively explains the nature of his colleagues. He shares that funders often lack the long-term focus that coalitions require, even when success is being made:

> Some funders will only fund things for a year or a three-year period and then move on to something else. They will say, "Great, we made third-grade reading." Really, it's no surprise we have to keep at it, since we have second graders next year and we have to make it happen again. (Pennsylvania)

But funders are not entirely up to their own volition in such cases. Providing long-term funding to a single coalition can be a double-edged sword since, as one funder explains, "You would likely see push back from nonprofits if the funders focus on one thing."

Agencies that are publicly funded, on the whole, receive funding without having to apply to numerous funders. They don't have to constantly make the case for the work, justify their existence again and again and do not provide services at the pleasure of a foundation board. For many nonprofit coalitions, funding dilemmas keep the organization in a lifeboat, never secure and confident that they can sail freely. This is a challenging way to sail a boat and stay afloat to say the least. Coalitions, and many other nonprofits, really run two businesses under one roof by developing both the funding for services and providing the services. This is very different from a for-profit model in the business world or the systems funded with our tax dollars. A business develops a product that matches a customer's need and the customer pays for it. In the nonprofit world, it is typically not the customer that pays for the service or product and this is especially true of an intermediary organization like a literacy coalition. One coalition director reported that she had over a hundred different funding sources to build her budget every year and each had to be nurtured, appreciated, and reported to. Another reported that the one funding stream that maintained the organization was about to fund another issue area—they were preparing for a crisis situation. While some seek backup funders, this is easier said than done:

> Funders often have their own silos within and among themselves. And some funders will not get involved if others are already involved. They say, oh, they've already got that covered, I don't need to get involved in that. Funders want to stand out from others. If the larger funder gets involved, others might stay away. The community needs to do a lot of work to get multiple funders involved. (Ohio)

While funders are critical, coalitions are loath to rely too heavily on them. A funding system that relies only on charitable contributions from private funders is in many ways seen as dysfunctional, and that drives a level of dysfunction within the organizations. For instance, consider a scenario in which a coalition outlines three key goals in the annual strategic plan but manages to fund just one of the goals. The plan is driven by what is funded, not what is needed. Some coalitions spend valuable resources hiring a development director and funding the organization's development machine. The development director's first job is to fund the operations of the organization so that the staff and structure are in place to do the work. Many funders do not like to fund operations and staffing; they would rather fund programs that have direct measurable impacts that they can share with their boards. It is the chicken and egg scenario because programs cannot be successful without the infrastructure to support them.

For many years, funders looked for and complimented coalitions for unrealistically low operating expenses. One funder was delighted with a 12 percent operating expense figure for a coalition. Creating a budget with that low figure required very careful juggling to ensure every staff member had a programmatic role as well as an administrative role. The funder was delighted that such a large amount of funding went to direct services and continued to make large contributions. This kind of unrealistic expectation from a funder encourages creative juggling from coalition staff. Some coalitions, driven by funder expectations and the drive to impress funders and meet their requirements, sacrifice more efficient ways of doing things out of fear of losing current funding. This creates artificial, even dishonest relationships between funders and coalitions. Over time acceptable rates for overhead and operating expenses have increased to 20 then 25 percent, but staffs must raise those funds in a process that may take hundreds of hours with uncertain results.

Once funding relationships are on a firm footing, it becomes easier for a coalition to stand up for itself and negotiate for perceived community needs, but the coalition is always at risk of incurring the funder's wrath, which could be catastrophic for the organization. The dynamic between funders and funded is delicate and has caused coalitions to flourish or fail.

## A Diverse Portfolio: How Coalitions Negotiate Rough Waters of Funding

Over time, coalitions have had to become creative in the ways they use funding to best impact their partners. Increased flexibility, creativity, and coordination can maximize resources. No one funder or system can provide resources for all the services that coalitions and their partners require for success.

Amid these complex relationships, new concepts are emerging, known as blending and braiding funds for coalition development to encourage the use of increased alternative funding strategies. Blending refers to mixing together a variety of funds into one pool so that a variety of services can be funded and managed under one account. Public funding streams often prevent funds to be mixed in this way, because it could be considered double dipping, but where it is permitted by law or policy it may allow for greater stability of services. When funds are blended in this way however, it becomes impossible to report on where specific funds were spent and coalitions can only report on the community outcomes achieved.

Braiding, on the other hand, maintains the separate nature of the funds and allows for a variety of funding streams to support a specific project but requires that, for reporting purposes, each dollar can be assigned back to the original funding stream. This requires more documentation and careful accountability to ensure that each funding stream supports only eligible activities. Even though this approach sometimes requires waivers and additional approvals, staffing time, and careful monitoring, braiding often brings more resources to the coalition.

Even with these challenges, braiding and blending can be mutually beneficial to the community, and coalitions play a crucial role as intermediaries in bringing the various components to the table.

*Intermediary funding.* Coalitions providing direct services have sometimes been more successful at accessing funding as intermediaries. Coalitions acting as intermediaries often have different measures for success than they do when serving the role of a direct service provider. For instance, one coalition, with support from the mayor, successfully negotiated a portion of the federal adult education grant that had traditionally gone to the local community college. The mayor, in cowboy hat and reclining with boots on his desk, asked the college representative if he was willing to negotiate with the coalition so that a portion of funds could flow through the coalition to the nonprofit service providers. The college reluctantly offered a 30/70 split of the funds. The mayor asked the coalition director if she would accept the 70 percent. She replied that she certainly would, but she felt a 50/50 split would be more equitable. With that agreement, the coalition increased services and quality of its programs.

Another funding success story comes from a Philadelphia adult education program. There, the Mayor's Coalition for Literacy received funds as the intermediary with a network of providers. This arrangement allowed central coordination and shared professional development as well as outcome and results tracking for program improvement. The city council negotiated for the coalition to act as the fiscal intermediary in allocating county grants for

English language services. The council valued the expertise of the coalition, its knowledge of the community partners, and its track record for professional services. The coalition managed the funds and implemented a strong accountability model.

As backbone intermediaries, coalitions help members negotiate relationships with funding partners, explore intermediary roles and responsibilities, review impact measures and outcomes, and advise on strategies for collaboration. Often coalitions identify gaps in services and determine how best to fill those gaps. Some coalitions insist their role is purely intermediary, while others as strongly insist that direct services that fill gaps are good for everyone. A coalition that provides gap-filling services that have been agreed upon and designed with the help of partners is more likely to succeed in those services.

Over time, community foundations in particular, because of their strong start-up support for coalitions, have been both the success and the bane of some coalitions. Coalition leaders will report that these funding partnerships are powerful and positive but sometimes the support does not transfer over time. In one community, for example, the community foundation provided only seed funding, including the start-up salary for an executive director and office space. After the first two years, the foundation withdrew its support for the project it had envisioned and nurtured. The coalition had not succeeded in replacing the seed funding with other support and had not secured alternative space. The burden fell back on the literacy providers who reorganized, secured other funding, purchased a building (and leased some of the space for an additional income stream), and built on the remaining elements of the dying coalition.

*Investing in entrepreneurial initiatives.* To create a sustainable coalition, not having all of the effort's eggs in one basket helps. Raising funds not just from multiple funders but also from multiple types of funders offers stability. Getting written into line item budgets at local, county, and state levels is also very advantageous. Finding innovative strategies also can keep coalitions running. One literacy coalition opened a bookstore and published a book. The book features short stories, essays, poems, memoirs, and even puzzles and a play, all donated by twenty-nine area authors. The works focus on reading, writing, bookstores, and a love of books. "It has received very positive reviews and continues to be the best-selling book at our store," one member of the coalition said. The organization used a generous grant from the estate of a major donor to publish the book, and all sales proceeds support the organization. "One of the great outcomes of having published this book, and having the bookstore, is that we have been able to become a significant force in promoting local authors to a wider audience," the coalition member said.

Although each community takes advantage of opportunities in different ways, this example highlights the importance of openness to creative new ideas.

*Spelling bees.* Activities that promote the mission, increase visibility, and raise funds are not always easy to find, but starting in the 1990s the concept of the Great Grown Up Spelling Bee was born. Usually citywide events, organized by a host committee of local leaders, and following the rules of the long-running Scripps Howard competition, spelling bees across the country fostered business competition and sometimes cutthroat fun as companies vied to become spelling champions. Teams brought out their mascots to support them and invited guests to cheer them on. In some communities, the team fee was $2,000, and some events raised money with guest tickets and dinner fees. Some of these spelling competitions raised more than $100,000. Palm Beach County, Austin, Nashville, Boston, and Houston have been raising money through spelling bees for years, and their bees are a fixed institution on their communities' annual calendars. Annual dinners hosted by the mayor or a major sponsor, walks, and runs, Scrabble tournaments, and even old-fashioned bake sales raise money to support literacy coalitions. Some programs are successful, and some are not, but all take hours of preparation and are very volunteer-intensive, which often adds a team-building element for the coalition and its partners.

*State lotteries.* Texas tried a new idea as state lotteries grew and gained traction. The literacy coalitions around the state introduced, through their champion Senator Rodney Ellis, a lottery for literacy—The Texas Lotteracy. The idea, spearheaded in the Texas legislature, was to use a portion of state lottery funding for literacy coalitions. The bill got traction in both the house and the senate, but finally was overturned and chalked up as a good marketing strategy to raise awareness about literacy. Many states have lotteries and many of those lottery funds are designated for education. Perhaps coalitions have an opportunity here.

## Emphasizing Impact in Collective Impact: Funders and the Push for Results

In the following chapter we will explore how coalitions measure success, but before doing so it is critical to see the role that funders play in pushing coalitions to define and measure success. To cut to the heart of the matter, it is the impact that coalitions can have that draws most funders to collective impact. As this interviewee explained, it is this impact that "puts some meat and teeth" behind the effort.

> The way funders perceive literacy is as the First Lady's hobby. They said until you can put some meat and teeth behind it and show the return on investment, they

don't really care that everyone has the right to read. We have to be able to speak the speak of those corporate funders and that is a big shift to corporate language.

Within the coalition field cautionary tales exist about what can happen when impact is not achieved and there is no identifiable return on the investment that funders make. As one coalition builder recounted:

> In our community, the funding model was different but not unique; the workforce investment board, the school district, and the city provided the seed grants. This model was essentially a public funding triumvirate that was initially highly successful [but] the founding leaders were not fully invested in developing the work. The funders saw a great deal of intensive planning and partnership development but did not see that transfer into measurable education change in as timely a manner as they hoped. When the funding came to an end, so did the coalition. (Connecticut)

Scary to coalition directors to say the least, this form of cut and dry, "results or perish" approach understandably encounters resistance from coalitions. Getting results and impact, as the following interviewee shared, might require thinking outside the box.

> My biggest takeaway as a funder is knowing what you are getting into and that this is a marathon and not a sprint. Just be honest about it: Is the work going where you want it to go? I was expecting my community foundation to be a partner as well as a funder, and eventually they started to be just a funder and all they wanted was results and impact numbers. When you are running a coalition, it is hard to deliver all of that in one grant cycle and show real change. I never found a good way to do that. I think a funder has to look at a different funding mechanism for a coalition of a collective impact initiative. They need to understand that it takes longer to show results, a different type of measurement than maybe people are used to.

While such urging may be welcome to coalitions, this does not always mean it is easy for foundation staff simply to acknowledge that measuring success is difficult and move on from there. One funder offered an inside perspective:

> One of the frustrating things about being a funder working with a coalition is the lack of results, feeling like you want this community initiative to be involving lots of different people to do the work, but you have your own board to answer to so you want to see the coalition making strides and stepping out of the shadow of the foundation and you want it to be done in a really professional and strategic way. As a foundation professional that was a hard balance to strike

because there are a lot of people involved. It is a messy process and it is a new process. We were pretty much the only collective impact approach in town, so it was new to get people together to talk about an issue without any grant money attached. You wanted to keep people together and do things, but you don't want to do it all yourself.

This funder's sense of feeling alone in measuring progress is also shared by some coalition staff when it comes to data and impact. One staff member shared:

I've looked at other communities and wished that I had a data expert and person at the foundation who was a partner who could soundboard ideas and help guide the work, but through data and real information, not just through anecdotes and emotions. It doesn't have to be the same person at the organization who acts as a partner and organizes the data, but they are unique pieces that are needed. The partnership is probably more important than the data. A lot of foundations are understaffed and their program people are focused on making grants, but having a person at the foundation who can be more of a specialist in strategic initiatives and can devote time to the coalition or collective impact structure is important. You cannot make collective impact grants the way you would do a regular grant cycle. It is just not the same thing.

Expressing a similar sentiment, a funder criticized other colleagues for trying to run collective impact projects the same way typical grantmaking operates. "Funders sometimes show up at the beginning and say this is what they want to see happen but then they disappear until the final report is due," he said.

Perhaps in response to this pressure and these challenges of measurement, coalitions often resolve to find ways to show their impact, even if it means providing fewer services overall because they must shift resources to demonstrate effectiveness.

One of the reasons we have not been able to create this systematic approach to adult and lifelong learning is that we do not have enough money and we try to be everything to everyone. I think what you need to do is focus in on one thing and do that very well. There is not even enough money in adult education alone, let alone trying to do everything. We need to do that really well and collect the data and show the impact to get wins and then longer wins. We were doing so many things for so long that we did not do any of it very well.

One group that has devoted considerable attention to focusing on fewer indicators of success and measuring them well is the purveyor group. There is some evidence that affiliates of the Strive network tend to publicly track more indicators (or measurable outcomes of their efforts) than other types of collective impact efforts.[27] One purveyor that has set out from the beginning to be measurable is the GLR Campaign:

We said by 2020, a decade at the outset, we should see states and movement at a population level. We should see a critical mass within the states that are doing enough work that we start to see a population movement. We don't have a lot of examples of population-level change to look to outside of the health field. We saw concentrated efforts to reduce teen pregnancy and increase paternity establishment and increase child support, but we do not have a tight image of what population change should look like. This in part takes Stephen Covey's figuring out leading and lagging indicators [leading indicators are often things that can be measured up front and in a timely fashion while lagging indicators are the longer term result of these]. Grade-level reading is lagging, so can we see movement on the leads. If people in coalitions can do things powerful enough to move the leads, we are going to see movement in the lags.

And they have seen movement; as of 2015, the Campaign has noted at least one hundred communities showing progress in one of the areas of their focus and more than fifty communities in fifteen states showing progress in at least two areas.[28] In the following chapter, we dig deeper into what success looks like within individual communities and we explore further what it means to ask whether coalition communities are better off.

## NOTES

1. Peters, G., & Wooley, J. T. (1988, August 18). "Address Accepting the Presidential Nomination at the Republican National Convention in New Orleans." Retrieved April 3, 2017, from http://www.presidency.ucsb.edu/ws/?pid=25955.

2. Peters, G., & Wooley, J. T. (1988, August 18). "Address Accepting the Presidential Nomination at the Republican National Convention in New Orleans." Retrieved April 3, 2017, from http://www.presidency.ucsb.edu/ws/?pid=25955.

3. Early Comprehensive Childhood Systems Impact (ECCS Impact). (n.d.). Retrieved April 3, 2017, from http://www.grants.gov/web/grants/search-grants .html?keywords=ECCS.

4. "Obama Administration Announces Eight Additional Promise Zones to Build Community Prosperity." (2015, April 28). Retrieved April 3, 2017, from http://www .usda.gov/wps/portal/usda/usdahome?contentid=2015/04/0116.xml.

5. (n.d.). Retrieved June 27, 2017 from http://communityfoundationatlas.org/.

6. (n.d.). Retrieved April 3, 2017, from://grantspace.org/tools/knowledge-base/ Funding-Resources/Foundations/health-conversion-foundations.

7. (n.d.). Retrieved April 3, 2017, from http://www.jmsims.org/about/history .html?cv=1.

8. (n.d.). Retrieved April 3, 2017, from https://www.unitedway.org/blog/charting -a-course-for-change.

9. (n.d.). Retrieved April 3, 2017, from https://www.unitedway.org/blog/charting-a-course-for-change.

10. Some of this info from an interview is also available on the following website: (n.d.). Retrieved April 3, 2017, from http://www.unitedway.org/about/history.

11. Venture Capital Guide: The Guide On Venture Capital And Getting Funded (2016). Retrieved from http://www.venture-capital-guide.com/using-angel-investors-to-fund-a-business/.

12. (2012) Retrieved June 27, 2017 from http://www.legacy.com/obituaries/houstonchronicle/obituary.aspx?pid=155939829.

13. Frey, Lohmeier, Lee, & Tollefson, 2006.

14. Ridzi, Carmody, & Byrnes, 2011, 114–116.

15. Ridzi, Carmody, & Byrnes, 2011, 114–116.

16. Oosthuizen & Louw, 2013.

17. Some of this info from an interview is also available on the following web site: (n.d.). Retrieved from http://national-coalition-literacy.org/about/history/.

18. The Campaign for Grade-Level Reading: Midpoint Snapshots. (n.d.). Retrieved April 8, 2017, from http://gradelevelreading.net/wp-content/uploads/2016/04/MidpointSnapshots_Apr12.pdf.

19. The Campaign for Grade-Level Reading: Midpoint Snapshots. (n.d.). Retrieved April 8, 2017, from http://gradelevelreading.net/wp-content/uploads/2016/04/MidpointSnapshots_Apr12.pdf, 3–4.

20. The Campaign for Grade-Level Reading: Midpoint Snapshots. (n.d.). Retrieved April 8, 2017, from http://gradelevelreading.net/wp-content/uploads/2016/04/MidpointSnapshots_Apr12.pdf, 3–4.

21. Ridzi, 2009.

22. Hart, & Risley, 1995.

23. (n.d.). Retrieved April 4, 2017, from http://hfrp.org/family-involvement/publications-resources/family-literacy-a-review-of-programs-and-critical-perspectives.

24. (n.d.). Retrieved April 3, 2017, from www.barbarabush.org.

25. "A Science-Based Framework for Early Childhood Policy." (n.d.). Retrieved April 3, 2017, from http://developingchild.harvard.edu/wp-content/uploads/2015/05/Policy_Framework.pdf.

26. Some distinction should be made between a Literacy Coalition that is also, and perhaps primarily, a service provider/program, and a Literacy Coalition whose existence is to seek systemic change.

27. Henig, Houston, Rebel, & Wolf, 2016.

28. The Campaign for Grade-Level Reading: Midpoint Snapshots, 2015: 6.

*Chapter Three*

# Are Collective Impact Coalition Communities Better Off?

## *Understanding Collective Impact as Part of a Virtuous Cycle*

The implicit assertion of those who build and fund collective impact community coalitions is that people are better off as a result of these coalitions' work. In the following pages we explore the question of whether communities that have collective impact coalitions are better off. We begin by surveying coalitions about their measurement practices and their perspectives on evidence of their impact. As we saw in the previous chapter, coalitions face considerable pressure to demonstrate their success. Relying on interviews and case studies, we explore both local and national experiences with the challenge of measuring outcomes as well as efforts to develop shared data systems that can accomplish this task. While these developments will surely take time, perhaps decades, we consider what is knowable from existing data sources, even with all their caveats. As some have asserted, a major role that coalitions can play is in tracking the outcomes of partner programs, both of individual partners and the coalition as a whole.[1] In a time when performance management is seeing greater emphasis on the national level, including the federal government, this is a key area in which coalitions have a clear added value, since, to paraphrase the saying, "It takes a village to measure a program." This is so because each program is limited in its data collection by the fact that clients often move on after receiving services and programs must rely on the groups working with those individuals months or years later to obtain data on how well their lives have turned out. Furthermore, the value of programs cannot be fully appreciated until they are placed in the context of other programs and their outcomes are compared. This requires a level of data sharing that is not possible without the type of collaborative community ecosystem that coalitions nurture.

The goal of community coalition measurement is not only to assess whether a community is improving as a whole, but also to seek clues as to whether and why certain practices do or don't work. It is only through this work of measurement and evaluation that coalitions can seek to maximize their impact. When it comes to analyzing impact, there are several options for level of analysis. These include the literacy effects for: clients of each single program in the community; all clients served by the coalition, regardless of which program(s) served them; all citizens in the community, regardless of whether the citizen received any help from any coalition partners; and all citizens in the country broken out by whether or not the community had a coalition. In this chapter we will go about exploring evidence on all of these levels. For the first three options, we utilize case studies that exemplify this type of work. For the final option, we use national data to ask whether coalition communities are indeed different from the national norm. Finding that they are correlated with more positive community outcomes, we then seek to discern how much of this favorable status might be attributable to the presence of coalitions. We do this by controlling for a host of other potential explanations for why coalition communities could be better off. Then we seek to examine whether these coalition communities simply started out better off in the first place, or if the creation of a coalition is in any way correlated with community-level improvement. Overall, the data that do exist are not adequate to make any statements about whether having a collective impact coalition causes a community to be better off. Rather, what they do accomplish is help to establish the presence of such coalitions as part of a virtuous cycle in which positive community characteristics seem to mutually reinforce one another. While more and better data are needed to run such models with confidence, this preliminary analysis offers a hint of what such further analysis would find.

## WHAT COALITIONS MEASURE AND
## MONITOR ON THE LOCAL LEVEL

Measurement is an important part of what many coalitions do. Whether surveying local literacy providers, tracking attendance at literacy conferences and training events, collecting feedback forms from participants, or examining the amount of training that coalition members implement, coalitions are deeply involved in measurement. Much like funders, coalitions tend to measure on four levels: the individual, organizational, inter-organizational, and the community.

At the individual level, evaluation tends to be of the programs run by a coalition rather than of the coalition itself. For book distribution programs, coalitions track outcomes such as number of book giveaways or number of books distributed. For adult learners, coalitions may track numbers of learners who attain their GED or who are making progress toward educational goals. One coalition explains:

> We track the number of GED graduates within the programs that are members of the coalition, and number of clients served through our Learner Web grant. (Louisiana)

One community in Iowa has invested in the Decatur, Illinois database and has been using the Surveillance of Wellness of Young Children (SWYC) to measure progress. While many coalitions count the number of people served, some go even further, such as conducting interviews with students and tutors annually. For data on school-age children, they often rely on the local school district's formal assessments to gauge progress. As one coalition leader explained, "Each program has its own evaluation system."

When it comes to organizational level measures, coalitions that track these use such approaches as number of referrals to literacy providers, number of instructors trained in professional development, or number of inquiries for volunteer opportunities. As in the following example, the focus tends to be on building capacity to implement best practices:

> We record the number and percent of staff persons from literacy service provider organizations that have received professional development support in usage of common performance measures and client tracking to enable member organizations to articulate the full impact of literacy services in our city and make a compelling case for increased funding based on clear results. (Georgia)

Another coalition shared similar capacity-building goals:

> We assess through surveys of attendees at our conferences. These conferences are aimed at advancing professional development so we use assessments in the form of pre/post training evaluations to indicate that they have advanced and are implementing the tools and curriculum. (Texas)

Yet another coalition explained that their goal is an increase in the "number and percent of literacy service providers [that] have increased their proficiency in tracking the progress of low-level reading adults receiving literacy services from their organizations."

When it comes to the inter-organizational work that coalitions attempt, the emphasis for evaluation tends to gravitate toward seeing continued existence as a key indicator of persisting relevance and collaboration. As in the following case, such existence combined with key milestones of collaboration (as documented in some of the literature) is the extent of measurement practicable given the frequently limited resources of a coalition.

Measures include: 1) simply continuing to exist, with a combination of new and returning board members, for close to a decade without any paid staff. 2) Similarly, collaboration in the establishment of a Literacy Resource Center with partners that do provide direct services is a measure of success. 3) Creation and now maintenance of a website that continues to receive new and returning visitors on a monthly basis. 4) Convening an event or two every year. (Connecticut)

Another coalition explained that it measures success not only by continuing to exist but also by growing membership:

Increasing the coalition's membership by recruiting at least six new organizations annually to join the coalition representing a 20 percent increase in membership, thereby strengthening our sustainability. The coalition tries to leverage the support of our single donor by raising an additional $75,000 annually to support programming and organizational infrastructure. (Georgia)

Listening to an inventory of all the measures coalitions can collect, as in the following example, it becomes apparent how unique local measures are to the local priorities that each coalition sets. Measures can range from attendance at coalition meetings to the number of editorials coalition members write for local newspapers. As one coalition reported:

We track:

1. Number/percentage of attendance at [coalition] meetings.
2. Number of trainings produced on key literacy topics and professional development sessions for literacy providers and community literacy volunteers.
3. Proceedings from our Literacy Summit.
4. Number of events facilitated by coalition.
5. Materials (press releases, sign-in sheets, notes, etc.) from each event.
6. Number of public literacy messages by coalition non-profit participants.
7. Number of resources the coalition provides for tutors to use to enhance skills.
8. Percentage of participants that report high satisfaction and usefulness of trainings and summit (via surveys after trainings and summit sessions).
9. Number of new collaborations or partnerships among coalition participants.
10. Number of instances in which [the coalition] hosts and/or convenes coalition participant organizations meeting with each other.
11. Percentage of editorial pieces published locally regarding literacy written by coalition participants.
12. Number of letters to the editor published locally regarding literacy written by coalition participants.
13. Number of contacts regarding literacy with government officials by coalition participants.

14. Percentage of coalition participants participating in community initiatives to advocate for literacy issues/policies. (Tennessee)

For most coalitions, coalition-level measurement is a work in progress. One coalition clarified a dominant theme that coalition measures are not as strong or as easy to conduct as evaluating programs.

> For programs, we have a number of participants in the programs represented, standardized test scores. We are still working on measurement issues as a coalition. (Colorado)

This theme points out a weakness many coalitions experienced. As one admitted, coalitions have "limited ability to formally measure success, so we try to capture number of trainings provided, number of partner organizations, etc." (Minnesota)

Nevertheless, most coalitions seek to eventually make a noticeable difference on the community level, such as increasing community awareness, mobilizing volunteers and other resources, and ultimately, increasing literacy levels.

> Ultimately, we would hope that the coalition could contribute through a significant media/public awareness campaign to the generation of a substantial increase in the number of literacy volunteers and eventually measurable improvement in area literacy levels. However, with an annual budget of approximately $5,000 (even less in some years) and with zero paid staff, the coalition needs to be realistic about what it can accomplish as a group of volunteers. (Connecticut)

Funding levels are very significant differentiators for coalition outcomes and measurement. With budgets ranging from $5,000 to $5 million, the scale of accomplishment often matched the scale of investment. While funding is one barrier to more rigorous evaluation, there is also an acknowledgement that by their very nature, what coalitions do is hard to measure. As one coalition participant shared:

> We just submitted a proposal to the local United Way to launch a collective impact approach on a targeted community, but it is hard to measure impact because it is so broad. We have a vision of 100 percent literacy through 100 percent literacy infusion. (California)

Another coalition leader explained that there can be a disconnect between coalition work and typical approaches to measure.

> There is this sneaking fear that we are not impacting things by actually convening. There is that measurement piece but even what you measure may not be related to the coalition work. (Michigan)

Coalition leaders share a general sense that publicly available data sets are weak and often not helpful. To make them relevant you have to stretch them to make connections that require some degree of contextualization.

> There are some very old statistics out there. When we worked with the Bush Foundation we found there is no way to determine literacy rates in adult education (you can in school.). So we had to use dropout rate, poverty rate, unemployment rate. Do not throw out data without a good source because when they ask where you got that you can't just say, "Someone said that." You need to know where that number came from. I tie education data for early learning to adult education so people care about adult education. We talk about our next generation of college graduates. Although we do not work with early childhood and school-age programs, we tie it to adult education to paint a fuller picture so people care.

While some coalitions try to leverage existing data to create a broader picture of their community, others have sought to collect their own.

> In 2014, the mayor launched a centralized registration and enrollment place for adult learners across the city. We know how many and their level of skill since we assess them and then where they go into the community for learning. The coalition set this system up. We have very formal partners in this approach and then we have this broader alliance of providers, some of which are not enrolled in this program but are able to improve. (Pennsylvania)

In addition to measures of community learners, coalitions also shared that one way they measure their success is by creating a culture around literacy. As one leader explained, this can take time:

> Seven years ago, we brought a group of literacy coalition directors together to try and figure out what we should be doing. We had to push our way into meetings and it seemed like we weren't wanted around the table, but now people come to us and ask, "What do you think about this. Are we focusing on literacy enough?" So, one of the messages is persistence. The stars are starting to align around literacy. It no longer is a dirty word. It used to be a conversation stopper. (Ohio)

## COALITION PERSPECTIVES ON EVIDENCE OF THEIR OVERALL IMPACT ON THE COMMUNITY

Since, by their nature, many coalitions formed in response to needs as identified in community-level outcomes, a number of coalitions have sought to keep track of community-level progress by developing a "community scorecard" or other mechanism that focuses on progress of learners in the community along the developmental continuum. This can be quite complex. As one coalition shared, they use "four primary quantitative indicators, ten secondary quantitative indicators, and one hundred tertiary indicators." However, most coalitions reported using academic gains, grade-level reading, graduation rates, transition to post-secondary education, and completion of college or other higher level of training/education. While these are the easiest data to obtain, they are not necessarily easy to effect change in. Many census and school district level data sets operate on a scale that requires considerable sustained impact in order to create a noticeable effect. Reflecting on this reality, one coalition leader suggested that "moving the needle" may take more than just local effort to avoid frustration.

Funders get frustrated because the "needle" isn't moving. Local coalitions need to be broader at both the local and national levels to be more effective. (Maryland)

Encouragingly, the work of many coalitions dovetails nicely with efforts made on the state and national level to better measure the impact of their work. As one explained, efforts are under way to develop a single statewide data system to track core outcome measures and demographic data.

This is an issue. We are working with a company to try to bring our literacy members on to one statewide data system that tracks their core outcome measures and demographic data and allows our state office to access it via web to report state data to funders and legislators. There are no good database management systems out there for literacy providers to all "speak the same data language" and report along NRS (National Reporting System) standards so we can have a better idea of our progress in the field. [One national organization in particular] does not have the staff capacity to take the lead on this issue—we've asked lots of times. The Council of State Organizations, a coalition of executive directors of state coalitions, has formed a committee to look at this issue, but after two years we really don't have any progress that would work in all states. Each state is trying to address this individually and no one has proposed anything that has potential to move ahead. Even Verizon and the American Library Association took a crack at it about four or five years ago and that system only works for library-based programs. This is a huge need in the field if we want to report appropriate outcomes and compete for federal funding. (Wisconsin)

They are not alone. Arizona, Georgia, and Arkansas are all taking a state-level approach that helps to ensure that all clients served are being supported by measurement and analysis. Clearly, though, many states are not taking a statewide approach. While optimistic, as seen in the above quote, there are also many barriers to moving forward and, thus far, the best hope lies in development. In the meantime, several coalitions have set about encouraging data sharing as a first step toward a comprehensive system for measuring community literacy progress. As one coalition explained, data sharing is a part of their community planning process.

> We are currently identifying benchmarks and metrics as part of our local grade-level reading campaign. . . . We track student achievement data as part of our Literacy Zone pilots at three schools and encourage data and information sharing through an evaluation matrix where each of our partner literacy organizations shares information about their assessment system and intended outcomes. (California)

While there are hopeful signs, the nation overall has yet to develop a system for tracking the impact of coalition programs and efforts at the organizational and inter-organizational level to create community change. If the coalition phenomenon is to grow to its full potential, eventually, greater evidence of their impact will be needed. This challenge is further complicated by the fact that coalition capacities and effectiveness can be assumed to vary across a coalition's lifespan and across communities. As one funder explained, coalitions are like "civic muscle."[2] It stands to reason that some communities are more in shape than others. Indeed, national data bear this out.

## EFFORTS TOWARD STANDARDIZING LITERACY OUTCOMES

As the collective impact movement has grown, an increasing number of coalition success stories have emerged. Since there is no single agreed upon way to measure coalitions, and it is up to coalitions themselves to discern how they will measure success, it is often very difficult to tell whether one coalition is more impactful than another. At the heart of this is the question of whether coalitions should define their success at the level of organizational collaboration or community member outcomes. As one coalition explained, looking at student outcomes is politically problematic:

> Our main customer is the agency; if we focus on the student then we would be competing with our membership. Success for a coalition is different than success for an agency; we have to define our customer. I know we move the needle in how many classes our agencies are able to offer, and also the number of pre- and post-tests our agencies have been able to use, and in evidence-based professional development across the city . . . we have moved the needle on number of contact hours and number of classes offered. Now the agencies can prove that they have made differences where before they could not. Ultimately,

we would measure the success of a coalition by more people getting high school equivalencies, getting English they need for their jobs, getting promotions, and pay raises; there are a lot of things. It is a lot different than it is for children. I am becoming a more educated employee and parent. It is not only educational attainment, it is life attainment. (Texas)

This perspective highlights that this challenge is not so much a difference in ultimate goals, but rather one of a clearly articulated division of labor. The coalition focusses on improving the performance of its member organizations and those organizations, in turn, use that improved performance to bring about positive community change among the residents of the community. In the end, if all goes well, we should see a population-level improvement.

In order to help to clarify this division of labor, in 2010 the National Community Literacy Collaborative, a partnership between ProLiteracy and Literacy Powerline, drafted a series of accreditation standards for literacy coalitions and statewide literacy organizations.[3] The goal was to promote high-quality services with rigorous management guidelines that would "evaluate strengths and weaknesses, bring about continuous improvement of operations, facilitate long-term sustainability, enhance credibility, and increase public recognition of the coalition's services."[4] Though not regulated by any particular governing body, the collaborative offered these standards as guidance to coalitions across the country:

- Standard One: Governing Body Responsibility
  The coalition has a governing body that forwards the mission of the coalition and demonstrates the following indicators . . .

- Standard Two: Organizational Planning
  The coalition uses community input in planning processes that articulate its mission and set the direction for the coalition . . .

- Standard Three (a): Fiscal Management
  The coalition has board-approved budget policies and procedures for oversight and management of its financial resources . . .

- Standard Three (b): Coalition as Fiscal Agent
  This standard only applies to coalitions that serve as a fiscal agency and provide or manage funds for member organizations. Organizations that don't serve as a fiscal agent and provide or manage funds for member organizations may skip this standard . . .

- Standard Four: Employee Management
  The coalition has a system to recruit, train, supervise, and evaluate employees . . .

- Standard Five: Members or Participating Organizations
  Coalitions may have a formal membership process or an informal structure that allows organizations to participate. The coalition has a system in place to recruit new members or participants, has clear expectations of members or participants, and communicates expectations to members or participants . . .

- Standard Six: Capacity Building Activities—Direct Support
  The coalition seeks to strengthen the capacity of literacy service providers to deliver high-quality, effective programs that meet the needs of learners . . .

- Standard Seven: Capacity Building Activities—Indirect Support
  The coalition helps its members build capacity by providing indirect support . . .

- Standard Eight: Leveraging and Coordinating Resources
  The coalition leverages and coordinates resources for member organizations and key stakeholders . . .

- Standard Nine: Increasing Awareness
  The coalition increases awareness of literacy needs and resources in the community and engages new supporters through marketing, being a community resource, and raising awareness in the community . . . [5]

Basing much of their self-assessment on such standards, it is not uncommon for coalitions to emphasize the goals the membership desires for itself. Asked about how it measures impact, one coalition shared:

> We surveyed our members in terms of the interests and needs they have as members of the coalition. This is done once in a while to figure out if there are services needed. There has been a big push around advocacy. As a group of agencies, what kinds of things should they be doing together? (Pennsylvania)

Though helpful in articulating the goals of a coalition, some note that these standards and the measures that typically follow do not address measurable change in the community when it comes to actual literacy learners. This is a significant challenge since coalitions largely derive their identity from serving the organizations, not individuals. If they were to try to measure the impact on individuals, they would have to ask the organizations they serve to supply those data, which would be cumbersome to say the least.

Measuring outcomes is further complicated by the fact that many states and localities use a plethora of tests, making it unfeasible to choose the same measures even if communities wanted to. It is perhaps this precise dilemma that the Campaign for Grade-Level Reading (CGLR) faced. The project of the Annie E. Casey foundation initially intended to include a handful of communities that would sign on to setting a clear objective– using collective impact approaches to move the community toward a goal of increasing the percentage of children that were reading at grade level. Allied with the National League of Cities, the CGLR planned to select communities with the best plans to improve reading and award them with the All-America Cities distinction. The plan was then to revisit these communities in five years and award another set of All-American City designations based on which communities made the best progress. As Ralph Smith, managing director of the GLR Campaign, explained, "the best laid plans" don't always work out. Rather than the small handful of communities the organization expected, Smith was surprised when the GLR Campaign received more than 120 applications.[6] That summer, at the 2012 CGLR conference in Denver, campaign communities began to ask, "How exactly will you be measuring progress?"

Leaders of the campaign were as open-minded as they were overwhelmed with the prospect of measuring progress for more than 100 communities across the nation. They invited campaign communities to offer ideas and engaged in discussions ranging from community-wide data systems (such as Efforts To Outcomes/ETO's Social Solutions) to individualized approaches. After considerable discussion, the campaign began partnering with the Results Scorecard (now Clear Impact), which offered an introductory plan at highly reduced prices to all coalition members. From there, the network of system users has been expanding. Key to this system is that each community enters its own data, sets its own goals, and tracks its own progress. The system allows member communities to select indicators from a list of commonly shared measures that the campaign and its many helpful primers and manuals have endorsed. This is a helpful development in moving toward shared outcomes. While this has the appeal of being voluntary yet standardized, it remains to be seen to what extent its usage will catch on and the degree to which communities end up measuring shared indicators the same way. This will be the true test of this approach's ability to encourage common measures. Of course, the next challenge will be comparing these communities to others that are not engaged in the campaign.

The challenge of shared measures and the critical need to use common metrics is a theme that others have also taken up. Perhaps the most ambitious has been the National Results and Equity Collaborative (NREC). This group began as an informal gathering of membership from many of the more than twenty collective impact initiatives with a national scope discussed in the previous chapter. As a group, the NREC has set out to standardize results-based approaches:

> NREC aims to 1) accelerate positive results for vulnerable children throughout the country by creating a national network to align results-based TA [Technical

Assistance], measures, effective strategies and solutions across multiple national and local initiatives; and, in so doing, 2) promote consistency and greater
impact in the use of results-based methodologies at the federal, state, and local
levels. As these elements are developed and tested, the collaborative will function as an open source peer network, with ever expanding circles of leaders testing and using this approach and sharing what they are learning with a network
of peers throughout the country.[7]

Of these, literacy coalitions are just one of many such networks, including
Promise and Choice Neighborhoods, Strive, and many others. These groups
gathered together and created a list of communities where they were located
and looked to see where there was overlap (for a list of NREC initiatives refer to table 2.1). From this discussion a new agenda emerged in which a core
nucleus of national actors involved in these initiatives sought to bring about
a game-changing approach that would lead to faster results for vulnerable
children and youth.

As one of the group's leaders explained:

> This was not meant to be all the indicators; this was meant to be a starting
> point . . . We were a group of people from different programs meeting who
> liked each other and we had no egos, no power problems. And we said, "Well,
> we are all measuring the same things but slightly differently. Wouldn't it be
> nice if we measured things the same way?" We decided to also use the same
> tool, Results Scorecard (now Clear Impact), since many were already using it
> with the CGLR.

One of NREC's innovations was not only to identify a core set of measures,
but also to emphasize the idea of proxy power, or an understanding that certain indicators are useful because they are proxies for other important things
that tend to accompany them. This concept helps to address the issue that one
coalition member shared as she lamented that many important data points are
simply not collected.

> It wasn't until I started taking a child to school every day that I knew how much
> effort was attached to taking a child to school. I was thinking that would be a
> better measure because to take a child to school means you have to wake them
> up and whatever, so you are moving them along toward being a better person. I
> am saying strong families take their children to school.

This foreshadows the NREC's use of the concept of proxy power, in which
a specific indicator is valuable not only for what it represents, but also for
the things with which that indicator is likely to be correlated. A participant
explained:

Right now we are measuring apples and pineapples so we are hoping this will be a start to measuring things the same way. Proxy power means if you are doing this, then it means these other things must have happened. We started birth through eight, but the commitment is that eventually it will be cradle through career. There is a new evolution in data collection. Evaluation has been used to decide whether you get the funding or not, but, really, it should be used to figure out how you can do things better.

The purpose of the NREC was to accelerate positive results for children by promoting consistency and results and broadly sharing those results with peers. To achieve this goal, the group convened for a conference in Washington, D.C., to hash out a common framework, with shared tools, a common manual, and a common set of birth through eight measures. This task proved to be more difficult than expected, but, in the end, the group produced a manual and a set of shared guidelines. Here is what the group came up with:

Core B-8 Results and Indicators

RESULT: Families are strong and supportive

INDICATOR: Families read regularly to their children

RESULT: Births are healthy

INDICATOR: Infants are born at healthy weight

RESULT: Children are safe, healthy, and developing on track

INDICATOR: Children are free from unintentional injury

INDICATOR: Children have access to a consistent primary health care provider.

INDICATOR: Children with developmental concerns identified through screening who access needed treatment or services

RESULT: Children are emotionally, socially, and cognitively ready for school

INDICATOR: Children enter school ready to succeed

RESULT: Children perform on grade level

INDICATOR: Children attend school or pre-school regularly

INDICATOR: Children are reading on grade level

INDICATOR: Children are performing math on grade level[8]

While this moment is somewhat akin to the standardization of railroad gauges, it remains to be seen the extent to which these national standards are taken up and utilized. Furthermore, the literacy community still needs to address a lack of data on the part of communities that decline to sign on to the protocol. After that, the protocol would need to be expanded to adult education goals as well. Though this group has struggled to maintain funding to carry out its work, it has been successful in convening representatives from many of the national purveyors mentioned in the preceding pages to forge a starting point for measuring success, defining the gold standard for community impact measurement. While this list ends at age eight, the implicit conclusion is that attaining these indicator standards will eventually result in an increase in high school graduations and foster a "cradle through career" measurement standard. As one coalition articulated, given this long-term goal of high school graduation, local efforts to work on youth literacy often persist even despite challenges with measuring more immediate outcomes:

> We have a set of main measures that are enterprise-wide. Then each of our teams, such as the pre-K team, is working toward a very long-term outcome of high school graduation, but they also attempted to measure in the interim with kindergarten readiness. We had some difficulty measuring that and an intermediate being third-grade reading. Our new director of schools came on board July 1 and his major push is literacy, so we are reorienting and third-grade reading will be a priority and working on kindergarten readiness, but at the moment we don't have a good measure. Our main measure has been high school graduation. And we know that if we are doing kindergarten readiness that will eventually impact high school. (Tennessee)

Although this group was admittedly youth centered, when it comes to adult groups, the goals typically also include a high school degree or a high school equivalency (HSE, often referred to as GED). For instance, one coalition focusing on adult education shared the following benchmarks in the form of a pipeline that mirrors that of coalitions focusing on early childhood. In this scale, the higher the number, the better off an adult is when it comes to literacy.

Education, Adult Survey of Thriving

1. In Crisis: no high school diploma or GED and not pursuing diploma or GED
2. Vulnerable: working on GED, improving literacy
3. Stable: high school diploma or GED
4. Self-Sufficient: pursuing needed training/certifications
5. Thriving: has needed training or certification for desired employment

While many communities have set their own benchmarks for adult education, we highlight this one because it helps to avoid many of the challenges that communities face when they begin to set goals. As one coalition staff member shared, looking at communities across his state reveals a variety of adult education foci.

> Some focus very much on functional literacy, such as reading directions or applying for food stamps. Others work mostly on health outcomes and being able to navigate the health system well. (New York)

Even though most focus on educational gains in the three areas of adult basic education, high school equivalency (GED), and English language learning, communities often end up debating the purpose of literacy. Some say it is to find gainful employment, but others insist it is to be better able to manage one's health (i.e., health literacy) or finances (i.e., financial literacy). As one adult-focused coalition shared, jobs are often important:

> Most of our members are working on achieving a level of success, in terms of educational gains: get a commonwealth diploma (i.e., pass the GED), get a job, keep a job, helping them pass an HR test (Human Resources), to get into college, or some sort of training. (Pennsylvania)

Still others insist that plenty of adult learners, especially those of retirement age, are seeking enjoyment and greater personal fulfillment by striving to gain access to the vast published worlds of literature, philosophy, theology, and self-help. In some communities, these differences of opinion have become roadblocks to establishing the shared vision and agreed upon measures needed for collective impact to take place. In the above example, however, there is a clear linear hierarchy of the levels to which a person has achieved literacy. Interestingly, high school graduation appears as a middle ground that includes further certifications and other higher educational pursuits. Perhaps unsurprisingly, high school graduation (or its equivalent) is central to this set of indicators, just as it is with other collective impact initiatives focused on younger populations. For instance, the GLR Campaign, while focusing primarily on third-grade reading, has framed this as a reasonable starting point for later success, including high school graduation and eventual career success. In their communications, the goal of early reading is a milestone on the way to graduation: "Reading proficiency by third grade is the most important predictor of high school graduation and career success. Yet every year, more than 80 percent of low-income children miss this crucial milestone."[9]

This focus on education level is also seen in coalition literature on performance management, such as the one developed by Hatry and Morley (2008), which proposes that one measure could be the: "Number and percentage of adults who have completed fewer than "X" years of school. ("X" would be the number of years chosen by the community. The indicator would be calculated from the census data so that only adults are included in the calculations.)"[10]

## EXEMPLARS OF LITERACY OUTCOMES

As noted earlier, when it comes to analyzing impact, there are several options for level of analysis. These include the literacy effects for: clients of each single program in the community; all clients served by the coalition, regardless of which program(s) served them; all citizens in the community regardless of whether the citizen had received any help from any of the coalition's partners; and all citizens in the country broken out by whether or not the community had a coalition. Our analysis of coalitions across the nation reveals exemplars for each level that serve not only as proof points of the potential effectiveness of coalitions, but also as pioneers of technologies that make performance measurement possible.

In her very influential book on nonprofit lifecycles, Susan Kenny Stevens outlines the continuum of nonprofit success as beginning in organizational capacity or competence with its core activities or service delivery. Moving further on a continuum of maturity is performance, or the ability to achieve measurable goals or objectives. Both are antecedents to the overall goal of effectiveness, or ability to have an impact on members of society.[11] The preceding pages discuss ways in which coalitions assess their competence in developing a culture of collective impact (organizational capacity). It is this sentiment that is at the heart of comments such as the following from coalitions that focus their assessment on capacity building:

> When you talk about moving the needle as a coalition, you have to think about what your job is as a coalition. Is your job to serve the student, or to build the capacity of the agency? Our job is to build capacity. We have been able to prove we have built capacity by having the agencies have a database at no cost and now they have been able to raise more money. They have been able to open more classes based on the data we have been able to provide. So now they have more funding and more students and we are doing more advocacy work to get more funding for them, which we can do because we have the numbers. Helping organizations, I know the needle is moving, but I am not sure we have enough data to show that the needle is moving for learners. Our organizations are saying our needle is moving. The needle that is moving is serving more students, the ability to reach more students and the ability to consistently place students in appropriate classes with testing and teach more effectively. (Texas)

As they allude to, measuring the building of organizational capacity and charting the progress of learners are two different ways to approach accountability that address different levels of Stevens' continuum of success.

## Coalitions Examining Clients of Each Single Program in the Community

Moving further along Stevens' continuum (Capacity → Performance → Impact), analyzing impact on the level of clients in a single program falls squarely within the realm of performance. Some coalition communities have leveraged their collective influence to carry out evaluations of literacy programs that would not be possible without the collaborative environments that coalitions encourage. For instance, a group of coalition communities emphasizing early childhood literacy in states including South Carolina to New York have found that implementing Dolly Parton's Imagination Library program has been a good fit for their larger impact agenda. This program, which mails one age-appropriate book per month to each family in a targeted location, is relatively easy to implement and cheap to fund. As a result, coalitions have found that they can use this program as a means to practice and model working together in the hope that overall collaboration across the board will increase as coalition member agencies become more comfortable with each other. However, in the process, these communities have used this opportunity to rigorously measure this direct service provision and thus demonstrate to their communities that there is a concrete positive community impact to their work. Coalition-led research on this program, including some that has involved the authors, has found that families end up reading more to their children[12] and children show up to school more ready for kindergarten.[13] In addition, there seem to be positive results for refugee and immigrant families who use these books to develop a culture of reading at home.[14] Key to this analysis was the ability to disaggregate data by specific subpopulations such as low income, non-whites, and speakers of languages other than English. Many, including the CGLR and the National Institute for Literacy have emphasized the importance of this when locating areas of need in the community,[15] but these experiences point out that disaggregating data is also important when determining which subpopulations are seeing improvements associated with program implementation and which are not.

Programs such as this can be a source of inter-community collaboration as well, with several communities across New York and parts of South Carolina sharing modified versions of the same database and working with partners from a variety of academic institutions to further a research agenda around this program. This has required innovations in relational database development that allowed coalitions to pair data collected from program participants with data on address changes from the post office, data from the school district on child performance, and data collected by collaborating college students conducting surveys of families about their behaviors while participating in the program. Here the great advancement is not so much in the technology, since this has been largely done using desktop applications such as Microsoft Access and Excel. Rather, the major advance is in the way the coalitions have been able to build trust among partners to secure data sharing and then to collaboratively transform this trust into a finished product that has credibility not only among the many community members involved in the data collection and analysis, but also within the academic realm. In some cases, the knowledge produced by these agents of the coalitions has met the rigorous standards of academic peer review and has subsequently been published in academic journals, hence making a contribution to the broader base of knowledge shared on an international level.

Indeed, in the realm of evaluation, partnership with academic institutions has been a source of strength for coalitions. Relationships between academia and community groups have been in existence dating back at least as far as 1990, when the Carnegie Foundation for the Advancement of Teaching published Ernest L. Boyer's "Scholarship Reconsidered: Priorities of the Professoriate."[16] This report argued for a stronger connection between academic work and efforts to solve the social and environmental problems that face communities across the nation. In many ways, coalitions have tapped into this sentiment and offered a compelling product to those in academia who are positively disposed to this approach.

Coalitions offer advantages that help to address some of the inherent challenges to community-academic collaboration. Whereas individual nonprofits and faculty can and certainly do engage in mutually beneficial interactions and forms of applied scholarship, these relationships are often fraught with problematic aspects. Among the hurdles is lack of compatibility. Since these arrangements are often based on interpersonal relationships, changing staff at a nonprofit (which is typically more frequent than is healthy) or shifting courses taught or taking leave on the academic side can often lead to the end of a community-academic collaboration. In addition, these relationships face the challenge of a lack of depth such that a single institution and individual faculty member may eventually run out of recognizable common interests on which to collaborate. Finally, it can be exhausting for both nonprofit staff and faculty members to carve time out of their already busy schedules to keep meeting and sharing ideas to maintain a working relationship. Coalitions help to solve these problems, most notably through the establishment of data or research committees, sometimes called Measurement Action Teams or Performance Measurement Action Teams. These teams are typically seen as support teams (often along with other support teams such as fundraising and communications) that exist to serve other committees or action teams that focus on specific community need areas (such as early childhood, school age, and adult literacy).

Measurement or Performance Measurement Action Teams help to address the structural problems of applied scholarship in several ways. First, they build in redundancy. Rather than a one-on-one relationship between an organization and a faculty member, these teams facilitate a many-to-many relationship in which multiple agencies working on literacy begin to form a collaborative relationship not only with each other but also with multiple faculty members, even from multiple higher educational institutions. As a result, a group relationship is cultivated that avoids burnout because it can withstand the departure or hiatus of any few nonprofit staff members or faculty and maintain a robust agenda that pushes forward community data sharing, analysis, conclusions, and action, much in the fashion of a team relay race. This structure also helps to build a broad base of questions that need answering and academic worker bees that can help the community while simultaneously fulfilling their academic commitments. In the best scenarios, coalitions can help faculty members in their full portfolio of teaching (through opportunities for service learning such as collecting surveys from coalition clients), research (through offering topics and data that address areas of critical community importance), and service (through opportunities to serve on the committees of the coalition).[17] In some instances, such as two coalitions in Michigan, the coalition staff is made up of employees of local colleges. Some coalitions, such as two in New York, have even worked with national research institutes such as American Institutes for Research (AIR). Often partnerships with academia can be helpful in figuring out how to get things to work better. As one coalition working with adult learners explained:

> The University of Penn graduate students are helping us work on our telephone script for when a person calls us to make an appointment. About 50 percent of our people drop off and do not show up for their first appointment. As part of Wharton's Behavioral Economics, their work with us is to see, if we provide that information in a certain way, will that affect whether they show up or not? (Pennsylvania)

As a coalition in Kansas shared, "We use data to both track our progress and prove things." As part of the CGLR, a national initiative that has put an emphasis on measuring progress, this coalition stands out as a community that has put this imperative to work to institutionalize their efforts. They did this by hiring a university research firm to assess whether students' participation in their community's summer learning programming was making a difference. Their initial research found that children experienced less summer slide (i.e., a decline in scores between June and September due to a dearth of learning over the summer) when they participated in summer schooling. As a result, the community committed to doing even more by extending their reading curriculum through the summer. Another key learning from a study they sponsored was that there is a high level of churn such that students move around and in and out of school districts frequently. Their findings suggest that in any given school, when comparing the beginning of the year with the end of the school year, as high as 60 percent of the student body could be different. While this finding alone might cause someone to question the validity of school testing for measuring teaching quality, a lesson that this coalition took was that it needed to do something to minimize the lost school time during such transitions. Once again, data were helpful in accomplishing their vision. By appealing to lost school aid due to reduced average daily attendance, they were able to form a partnership between the school district and the utility companies, since utility bills are a key document that school districts use to verify residency before they allow new children into their school district.

Such academic-community relationships fostered by literacy coalitions have helped not only to evaluate whether programs are working, but, just as importantly, where specific programs are needed. As one coalition explained:

> We worked with Texas A&M on a research project on ROI and examination of gaps in services looking for neighborhoods with high need and low services. We brought in the mayor and city council member and explained zip code by zip code, this is what we are doing with literacy. We use this and reports we commission from the Bush School of Government and Public Services to springboard the effort. (Texas)

Others have worked with local universities such as one that worked with Syracuse University and Le Moyne College staff to use open-source platforms to develop apps that could be used to view critical data on the web or on people's smartphones. One app in New York allowed funders to select age groups and zip codes to see how many children were involved in programming and how much it would cost them monthly to provide services. Another app in New York allowed community partners to track progress on CGLR results by census tract neighborhoods to see where their collaborative work was making a difference. In Texas, one coalition used the same open source computer coding technology in a literacy hackathon (a collaborative computer programming event). The result was a web-based community map that displayed not only the location of all the relevant organizations, but also the related census data for the neighborhoods where those organizations reside. As a result, the community shared,

> It is helping us make more informed decisions using data, rather than saying, "We think this is a rough neighborhood that needs services, we can know that from the map." (Texas)

Epitomizing the hackathon approach but at a much larger scale, the Barbara Bush Foundation has worked with local coalitions in Pennsylvania, such as Philadelphia's Mayor's Commission on Literacy, to launch the Adult Literacy Xprize, "a $7 million global competition to transform the lives of low-literate adults."[18] This approach fosters competition "to develop mobile applications for existing smart devices that result in the greatest increase in literacy skills among participating adult learners in just 12 months. The solutions will overcome key barriers to literacy learning by improving access, while increasing retention, and scaling to meet demand."[19] Through combining such tactics with others, these coalitions are able to take an approach sensitive to the community by focusing on need, then combining that with specific strategies to deploy programming in targeted neighborhoods.

Coalitions that focus on specific geographies of high need can better deploy their limited resources in those target areas and, as a result, can spend more time measuring their targeted interventions because they are smaller and more manageable. That means they can use their extra time to improve programming and measurement. For instance, one community selected a specific neighborhood and targeted it with specific book distribution programming and developmental screening:

> One of our schools has identified school readiness as its top priority and is looking at five census tract blocks and working with groups to support children who might be preschool age with programs like *Raising a Reader* and developmental screening to catch those issues early. (Arizona)

Another coalition, in a major city in New York, has developed somewhat of a vertical monopoly by connecting programs that reach learners from birth to third grade. This was possible because the coalition has limited its reach to a single high-need neighborhood (rather than the entire city) so it has the resources to administer a book distribution program, a child care program, a pre-school program, and intensive work with an elementary school. Specifically, their work involves paid staff and AARP Foundation's Experience Corps Volunteer Tutoring program to provide embedded support working directly with teachers in the context of the classroom, support for the collection of student assessment data and progress monitoring, and support in planning and reflection to meet program, classroom, and individual targets. The result is a battery of high quality evaluations of program participants that demonstrate high levels of age-appropriate development among children at the child care centers, improvement in child care site environments and improvements in vocabulary for children in prekindergarten, kindergarten, first grade, second grade, and third grade.[20]

As can be imagined, such measurement also entails technological advances that can range from a series of databases, one for each program being administered, to a shared system across many sites administering the same program. One coalition, for example, reported it has a single system into which many different sites offering the same program can report (or "roll up") their data.

We have a tutoring program through AARP and they are tracking their reading level and that folds up into ours. (Arizona)

In addition to focusing on overall program effectiveness, these same technologies can be used to improve teacher performance. One adult-focused coalition is developing ways that the data it collects can feed back directly to frontline service providers.

We are continuing to develop a portal into the data system for teachers, with specific information for teachers who can see areas students are having difficulty in. Similar to what we are doing with teachers, we want to create a case manager portal that would allow case managers to track the work they are doing and the impact they are having. (New York)

Such technologies can be helpful, regardless of whether there is a targeted neighborhood approach or a broader city or communitywide emphasis. As one community reported, such data systems enable direct communication between providers:

Prior to me taking over the program, my supervisor was working toward developing a statewide longitudinal data system. We have a mandate to have usable data. If we could have useable data, we thought they would keep us funded. In our student application for family literacy, we have a family unit application, an adult application, and an infant toddler application. On the adult intake we made sure that mapped to our adult education database. We had a data matching agreement with the Department of Labor, so we backtracked to make sure our data matched. We had to be patient and understanding of our partners' limitations. Labor will never give us back disaggregated data on an individual level so we could track back. But we don't need that level data; we just agree to treasure what our partners are measuring. We have learned how to make their data meaningful to us. . . . We created a triangulation between data partners so if I say, "Did your child receive all immunizations in the last six months?" then I take name, address, etc., and send that to family services and they send it to health services and they say, "Oh yes they are immunized." So we are all happy. But the biggest effort we had was that we are doing this statewide. We have the student sign a waiver to get around HIPPA. If we are going to give high quality services, there are mandates for developmental benchmarks and initial screenings during the application process. We have created a data dictionary so if I call about immunizations, then I need to ask it the same way. In our school readiness program, it was a big lift. We had to work with our department of education to make an MOU. They had to pre-establish MOUs with each school district and use whatever their kindergarten screening tool was as our exit test for our kindergarten readiness programming. So they enter the student and whenever K–12 says, "What is the readiness on this kindergartener?" we dump it out to them as a data extract. Every time a parent fills out a form they know this can be shared with K–12, Department of Labor, etc. (Wyoming)

Among coalition communities, those that have statewide systems are often the envy of other communities who may feel left behind in data discussions and even stuck on square one trying to gain access to useful data. This seems to be more common in the legacy and coastal cities that populate such places as New York and California. But here, expressing this frustration is one coalition from the south:

I like this idea of using the same measure, but the measures here are not mandated, so while I would like to use them, the school district is not mandated so it would be just me and I can't make them. (Louisiana)

As noted by the adult-focused coalition below, in the absence of a shared measure, a database can be structured to collect a wide variety of information from many community providers.

Our database is wide, not deep. We can track the professional development taken by the staff, student attendance, student hours, and each agency has the ability to put the test they are using (TABE or BEST, etc.) and then they can put in pre-test and post-test scores. We also have demographics. We offer it to the coalition members at no cost. (Texas)

Like programs noted earlier, the ability to track by demographics is critical since outcomes for clients as well as professional development can often vary by socially consequential characteristics. Systems must disaggregate so that trends for effectiveness are not lost in the noise of a data analysis that combines all data without paying attention to demographics. Sometimes disaggregation occurs less by demographics and more by literacy level, as in the program below that was developed by a coalition to fill a community gap.

We didn't want to be competitive, and as far as I know, no one else was offering cohort-based and facilitated online classes for those assessed at fourth-sixth grade level. We also created an online class designed to help individuals understand what it means to be in adult education. It can go from three to twelve hours depending on their reading and technology skills; we built into it how to use a computer. It is self-paced. When you complete the intro course then you discuss with the learning coach the next steps. Here the learning coach will register you to take face-to-face classes and/or you can take online courses. If you are between a fourth and sixth grade level, you can do the online courses. They are cohort-based, seven-week classes that are facilitated. At first they were fully online, but now we are building in opportunities for the learners to meet. We wanted to pre- and post-test on TABE, but since it is online it is hard to get

them to come in to take the post-test so we are starting to build in the assessment
at the pre- and post-now. We built the program on college and career readiness
but were using pre- and post-test on TABE and we weren't seeing the gains we
expected, but we then realized that the TABE does not measure college and career readiness so we had to backtrack and pick a better measure. We could see
Suzie was writing better in her online classes but we were perplexed with why
is it not showing up on her TABE scores? (Pennsylvania)

As this experience reveals, coalitions have often learned in hindsight that
picking the right measures to track can be trickier than it would appear, even
when using standard measures. In addition to conducting research from
scratch, coalitions can be helpful in making sense of existing data to discern
what is working about current programs. As one coalition shared:

We had all of this data, but were having trouble telling what it meant, so this
mapping tool helped us get a feel for what this data tells on a local, or regional
level. Our communities could use the data to drive their planning and decision
making. Just yesterday, some of our local communities gave feedback on what is
working and what they would like to try to do in the future. Having data analysis
training workshops has also been helpful because what we found is that it wasn't
enough to just get them the data and make sure they had access. The analysis of
the data has become a very important piece. For instance, at the state level we
did an analysis of the three things most impeding reading. (Arizona)

A variety of communities are emerging as exemplary when it comes to
evaluating individual program participants. However, not all are this sophisticated. While some have partnered with researchers to produce local knowledge, many coalitions simply scour the Internet for best practices that become
published and then make that research available to their membership.

## Coalitions Examining All Clients Served by the Coalition, Regardless of Which Program(s) Served Them

In March 2010, FSG Social Impact Advisors, the original purveyors of the
collective impact approach nationwide, presented "Shared Measurement System for Literacy Coalitions" at the National Community Literacy Coalition
Conference.[21] In this presentation, they discussed a continuum of shared measurement systems that could be deployed to meet the needs of coalitions, including an "infrastructure needed to strengthen the services and partnerships
vital to the success of a coalition." All these options included common online
platforms for data capture and analysis. The first allowed for the recording
of performance or outcome indicators that were specific to the literacy field.
The second did the same, but ensured that the outcomes and indicators would

be defined and collected in uniformed ways across all participating organizations. The third focused on collective measurement, learning, and coordination of efforts to improve performance. Although a national database such as the one being proposed has yet to be built, our interviews and observations indicate that variants of each of these three approaches have been deployed in communities across the nation to examine all clients served by their coalitions, regardless of what programs are serving them.

## Platform for Recording Literacy Related Data

While it seems the least sophisticated at first blush, establishing a database that only meets the first level of the continuum laid out by FSG (by collecting any literacy-related data, even if they are not uniformed) can be quite powerful. Though the data can be as diverse "as apples and oranges," compiling them in one place can have a noticeable impact and can still allow for the aggregation of similarly measured data such as demographics, retention rates, and learner gains. Doing so helps to develop an understanding of the breadth and quality of services being offered. Some coalitions, such as the following, have used this type of data as leverage when it comes to lobbying elected officials for additional funding to carry out the work of literacy building. For them, collecting data on those served and their outcomes is needed to advocate on behalf of the entire literacy industry:

Actually having hard data has informed a lot of things we are doing and it helps when I have conversations with the mayor and city council; they are interested in what the data is showing us. When I show them the data, it validates many of the issues we see happening in the city. (Pennsylvania)

As another coalition elaborated:

We told the literacy providers that our job was to advocate for literacy in our city, but we couldn't do it without the armor. Legislators and all said we need data. At first, agencies were hesitant to use the database, so it took a few years for trust to be built. We said we need aggregate data to be able to get funding. Some people resisted, but as some people used it and raved about it and it is on the cloud and free, as their database got old, and they couldn't afford a new one and ours was free, they naturally moved over to using it. We have access to everyone's individual client data, we can go in and see it, so we can see and track people if they move across town and take a different GED class. We don't care about their student data individually; we care in aggregate. We work to support all adult education agencies in the city, whether they are federally funded or not . . . I think that should be the role of a coalition. If we are going to advocate, we need to know what is going on with them. We were able to go to the mayor and say we have the value. It really isn't about the funding, but it really is about the funding. Companies that don't produce great products don't get invested in. (Texas)

Once in this position, such coalitions can also play a role in data collection aimed at quality control:

> We are a funder, with a small amount of funding, and we endorse agencies. There are seventy agencies in the city, and they can all get support, but only endorsed agencies can get our funding. It is like the Better Business Bureau. They must use the database system, give us their IRS 990 forms and lists of board members. We make sure they are fiscally healthy and we do a site visit. We have not gone deep into the quality of the instruction they are providing, but we have given them the tools and monitor it with site visits . . . Our system was funded by a private funder to create the system and a different funder to have staff to manage it. We had to create a marketable product with a user's manual and training so we could sell it to the funders. We go to the mayor and city councilors and state legislators . . . In the past, all we had was NRS data, but now we have additional data.

## Using Uniformed Indicators

Further along the FSG continuum, creating a platform for literacy-related data requires or ensures that data being compiled are collected in a uniform manner. This allows for a more robust comparison across programs that could help to identify which programs are having the most success and could be a key avenue to developing evidence-based best practices. As one coalition shared, by using the same measure (Teaching Strategies Gold) across multiple child care centers, it was able to encourage certain more successful programs to expand to other areas of need:

> We are using Teaching Strategies Gold across multiple childcare centers. The idea is that one of our communities looks at this data and then they may decide to encourage their [more successful] programs to do programs at certain sites to build student readiness or decide what sites they may go into in a more intensive way. (Arizona)

While this approach may seem to be ideal from an outsider's perspective, it is very hard to accomplish and is a challenging approach for coalitions to take. As one coalition shared, "Just like anything, people do not like change and they do not like being told what to do." (Texas)

To address the challenge of getting agencies to all collect data in the same way, a coalition in New York, after failing to convince school districts to use a shared kindergarten screening measure, worked to collect data themselves through surveys of the clients of each of their partner organizations. This approach promised to offer insights into family behavior changes as a result of coalition programming through a wide variety of service delivery partners. This approach was encouraging in that it did not overburden the coalition members or require the school district to change its ways of doing things. In the end, however, the response rate was so small for certain providers that the data were not comparable.

## Coordinated Efforts

Ideally, to truly coordinate efforts, communities will have access to action-able information and can share insights with each other in real time. This is the concept behind shared community databases. While not common, they have nevertheless been successfully deployed in some collective impact initiatives by using such communitywide data systems as Social Solutions or Comet. For instance, one collective impact approach targeting four urban neighborhoods sought to coordinate efforts to produce a "coordinated, cradle-to-graduation alignment" for the 12,000 students involved. This included preschool, in-school, and out-of-school-time programs and related support systems. To measure this effort, they built a state-of-the-art community data system to track their work. The result has been a 23 percent drop in chronic absenteeism (35 to 27 percent since 2010).[22] In addition, their data suggest a 40 percent increase in the likelihood their participating students would remain within the school district.[23] Perhaps most notable in this case is that data helped to reveal a problem that the collective impact structure then went about solving. As shared in a publication about their work:

> For many years, the problem of chronic absenteeism went unnoticed, flying un-der the achievement gap radar. Historically adopted measures such as "average daily attendance," required by the state and federal education reporting entities largely masked the problem. This gave school districts inadequate metrics and therefore a false sense of success by glossing over, in some cases, a third of the population of students missing too much school.[24] (Michigan)

It was only once the community began, as they described, to "mine the data" using the Attendance Works' District Attendance Tracking Tool (DATT) and School Attendance Tracking Tool (SATT) (tools widely popularized by the Campaign for Grade-Level Reading) that the problem became apparent. Again, as with previous instances of data-driven action, disaggregation of data revealed key patterns by grade level, gender, and geography. The result-ing actions were as follows:

[We] mobilized more than 150 community and faith-based organizations by means of grants that embedded school attendance and chronic absenteeism metrics into each agreement. Forging an unprecedented Master Data Sharing Agreement (MDSA) with the district, we were able to support community partners in tracking and supporting families directly. As a result, community organizing entities on the ground had access to geo-coded maps highlighting neighborhood hot spots of chronically absent students for door-to-door engagement.[25] (Michigan)

Hence, data enabled not only coordination of efforts but an eventual community success that moved the needle.

Another community in New York, also working to implement a cradle-to-career pipeline through collective impact efforts, developed its own community database to monitor its efforts to roll out "comprehensive screenings for three-year-olds to identify needs in hearing, vision, dental health, language and speech, cognitive, and social-emotional development."[26] Rather than create an entire database system as in the Michigan example above, this community relied on academic talent at a local research institute to build a data platform that simply connects data from multiple community agency databases during a nightly sync. Careful to maintain confidentiality, this data infrastructure also allows for unduplicated data sharing and coordination of efforts in a way that would otherwise be unfeasible. The result has been a 26 percent (46 to 35 percent) drop in chronic absences among kindergarten through third grade students in targeted schools. Furthermore, they have seen a 49 percent increase (from 5.5 to 8.2 percent ) in third graders reading on grade level as of 2016.[27]

Though these exemplars are impressive, following in their footsteps is beyond aspirational for many communities. Creating a community database is daunting since the real challenge to making this work is not in the technology but in the trust with respect to data sharing. Nowhere is this more evident than in the case of one collective impact initiative that had been a leader in measuring its work until partners suddenly found themselves locked out of data when a new school district administration came to power. Similarly, other communities find themselves spending so much time in the legal weeds trying to negotiate data sharing agreements that their entire initiatives stall. While the difficulties of getting organizations to use shared measurements might seem to imply that the most advantageous level on FSG's database continuum is unattainable except in the rarest of cases, recent developments suggest that this may not be the case. People often default to thinking that there is a need to have a shared central database in the community, but this is not always needed to bring about coordinated efforts. Recent efforts among coalitions working in open source technology, such as the platforms mentioned in the section on individual programs, suggest that, soon, organizations will be able to share their data with each other on a near real-time basis without needing to worry about violating confidentiality simply by sharing their data in strategic aggregates. For instance, by geocoding their clients to census tract levels, organizations can not only share the number of individuals served each month but also the average scores on any assessments of interest. Furthermore, by plotting addresses on internal maps with this same technology, organizations can be extremely precise about where they will and will not outreach when it comes to coordinating services. Here, as in the other cases above, data sharing is only part of the issue, however. As this coalition shared, coordination will also involve developing plans that are workable for all involved:

> We have learned that coordination is really hard and how we are addressing this is having them not just come up with a plan but working through a planning tool to bring them together to coordinate at a different level. Coordination and alignment sounded good but it is really hard to put it into action. With this they go away with much better tools and it has upped the game in terms of alignment and integrating in each other's plan. There is actually a skill to that and building that cohesion. It is difficult if you are not constantly maintaining it. (Arizona)

Coordination is a theme in coalitions that focus on adult education, just as it is in those that emphasize early childhood. As one coalition explained, a shared system allows them to figure out if the services being offered communitywide meet the needs.

> We developed an adult education system in our city that started with three campuses and we are moving toward five campuses shortly. People who call us are scheduled for an appointment using our Student Information System. This SIS is cloud based and information about the learners can be shared among the campuses and the partners. When they arrive at a campus they work with a learning coach, set their learning goals, and all of this is maintained in the system. Currently we have 11,000 individual accounts. We find that 60 percent come to us scoring between the fourth and eighth grade level. We suspected that would be the case and decided to use a Learner Management System (LMS) to help us develop four online classes that run seven weeks and are cohort based and facilitated. Once the person has been assessed, they can either go to a face-to-face or online class. Those who assess at a fourth-grade level or higher can take their first course at the campus. This is a self-paced online class that introduces learners to what it means to take adult education classes and how to plan on achieving their goals. This online class also provides them the opportunity to develop digital literacy skills. Because of this system we now have some really good data not only on the students, but the nature of the system. It allows us to see what types of classes are being offered. In one of our partner meetings we looked at the profile of the learners coming to the system and where they were

performing. Then we looked at courses that were being offered and we saw that the highest percentage of courses they were offering were GED, which did not meet the need of the people coming through the system. We have begun to see the impact of these data on how organizations are planning and offering services. Providers feel that the retention is better among those who come through the new system. (Pennsylvania)

In these instances, as with the other data scenarios, data sharing is meant to help initiatives make the best decisions, but they will ultimately rely on community-level indicators to ascertain whether they, as a community, have accomplished their goals. In the words of the same coalition quoted earlier when referring to their data sharing tool, "This is not meant to be a reporting tool, but an informing tool, giving them the ability to make decisions, not take temperature. We have the progress meter to tell how communities are doing." (Arizona) In the next section we focus in more detail on how communities are using progress meters to examine whether they are seeing community-level improvement.

### Coalitions Examining All Citizens in the Community Regardless of Whether the Citizen Received Help from Coalition Partners

Concurrent with and quite complementary to the flourishing of collective impact community coalitions is the rise of the community indicators movement. This phenomenon coincides to some extent with collective impact community coalitions in its emphasis on using data to bring about change. Spreading across the nation, this movement seeks to make useable data about community well-being readily available to groups who will be inspired by such awareness to create efforts to bring about positive change in areas where the community sees a deficit. Typically including a wide range of data content including health, public safety, poverty, and civic engagement, the community indicator movement can be seen playing a supporting role to collectively impact coalitions, including health and safety, economic revitalization, and educational improvement.[28] In the case of literacy coalitions and participants in such efforts as the Campaign for Grade-Level Reading, there is often overlap with activity in the area of community indicators. Communities such as Spartanburg, South Carolina, have both CGLR and indicator activity, and, in fact, CGLR is prominently displayed on cnyvitals, Central New York's community indicators website.

Part of FSG's aspirations in its 2010 presentation regarding a comparative performance system for literacy coalitions was to capture and share data nationwide to compare communities with coalitions against those who lacked coalitions. Though this aspiration has yet to be fulfilled, our research uncovers a series of promising examples. In the next section we do a similar such nationwide comparison, but before that, we will look at exemplar communities to see what community success looks like. Such communities measure their work not by evaluating a specific program or cohort of individuals but rather by the movement of existing community indicators. As one coalition shared:

> We don't have a lot of resources about measurement and evaluation so we look for existing resources and we also look for what is proven. We look to see what programs are associated with positive outcomes and we don't follow a cohort of students. We just look to see if the scores are going up overall. It is not just that we know what each other is doing and we are all working together but we are looking to be more strategic—and that is how we are able to make the needle move. (Tennessee)

Articulating this dynamic of comparative success from a statewide perspective, a coalition builder celebrated some success:

> We are starting to see them move the needle, at the big level, at the local level. In . . . schools where that form of alignment is happening we have seen third-grade reading scores increase at an accelerated level, whereas at other schools they have not increased or they have dropped. Though we can't take all the credit and it could be that this just happens to be where improvement happened . . . We developed a progress meter, so we have a third-grade baseline and we also track for all students and we've identified a baseline around all groups and progress. (Arizona)

For those in the field of collective impact and community coalitions, such a statement is a remarkable testament to progress over time. Years ago such a statement would have been exceedingly rare, since few organizations were tracking patterns of community success.

In the more recent past, purveyors of collective impact have driven the permeation of a culture of shared measurement. Perhaps one of the best examples is the work of Results Scorecard, now Clear Impact, which is based on the Results Based Accountability Framework. In one online webinar, they shared how they have gained access to local communities through national organizations such as the Campaign for Grade-Level Reading and Promise Neighborhoods:

> Adam Luecking, CEO of Clear Impact, highlights how the Promise Neighborhoods Institute and the Campaign for Grade-Level Reading in the United States are using Clear Impact Scorecard software for collective impact. These national organizations are helping local communities and backbone organizations create a common agenda, mutually reinforcing activities, shared measurement systems, and continuous communication through use of the RBA framework and Clear Impact Scorecard.[29]

It is through efforts like these that communities such as the following from a site in Michigan can examine all citizens in the community, regardless of whether the citizen has received any help from any of the coalition's partners. The Michigan coalition built this report card (see figure 3.1) by conducting multiple surveys at each planning meeting it held, reporting feedback at

| ● R Children are succeeding at school. | Time Period | Actual Value | Forecast Value | Current Trend | Baseline % Change |
|---|---|---|---|---|---|
| ○ Proficiency % of 3rd Graders who are at or above grade-level in English/ Language Arts | 2015 | 17 | 17 | ↘ 2 | -59% ↘ |
| ○ Proficiency % of 3rd Graders who are at or above grade-level in Mathematics | 2015 | 11.40 | 11.40 | ↘ 3 | -47% ↘ |
| ○ Proficiency % of 6th Graders who are at or above grade-level in English/ Language Arts | 2015 | 14.80 | 14.80 | ↘ 3 | -59% ↘ |
| ○ Proficiency % of 6th Graders who are at or above grade-level in Mathematics | 2015 | 11.39 | -- | ↘ 1 | -17% ↘ |
| ○ Proficiency % of 8th Graders who are at or above grade-level in English/ Language Arts | 2015 | 14.16 | 14.16 | ↘ 1 | -3% ↘ |
| ○ Proficiency % of 8th Graders who are at or above grade-level in Mathematics | 2015 | 7.12 | 7.12 | ↘ 1 | -21% ↘ |
| ○ Proficiency % of 11th Graders who are at or above grade-level in English/ Language Arts | 2015 | 9.58 | 9.58 | ↘ 3 | -62% ↘ |
| ○ Proficiency % of 11th Graders who are at or above grade-level in Mathematics | 2015 | 7.99 | 7.99 | ↘ 1 | 33% ↗ |
| ○ Proficiency % of students who graduate from high school or attain a GED | 2014 | 68.25% | 68.25% | ↘ 1 | 21% ↗ |
| ○ Attendance % of young people who are chronically absent | 2014 | 55% | -- | ↗ 1 | -15% ↘ |
| ○ % of young people who are not in school nor working | -- | -- | -- | -- | -- |

| ● R People are prepared for and are succeeding in post-secondary education. | Time Period | Actual Value | Forecast Value | Current Trend | Baseline % Change |
|---|---|---|---|---|---|
| ○ Adult Ed % of high school graduates who enroll in post-secondary education (by graduation year) | 2015 | 56.3 | 56.3 | ↘ 1 | -25% ↘ |
| ○ Adult Ed % of students who enroll in vocational training/ certification programs (by graduation year) | -- | -- | -- | -- | -- |
| ○ Proficiency % of students who place into college-level English | 2016 | 76.56 | 76.56 | ↗ 2 | 13% ↗ |
| ○ Proficiency % of students who place into college-level Math | 2016 | 74.06 | 74.06 | ↗ 1 | 1% ↗ |
| ○ Adult Ed % of students who graduate from a college or university (2-year or 4-year) | 2010 | 36.95% | -- | → 0 | 0% → |
| ○ Adult Ed % of students who earn a vocational certificate or credential (by graduation year) | 2014 | 1.08% | 1.08% | ↗ 2 | 200% ↗ |

**Figure 3.1.   Scorecard.**

*Source:* Michigan example of scorecard: http://flintliteracy.net/about/results-and-accountability/ (Accessed December 29, 2016).

subsequent meetings and conducting interviews with key stakeholders. In all, they involved nearly 200 people in the process.

Evident in this excerpt from a community scorecard in Michigan is that coalitions are increasingly holding themselves to the high standards of attempting to bring about communitywide change. While results scorecards are certainly increasing in popularity, this is far from the only platform that coalitions are using to track progress. As a staff member of the GLR Campaign shared, "while more than 140 GLR Network communities are utilizing the Clear Impact Scorecard, more than half of the Network recently reported that they are using some type of data sharing platforms." One community United Way engaged in collective impact work shared that it has found Salesforce to be a helpful platform:

> Salesforce is a platform for crm [customer relationship management], grant-making and results measurements, project management, and the collaborative grants (all of our grants must now be collaborative)—this platform will allow all of them to manage their partners and clients so that the volunteers can see the results of what they are doing. We liked Results Scorecard. It just didn't have all of the other elements that we needed as an organization, including volunteer and donor management. (Pennsylvania)

Regardless of the platform, many of these communities have been urged to track community indicators because of national efforts of purveyors such as the Campaign for Grade-Level Reading (CGLR). For instance, in California, the Oakland Literacy Coalition's Oakland Reads has seen its third graders reading on level jump from 42.8 percent in 2015 to 46.3 percent in 2016 since it joined the CGLR.[30] Another community that has embraced what they are identifying as a "collective impact" approach as a means to setting shared community goals is a coalition in Iowa. As they shared:

> A wide network of local individuals and groups join [us] in understanding the importance of early literacy. We are also developing partnerships at state and national levels. In 2012 [we] helped form . . . a coalition led by United Way . . . We joined the national Campaign for Grade-Level Reading. (Iowa)[31]

Following these efforts, the community has noted that the percentage of kindergartners scoring proficient on kindergarten readiness improved from 38 percent in 2008 to 80 percent in 2013.[32] Yet another community in Virginia has focused on low-income children and seen the percent of kindergarten-ready children jump from 76.8 to 80.2 percent (2012 to 2014), chronic absence for second graders decline from 11.4 to 8.7 percent (2012–2013 to 2014–2015), and the number reading on grade level by third grade rise from

53.1 to 67.2 percent (2013 to 2015).[33] Ninety-four communities nationwide have seen positive progress on at least one of the CGLR's key indicators. Beyond this, forty-nine communities in fourteen states have seen their grade-level reading improve.[34]

Such gains are seen not only in collective impact efforts focusing on young children. Adult education focused coalitions have also seen some success. As one coalition staff member explained:

> There are two different ways to answer the question of impact. One answer is based on federal reporting measures; Are they better? And the answer is definitely better. The educational gain rate for adult education focused coalitions is significantly larger than the state at large. There are now fifty-one adult education focused coalitions in the state. As part of this project, their educational gain was 68 percent and the overall state gain was 64 percent. Since New York state is one of the highest, this is significant. The 64 percent has literacy programming but no coalition approach. NRS has a series of levels based on standardized assessments, and when you make it to the next level, you have made an educational gain. This is one of the more solid measures you can hang your hat on because they are based on the standardized assessments of TABE for adult education and Best Plus for ESL. . . . Employment numbers are also measured, but are more soft. I would anticipate this work would lead to greater high school equivalencies. High school equivalency is definitely one of the outcomes that are tracked by adult ed programs. (New York)

Here, once again, we are reminded that high school graduation, or high school equivalency (HSE) is a common ground where early childhood and adult literacy efforts converge. Indeed, it is not uncommon to see literacy coalitions that focus on adult education orchestrating communitywide graduation celebrations for anyone who has attained high school equivalency (GED). As one explained, this is a way to encourage success and advocate for the field:

> We now do a citywide graduation where any person who has gotten their diploma in the last year can attend a citywide graduation. We are trying to court a citywide effort and have people understand what it means to support a person with adult education. So we do a lot around advocacy. We have done the citywide graduation now two years and this last year we had about one hundred graduates express interest in participating. We invited people who attended GED classes and those who got their GED on their own. We hope it continues to grow; we had thirty people the first year. We contacted the GED testing sites and advertised and were able to work with the state and GED testing centers to get the word out. The state provides information on how many people get a commonwealth diploma, but we don't know who those people are. So we worked with all the testing sites, but they don't always know who passes. In

the past, many organizations had done their own graduation, but now there is an interest to try and get learners from various organizations to participate. We had the mayor, assistant secretary of ed, and police commissioners attend. (Pennsylvania)

While this example reinforces the critical role high school graduation or its equivalent plays in the field of adult-focused coalitions, it also reveals that there is no easy system for tracking adult graduations. Perhaps the best way to track this trend is the U.S. Census American Community Survey. It is much easier to measure school age graduation (than adult graduation). Here we can more easily see movement in the area of graduation (and the indicators leading up to it) in such prominent models that predate the Campaign for Grade-Level Reading, including StriveTogether, Say Yes to Education, and United Way, all of which endorse collective impact efforts (see table 3.1).

StriveTogether was first launched in Cincinnati, Ohio, and that community has seen increases in kindergarten readiness, grade level reading, and high school graduation. Strive communities take drastic steps to restructure how they do things and the network culls those communities that are unable to make the institutional changes required by its Theory of Action benchmarks, which include "community-level outcomes to be held accountable for improving."[35] Say Yes to Education has seen similar success in its first citywide launch site of Syracuse, New York. Say Yes also involves massive restructuring of the way that communities do business, including increased after school and summer supports, robust student monitoring and public accountability report cards, and the raising of millions of dollars to support scholarships to all city high school graduates that gain entry to a list of participating colleges. The United Way national office in its 2013 white paper entitled "Charting a Course for Change through Collective Impact" encouraged United Ways across the nation to help communities turn collective impact strategies into action.[36] Some, such as the United Way of the Salt Lake Region, were ahead of the curve, and just like Cincinnati and Syracuse, have already experienced improvements in kindergarten readiness, grade-level reading, and high school graduation.

While it has not been tracking kindergarten readiness and third-grade reading as these other communities have, one Tennessee coalition has seen considerable success in raising the end goal of high school graduation rates. As they explained, they too took the course of drastic community transformation:

With our high school graduation rate, we were looking at a dismal level and we knew incremental wasn't good enough so we needed something more transformative. We developed a vision for high school built around learning communi-

**Table 3.1.  Collective impact exemplars**

| Type of Project | City | Common Indicators | | |
|---|---|---|---|---|
| | | Increased number of incoming kindergarteners prepared for school | Increased number of K–12 students meeting proficiency standards on English and Language Arts (ELA) assessment | Increased high school graduation rates |
| Strive Together | Strive Partnership, Cincinnati, OH (The first Strive site) | Kindergarten Readiness increased from 45% in 2008 to 57% in 2014 (KRA-L) | 4th-grade ELA scores increased from 63% in 2010–2011 to 76% in 2015–2016 (Ohio Achievement Assessment) | 4-year graduation rate increased from 60% in 2010 to 74% in 2013 |
| Say Yes to Education | Say Yes to Education and Literacy Coalition, Syracuse, New York (the first citywide launch of Say Yes) | Kindergarten readiness increased from 36% in 2008 to 49% in 2014 (DIBELS-AIMS Web) | 3rd-grade ELA scores of low-income children in high-poverty census tracts increased from 8% in 2010–2011 to 13% in 2015–2016 (New York State Common Core) | Dropout rate decreased from 26% in 2008 to 16% in 2015; 4-year graduation rate increased from 45% in 2009 to 55% in 2015 |
| United Way Funded | Salt Lake Region—Promise Partnership Regional Council | Kindergarten readiness increased from 54% in 2011–2012 to 61% in 2013–2014 | 3rd-grade ELA scores increased from 60% in 2011–2012 to 65% in 2013–2014 | 4-year graduation rate increased from 68% in 2011–2012 to 70% in 2013–2014 |

*Sources:* published reports and coalition records.[1]

1. http://www.hbs.edu/competitiveness/Documents/business-aligning-for-students.pdf; The Promise of Partnership: Aligning Action for Results, 2014 Baseline Report of the Promise Partnership Regional Council, http://www.uw.org/our-work/reports-pdfs/2014-promise-partnership-brochure-vfmr.pdf Graduation Rates in the Syracuse City School District Continue to Climb Published on January 12, 2016 http://www.syracusecityschools.com/districtpage.cfm?pageid=3243.
3 Syracuse graduation rate reaches 55% for 1st time in 8 years. Published January 14, 2016. Syracuse Post Standard. http://www.syracuse.com/schools/index.ssf/2016/01/syracuse_graduation_rate_reaches_55_percent_highest_in_8_years.html  Standard.  http://www.syracuse.com/schools/index.ssf/2016/01/syracuse_graduation_rate_reaches_55_percent_highest_in_8_years.html and coalition records.

ties and the academy model. We transformed all twelve of our high schools. It really did engage all sectors of the community and engaged partners from every corner of our county and it completely changed what high school was like. You can see high school graduations skyrocketing and other indicators also on the rise. We had been with partners who were scattered and doing different things, but it wasn't coordinated. Using the academy model made them more coordinated. We used a federal grant of $6.7 million, but that wasn't enough to transform, but we were able to realign resources and it is now district funded. The academy model is a career pathway, or a school within a school, such as architecture and construction engineering, information technology. They are taking algebra and geometry in the context of the profession, such as architecture. With teachers, the real buy-in was understanding the value for the students and we spent a lot on professional development. We had a lot of buy-in from the business community and the depth of community buy-in convinced teachers this was not a program that would be gone within the year. (Tennessee)

As a result of these efforts, this coalition's graduation rate rose from 76.6 percent in 2012–2013 to 81.3 percent in 2014–2015.[37] 

While these communities certainly make the case that positive community transformation is possible, they fall short of telling us whether they are indicative of a wider pattern or are exceptions to the rule. In the following section we turn to this chapter's final level of analysis to examine whether we see a pattern when we look at all citizens in the country broken out by whether or not the community had a coalition.

## All Citizens Broken Out by Whether or Not the Community Had a Coalition

Literature suggests coalition communities should be better off on the national level. As evident in the preceding pages, much of the impetus behind building and funding collective impact community coalitions relies on an assumption that it will make communities better off as a whole. Indeed, it seems that coalitions are meant to create the communitywide change that individual programs themselves cannot achieve on their own. It is a simple tenet of faith that the whole of a community coalition is greater than the sum of its parts. Turning to a national perspective, we might envision that the collective total of each coalition's many local efforts will result in a better off community that has discernibly higher standards of living in the areas of coalition focus. In the previous chapter, funders emphasized interest in funding coalitions in part because of a potential for increased collaboration, increased funding resources, and improved community level outcomes. The literature on coalitions supports these expectations. Community coalitions have been noted in the literature to create a venue for collaboration among their memberships by virtue of both coalition structures and the programming they run.[38] By convening different organizations, community coalitions are seen as mobilizing community resources to address a common goal.[39] There is an expectation that this collaboration will also attract financial resources from beyond the community. Finally, we can anticipate that community coalitions, with their emphasis on the implementation of services at the local level[40] will capitalize on their collaborative framework to build stronger local service delivery systems that result in better outcomes for the community.

In the following pages we first review what others have done to evaluate the work of coalitions and then we explore both the process measures of coalition building (attracting funding) and the outcomes (higher standard of living in terms of higher high school equivalency completions).

## Evaluating Coalitions—Are They Better Off?

Looking at collective impact beyond the field of literacy, we find that, when it comes to evaluating coalitions, the literature is guided by the assumption that, "when coalition initiatives are well organized and delivered effectively, they should produce communitywide results that remain durable."[41] To measure such outcomes, the literature to date has depended upon several sources: surveys of key leaders, community surveys, and trend analysis of archival data.[42] Surveys of key leaders have been used to gain their perspectives on how well coalitions are doing in terms of community improvement, but one weakness of these measures is their subjectivity.[43] Since coalitions are often comprised of key community leaders, this approach can also face the problem of having coalition members evaluating their own effectiveness.[44] While this can be extremely helpful as a tool for formative evaluation, i.e., noting issues that should be addressed to make a coalition function better, they are less convincing to outsiders who may have considerable doubt as to the actual impact of a coalition structure.[45]

In other cases, researchers have moved beyond the cadre of coalition leaders to seek to measure the pulse of the community at large. In such instances, community surveys (i.e., paper or phone) are typically conducted of residents in parts of the community targeted by initiatives[46] and participants in programming sponsored by initiatives.[47] This helps to avoid the problem of having coalition members assessing themselves, but other problems arise. For instance, the general public is often not aware of the overall efforts of a coalition and would often find it difficult to say for sure whether a community is improving in areas that are beyond the scope of their daily lives. For instance, asking a grocery store worker if children are doing better in school in recent years due to literacy coalition efforts may yield only thin stereotypes and impressions at best. For this reason, the majority of studies along these lines tend to focus on participants or neighborhoods that have been the target of coalition programming and initiatives.[48] While this is helpful in many ways to ascertain real community changes, this approach has the weakness of being more an assessment of the programming coalitions run than an evaluation of the value added of having a coalition structure.

Perhaps the most ambitious efforts to assess whether communities are better off due to coalitions have resorted to trend analysis of archival data.[49] This has the advantage of looking at concrete community outcomes (such as graduation rates) rather than perceptions of community leaders or the general populace. In general, such studies look at a single community over time to see if major indicators of interest improve after coalitions are formed as compared with beforehand. This approach is the one the Urban Institute champions for use by individual communities to track their own progress once coalitions are formed. Specifically, they assert that U.S. Census data on years of schooling completed, collected annually by the American Community Survey, offers perhaps the best measure we have in terms of "examining overall community literacy."[50]

While trend analysis of census data is a strong approach, it is not without its problems. It requires considerable statistical analysis to distill the value added of a coalition. In the following pages we use a sample of 110 literacy coalitions identified by the National Center for Families Learning's Literacy Powerline, a group that has been the main convening site and conference host for literacy coalitions.[51] We then used these data to compare literacy coalition communities to all other communities in the nation. We first use county-level analysis to discern whether coalition communities are more likely to participate in national literacy-related initiatives. We then use zip code level analysis to ask whether literacy coalition communities are more likely to win literacy-related grant funding. Finally, we use a county-level analysis to ask whether these communities enjoy higher nonprofit financial health and level of high school graduation (see table 3.2).

## COALITIONS AS PART OF A VIRTUOUS CYCLE

Sometimes in blighted communities we see what is commonly called a vicious cycle, in which one negative indicator, such as low educational outcomes, is correlated with low employment, which is in turn associated with low wealth, and high poverty. In the complex ecosystems of a community it is hard to say which of these factors caused the other, but there is a sense that there is a continuing chain reaction in which each of these factors seem to magnify, increase, or at least reinforce one another. The result is that it is very difficult to figure out how to solve any one of these problems without solving

**Table 3.2. Collective impact outcomes**

| Hypothesized Outcomes Post Coalition Formation | | Question: Do coalition communities . . . | Finding | Data Used |
|---|---|---|---|---|
| Formative/ Process Outcomes | Participation in National Initiatives | Correlate with greater participation in national initiatives? | Yes, controlling for selected social capital variables | Data from National Results and Equity Collaborative Partner List of National Initiatives, by county[1] |
| | Win More Grants | Correlate with winning more competitive grants? | Yes, controlling for selected community characteristics | Data from U.S. Department of Education, by Zip Code |
| | Better Resourced Nonprofit Community | Correlate with better resourced nonprofit communities? | Yes, controlling for selected community characteristics | Data from IRS, by county |
| Summative Outcomes | Higher High School Graduations or High School Equivalency | Correlate with higher rates of high school graduates or equivalents? | Yes, controlling for selected community characteristics | Data from Census American Community Survey, by county |

1. We explore social capital and collective impact with data on all U.S. counties in 2010. There are 3,136 counties in the United States (and in our sample). Of these, 110 counties have Literacy Coalitions. (data acquired from the following web site: http://www.literacypowerline.com/literacy-coalitions/) We paired these data with county-level social capital data obtained from Rupasingha and Goetz (2008). We then geographically coded data collected as part of the National Results and Equity Collaborative Initiative (2013) that identifies which communities are participating in a series of national initiatives (see list in the previous chapter). An important methodological note is that, where initiatives were in cities that included multiple counties, all counties were coded as having that initiative. Additionally, when counties could not be identified the presence of initiatives was not coded.

Chart created by the authors.

all the others at the same time, since each is perceived as a cause of the other. Their constant loop seems to put a community into a downward spiral in which each component continues to worsen as the momentum builds. As the spiral accelerates, the hope for an external force to stop this cycle becomes ever more bleak since the force required to bring about change (whether it is a policy change, new program, or other initiative) must be ever more substantial and thus more costly. What we see in this chapter, however, is that coalition communities experience the opposite.

As we will explore in the following pages, by studying all counties in the United States, and in some cases all zip codes in the United States, we will see that coalition communities are better off when it comes to gaining access to national initiatives offering technical support, winning grants from the U.S. Department of Education, earning revenues and assets for their nonprofits, and succeeding in terms of high school graduation. However, the analysis presented in the following pages does not prove that the coalitions caused the positive outcomes we see. It could be something else that was co-occurring in all these communities but not in others, though we will try to control for whatever we think might rule this out. In the end, we can only conclude that we could have our logic reversed and it could be that stronger communities are more likely to form coalitions.[52] Regardless, we can feel fairly confident that coalitions are part of a virtuous cycle in which good things reinforce one another in a given community.

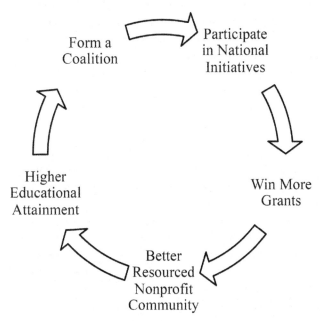

**Figure 3.2. Virtuous cycle of coalition communities.**
Graphic courtesy of the authors.

## ARE COALITIONS MORE LIKELY TO COORDINATE
## WELL ENOUGH TO JOIN NATIONAL INITIATIVES?

In recent years, emphasis on using collective impact and community coalition building to address persistent social problems have carried with them inflections of social capital.[53] As Butterfoss explains, the distinguishing characteristic of a community coalition is that a "structured arrangement for collaboration among organizations exists in which all members work together toward a common purpose."[54] Similarly, with respect to collective impact, much of the emphasis has been on constructing strong backbone institutions on which a community can build "a centralized infrastructure with dedicated staff, a structured process that leads to a common agenda, shared measurement, continuous communication, and mutually reinforcing activities among all participants."[55] At the heart of this effort, whether it be collective impact or community coalition building, is a focus "on preventing or ameliorating a community problem."[56]

Regardless of the approach, all theoretically seek to influence the social capital within a community. As Aldrich et al. point out, collaboration is an end in itself; while "interventions come and go, sustaining the capacity to collaborate means the community will always have a durable resource with which to address common concerns."[57] In the case of multi-issue advocacy, Jagpal and Laskowski write that all such collaborations "represent long-term efforts to bolster impact and address entrenched social problems to achieve lasting social change through deep relational engagement."[58] Given these investments, it stands to reason that working to build such social capital, or "civic muscle"[59] will both encourage and enable communities to make use of national resources such as civic campaigns working to benefit children's educational outcomes.

In the following pages we probe this relationship between social capital and community coalition/collective impact engagement by asking if literacy coalitions are correlated with a community's ability to organize itself to participate in national initiatives even after controlling for other forms of social capital present in the community. While more and better data are needed to run such models with confidence, this preliminary analysis offers a hint of what such further analysis would find.

First, how is social capital related to coalitions? Previous research has identified strong leadership, unity (or social capital) and communication as common elements of "effectiveness of coalitions."[60] In extensive research conducted by Joanne Keith, "unity refers to the strong sense of solidarity and togetherness that coalition members feel toward one another, and was assessed by over half of the coalitions as being an integral part of their effectiveness. By working together, coalition members deterred conflict and avoided duplication of services. Some coalitions used the word 'camaraderie' to describe the feeling among coalition members."[61] In this same research, traits of coalition members that were identified as contributing to the effectiveness of a coalition included open-mindedness, trust, "enjoyable involvement, personal commitment; and willingness to volunteer."[62] The study goes on to conclude that, "Trust, as pointed out by many coalition members, lays the foundation for cooperation and consensus."[63] Since these are many of the same characteristics that accompany areas of high social capital, we might expect social capital and coalition formation to be positively correlated.

Are communities that have literacy coalitions more likely to have higher social capital to begin with? Our hypothesis, based on the literature, is that counties with higher social capital will be more likely to form literacy coalitions. Before moving on to further analysis, we pause to examine this possibility. The results of our analysis were contrary to what we expected in that communities with higher social capital in 2005 were not more likely to form coalitions as of 2010. In fact, coalition communities on average had lower overall social capital than non-coalition communities. Furthermore, some types of social capital were correlated with coalition formation while others were not. Interestingly, perhaps the only forms of social capital that predicted coalition formation were fitness centers, labor groups, and political and professional groups. When controlling for the effects of all forms of social capital available to us at once,[64] we found that census response rate, political organizations, professional organizations, and labor organizations were all significantly associated with an increased likelihood of having a coalition. Next, we examined whether the presence of a coalition (even when controlling for greater social capital) is associated with higher participation in national campaigns aimed at improving children's educational outcomes. Our hypothesis, based on the literature, is that counties that have formed coalitions will be more likely to participate in national initiatives. As might be anticipated, we found that noncoalition communities joined an average of 0.2 national initiatives (i.e., initiatives listed in table 2.1) while coalition communities join an average of 3.9.

However, since coalitions are intended to create social capital, we further hypothesize that once social capital is controlled for, the presence of a literacy coalition will no longer be significantly associated with national initiative participation. Human capital (i.e., education), inequality, represented by the Gini Coefficient, being designated a High Creative Class area by the U.S. Census, and having a literacy coalition were all associated with launching more nationally affiliated initiatives. However, when we controlled for these variables in a preliminary analysis, presence of a coalition remained significant and associated with participation in more national initiatives.[65] While more and better data are needed to run such models with confidence, this preliminary analysis offers a hint of what such further analysis would find.

Quite interesting is the fact that having a literacy coalition remained statistically significant when associated with increased involvement in national initiatives, even after controlling for the other forms of social capital and other community characteristics. This suggests that having a coalition is in some way an indicator that the community possesses a distinctive form of social capital that is unique among the variety of social capital currencies. Somewhat similarly, Portes observes, "Lemann in *The Atlantic Monthly* and Pollitt in *The Nation* questioned whether American civic virtue is on the wane or has simply taken new forms different from the old-style organizations cited in Putnam's article."[66]

Intuitively, we might think of coalition formation as more of a "bridging" (i.e., bringing diverse social groups together) than a "bonding" (i.e., keeping a tight knit group together) variety of social capital, which would logically facilitate participation in national initiatives.[67] While we do not know whether coalitions actually create a form of distinctive bridging social capital, or whether they are the manifestation of a community that naturally has this quality and hence creates coalitions as an after effect, we can with greater confidence say that having a literacy coalition is a useful marker of a community that is more likely to be engaged in ways that facilitate involvement in national initiatives aimed at addressing "wicked" social problems in the area of education. As Putnam argued in some of his earlier work, communities that have not figured out how to work together appear "trapped" in their silos:

> Failure to cooperate for mutual benefit does not necessarily signal ignorance or irrationality or even malevolence, as philosophers since Hobbes have underscored. Hume's farmers were not dumb, or crazy, or evil; they were trapped. Social scientists have lately analyzed this fundamental predicament in a variety of guises: the tragedy of the commons; the logic of collective action; public goods; the prisoners' dilemma. In all these situations, as in Hume's rustic anecdote, everyone would be better off if everyone could cooperate. In the absence of coordination and credible mutual commitment, however, everyone defects, ruefully but rationally, confirming one another's melancholy expectations.[68]

What Putnam captures is that some communities are stuck in a vicious cycle because they have not figured out how to work together, or in other words, they have underdeveloped social capital. In the present research, we find that having a literacy coalition is perhaps a good indicator of communities that have figured out a way to escape such traps and work together toward the common good. This further suggests a role for philanthropy in building such coalitions in order to best leverage the resources available across the nation to address social problems.[69] Indeed, many coalitions bank on this possibility to fund their work.

## Are Coalitions Better at Winning Funding?

Key to the logic of coalitions is that, in order to bring about community change, they first foster a spirit of collaboration that enables community members to work together to both leverage existing resources and bring in more resources.[70] One of the key social capital building activities among many coalitions is collaborative grant writing. As one veteran coalition purveyor explained, such grant writing is critical because it avoids nonprofit infighting over limited resources by instead increasing the overall amount of resources that can be shared among them, i.e., "growing the pie."

> How do communities develop a funding plan where you say I love this idea of collaborating but don't take away my slice of the pie? But we know that the pie gets bigger and we all get more. It's the "how to" part that needs to be answered, we need a tool that helps communities put that funding piece together and make it work.

This is the idea behind collaboration, but does it work? Are coalition communities, by virtue of this collaboration, any better at actually winning competitive funds on the national scene? To answer this question, we looked at all of the 65,535 U.S. Department of Education grants awarded in 2010 to see whether competitive grants were more likely to be awarded in zip codes that have literacy coalitions. We found that, 9.3 percent of coalition zip codes successfully won DOE grant funding in 2010, as compared to 1.9 percent of non-coalition zip codes.[71] These results indicate that zip codes where a coalition exists are approximately five times more likely to win DOE grant funding than zip codes without coalitions.

In examining all zip codes (including those that won grants and those that did not), our data indicates that zip codes with a coalition won an average of $871,346.78 DOE dollars, compared to $22,771.36 for non-coalition zip codes.[72] Hence coalition zip codes won over 35 times more funding than zip codes without a coalition. If we restrict our analysis to only those zip codes that won grants, we find that the average coalition zip code won seven times more funding, or $9,410,545.20, as compared with the average non-coalition total, which was typically awarded $1,209,739.40.

## Narrowing the Grants

When we look with greater scrutiny at grants well suited to coalitions at the DOE we find that a total of 311 zip codes won these grants. We did this by using the list of grant opportunities that were compiled and distributed to coalitions across the nation in that year by a coalition purveyor, Literacy Powerline. We found that 5.56 percent of all coalition communities won at least one of the grants identified as most suited to coalitions. In contrast, only 0.65 percent of non-coalition communities won one of these grants, indicating that coalition zip codes are more than eight times more likely to win the grants identified as most suited to coalitions.[73]

In addition, coalition communities win more than twenty-five times as much money from the specified grants, on average, then communities without coalitions. Of the total "suitable" grant funding distributed, coalition communities won $157,817 on average, compared to only $5,954 in communities without coalitions. We also find that among only those zip codes that have won a grant, coalition zip codes win over three times more money than those zip codes without coalitions, $2,840,707 as opposed to $915,474. While more research is needed to determine the causal nature of these relationships, as well as further control for regional population characteristics, this inquiry presents a framework for hypothesizing how these relationships function.

In terms of increasing resources to address community needs, the focus of this section, current literature presumes that coalitions naturally create interdisciplinary partnerships that mobilize resources, particularly grant funding.[74] This "collective spirit" is believed to inspire donors and unite resources from multiple sources, ensuring that successful community coalitions will be able to identify new resources to sustain their activities and impact in the long term.[75] Based on our analysis, this is a plausible explanation.

## The Vibrancy of the Nonprofit Field

It stands to reason that more successful grant applications will result in greater nonprofit sustainability. The two key measures that are nationally available from Internal Revenue Service (IRS) data are nonprofit revenues and nonprofit assets. These measures are much broader than just looking at DOE grants as examined above. Rather than just education-related grants, they include all forms of income, including grants from other federal departments, private foundations, individual donations, and social enterprises. In this sense, it is a more holistic measure. However, it is also much less precise in that it includes a much larger playing field of all nonprofits in the community. Since the majority of coalition members are not schools, and since nonprofits focusing specifically on literacy comprise less than half of the typical coalition, this broader measure is perhaps still a valid measure, if somewhat diluted, of the overall community well-being in coalition communities. When we compare counties with coalitions with those that do not have them, we see that coalition counties on average received over twice as much revenue (per capita) in 2010 than non-coalition counties ($7,394 vs. $2,733).[76]

In order to distill what proportion of this advantage might be attributable to the formation of a coalition, we controlled for a host of factors including average household income, population density, racial ethnic diversity, immigration and language dynamics, household profiles, and local industry factors. When controlling for this series of variables, having a coalition was still significantly associated with higher average nonprofit revenue. While more and better data are needed to run such models with confidence, this preliminary analysis offers a hint of what such further analysis would find.

While less immediately related to funds received in the same year, a more long-term indicator of nonprofit vibrancy is nonprofit assets per capita. In 2010, nonprofits in coalition counties averaged nearly three times more assets ($6,036 vs. $17,278 per capita).[77] When controlling for the same series of variables noted above, having a coalition remained significantly correlated with a higher average assets per capita net of population density, diversity, wealth of the community, and local industry factors. Thus, not only do coalitions seem to be correlated with an advantage in winning competitive DOE grant funding, but they also seem to be correlated with more nonprofit revenue and greater nonprofit assets. While more and better data are needed to run such models with confidence, this preliminary analysis offers a hint of what such further analysis would find.

## Community Education Outcomes

While the findings above help us to speculate about the value added of coalitions to the process of raising funding to effect community change, and perhaps indirectly help us to see the value of collaboration, in the following pages we look for indicators of community change itself. As noted by Hatry and others, perhaps the best measure of this is community educational achievement. As shared in the previous chapter, this is really a proxy measure for many related factors. Nationally, the United Way sets the goal of increasing high school graduation in a way that is mindful of these interlaced factors:

> In any community, education, income and health are the building blocks for opportunity—individually and collectively. Education is essential to getting and keeping a job with a wage that can sustain a family and has health benefits. An income that can cover today and save for tomorrow builds a family's solid foundation. Good health helps children stay on track at school and adults be productive at work. Remove any of these building blocks and the other two topple. Build them all up and you have a cornerstone for individual and community prosperity. How should a community move forward in tackling any of those issues?[78]

They go on to explain in explicit terms:

> Every year, more than one million students drop out of high school. As a result,
> fewer young Americans are likely to earn a diploma than their parents, a dis-
> tinction not shared by any other industrialized country. That's why United Way
> is working to ensure that children and youth are: (1) ready for school, start-
> ing with the skills they need to succeed; (2) reading on track by fourth grade;
> (3) transitioning successfully to and from middle school; (4) graduating high
> school on time; and (5) working or in advanced education or training by 21.[79]

Conducting a similar analysis to the one above we find that coalition counties have an approximately 3 percent lower rate of adults age 25 or older with less than high school education (15 percent for coalition counties as opposed to 18 percent for non-coalition counties).[80] We then controlled for a series of variables, including population density, diversity, wealth of the community, and major employers. While more and better data are needed to run such models with confidence, this preliminary analysis offers a hint of what such further analysis would find. We found that, even net of these factors, having a coalition was correlated with fewer residents with less than a high school education.

## Examining the Dimension of Time

We have found evidence of a coalition effect such that being in a coalition community is correlated with a community being in a virtuous cycle of increased participation in national initiatives, strong DOE grant winning, wealthy nonprofits, and positive educational outcomes. However, as we shared at the outset, the direction of causality is unclear. Given this consid-eration, it is perhaps worthwhile to probe the chronology of coalition forma-tion and community outcomes. This, however, is also fraught with potential problems. First, we can no longer compare all known counties since we must rely on a smaller sample of only those counties that completed our survey of coalitions (i.e., 75 instead of the 110 known coalitions used in the above analysis). In addition, while the data we have collected on seventy-five coali-tions includes the year they were formed, qualitative evidence suggests that these are fuzzy estimates of the beginning of efforts because groups often begin to interact about an issue for years (even seven or more years) before they decide to formally call themselves coalitions. Furthermore, over time horizons that span in excess of forty years of existence, finding pre-coalition data to compare to post-coalition data is tricky, to say the least, and would include such confusing uncontrolled for factors as recessions, wars, and even the globalization of the world economy.

Nevertheless, if we look at the subset of national data for which coalition inception is available, we are able to pair these with decennial census data both pre- and post-coalition formation. When we do this, we see that, on average, coalition communities saw considerable improvement from pre- to post-coalition formation. In terms of people twenty-five and older completing high school, coalition communities saw average improvements ranging from 3.2 percent (for those launched in the 1990s) to 8 percent (for those launched in the 1980s), depending on the decade (those launched in the 2000s saw 4.4 percent improvement).

While this is initially encouraging for proponents of coalitions, this pre-post analysis also has its weaknesses. Foremost is the difficulty of ruling out other national trends that occurred during this same time period. Most notably, for a variety of reasons, the percent of U.S. adults age twenty-five and older with a high school diploma or higher in the dataset skyrocketed from just over 30 percent in 1950 to 80 percent in 2000. Much of this steep rise occurred during the years of coalition formation. So, while coalition communities experienced a notable improvement, from pre- to post-measurement, so did everyone else.

In general, at the pre-year of 1980, coalition counties had an average (mean) of 69.15 percent (median of 69.05 percent) of their population with high school diplomas or higher as compared to a non-coalition county mean of 58.48 percent (median of 58.45). By 2009, coalition counties had jumped to 85 percent and non-coalition counties had jumped to 78 percent. Coalition communities basically started out higher and ended up higher. While non-coalition counties improved more, this is partly because they had much more room for improvement, with many reporting pre-1980 percent of adults graduating from high school as close to zero. At best this is inconclusive.

## Controlling for the Starting Point

Given these findings, when examining how communities change over time, it is important to take into account where a community was in terms of people completing high school when it was first measured in order to understand its growth by the time it was measured again. As we have also explored, it is important to take into account other community factors, such as industries, population, and poverty. In order to do both simultaneously, we controlled for our starting point of high school at the initial point of measurement, 1980. To do this, we returned to the full national sample for larger numbers (all counties in the United States, not just the ones in the survey). Looking at high school in a preliminary analysis and controlling for starting point in 1980 we find that controlling for where counties were in terms of percent with high school or above in 1980 and a full barrage of other controls, having a coalition is correlated with a lower percent with less than high school in 2009–2010. Also, as we might expect, and as we see in our preliminary analysis, as the percent with high school and above went up in 1980, the percent without it in 2009 went down. This means that even though a higher number of high school graduates in 1980 predicts a higher percentage in 2009 (as we might expect), having a coalition is correlated with even better outcomes (i.e., more graduates) over and above what the 1980 rate predicts, even after controlling for the full host of community-level factors we described, including social capital. While more and better data are needed to run such models with confidence, this preliminary analysis offers a hint of what such further analysis would find.[81]

The above findings offer some evidence to support the literature's hypothesized impact of community coalitions. Namely, having a community literacy coalition was statistically significantly correlated with participating in more national initiatives, winning more competitive Department of Education grants, having financially better resourced nonprofits, and a higher percent of adults completing high school. While the robust nature of these findings, persisting even after controlling for a series of other community characteristics, may be encouraging to proponents of the coalition approach, they fall short of proving that coalitions cause these community outcomes. Rather, the findings paint a picture of healthy communities (literacy-wise), in which having a coalition tends to coincide with other desirable community outcomes. A much more robust research agenda that begins with local coalition data collection and extends to community outcomes is needed. One of the key issues is that much of the work that coalitions do and the social benefit that they produce are difficult to conceptualize in measurable ways, and when it is possible, often few indicators exist for such outcomes. Nowhere is this more evident than in the area of social capital.

## SOCIAL CAPITAL, COALITIONS
## AND EDUCATIONAL INDICATORS

Having confirmed that certain types of social capital are associated with coalition formation, and coalitions and social capital are connected with greater likelihood to join national initiatives, it is worth speculating whether coalition communities are indeed better off when it comes to educational indicators even after controlling for other forms of social capital. In the field of social capital research, perhaps the strongest relationship that has been identified is the one with education. Whether in international or domestic studies, as social capital increases, so does educational attainment.[82] As Iyer et al. explain:

> There is a range of possible explanations for this apparently robust result. First, education requires the development of social skills that enable the development of social capital. In some ways, education can be considered as providing the initial investment in social capital—working in groups, learning to cooperate, and understanding the needs and attitudes of others. Thus, it provides a stock of individual social capital that can be built on in the future—and the skills developed make it less costly or difficult to invest in additional social capital after formal education has ceased. Second, in education individuals learn that others can be trusted and that cooperation, networks, and engagement can provide positive benefits. To the extent that education is a societal activity, then individuals learn the benefit of being in a society. Third, individuals who are more forward-looking may invest in both social and human capital.[83]

When it comes to research, the vast majority focuses on what happens to education when social capital is missing. For instance, on the state level, state social capital indices are highly correlated with the Annie E. Casey Foundation's Kids Count index of child welfare.[84] States with higher social capital have better educational outcomes such that the social capital index is highly correlated with student scores on elementary, junior, and high school standardized tests, and rate of staying in school.[85] Social capital seems to be significant even after controlling for educational spending, teachers' salaries, class size, racial composition, affluence, economic inequality, adult education levels, poverty rates, family structure, religious affiliation, and size of private school sector.[86] While even Putnam admits that current research is unable to discern whether social capital causes these good outcomes, we can feel fairly confident that they are correlated. There are a host of other possible causes, such as parental education, poverty rates, family structure, and racial composition. As in Putnam's research, we try to control for these things and figure out if something else is causing both these things to happen. We find that these socioeconomic and demographic factors do matter, but so does social capital when we control for them.[87] In this fashion, we return to our community outcome indicator of high school education through this new lens of social capital. When we include the social capital variables in our analyses, we find that, even controlling for other types of social capital and the general variables we have mentioned earlier, having a coalition still has a positive and statistically significant relationship with high school education. While more and better data are needed to run such models with confidence, this preliminary analysis offers a hint of what such further analysis would find.

Coalition presence is associated with a lower proportion of citizens with less than a high school education. Thus, it seems that there is something about coalition formation (whether it is the coalitions themselves or something that co-occurs with coalitions) that is associated with better community educational outcomes, even after we take into account the importance of social capital variables. We find ourselves in a position strangely similar to that of Putnam when he writes: "What this admittedly crude evidence is saying is that there is something about communities where people connect with one another—over and above how rich or poor they are materially, how well educated the adults themselves are, what race or religion they are—that positively affects the education of children."[88] The present analysis merely extends this interest in crude evidence and expands the canopy of Putnam's conclusions to suggest that there may be reason to speculate that coalition formation is another medium of social capital that helps to predict good educational outcomes over and above the other measures of social capital that we have available.

## CONCLUSION

In this chapter we have learned that data show that many communities are better off if they have a collective impact coalition. These coalitions use the tenets of the collective impact common agenda, common progress measures, mutually reinforcing activities, communication, and a strong backbone organization to structure their work and measure their progress. Although we do not know if coalitions cause better community outcomes, we see a virtuous cycle moving communities forward toward desirable goals. Coalition building is a journey and the need remains to standardize data collection so that we measure apples and apples, not apples, bananas, pineapples and pears, to fully determine the impact of coalitions.

## NOTES

1. Hatry & Morley, 2008, 32.
2. David Laird of the Central Carolina Community Foundation.
3. National Community Literacy Collaborative. 2010. COALITION ACCREDITATION STANDARDS Revised March 9, 2010.
4. National Community Literacy Collaborative. 2010. COALITION ACCREDITATION STANDARDS Revised March 9, 2010.
5. National Community Literacy Collaborative. 2010. COALITION ACCREDITATION STANDARDS Revised March 9, 2010.

6. (n.d.). Retrieved December 29, 2016, from 3rd Grade Reading Success Matters: The Challenge http://gradelevelreading.net/.

7. (2016). Retrieved April 4, 2017, from http://resultsandequity.org/about/.

8. Turning Curves for Vulnerable Children from Birth to Age 8 Action Guide:Shared Results and Measures. (2014). Retrieved April 4, 2017, from http://re sultsandequity.org/wp-content/uploads/2014/12/NREC_Shared_ResultsMeasures.pdf.

9. Grade Reading Success Matters: The Challenge. (n.d.). Retrieved April 4, 2017, from http://gradelevelreading.net/.

10. Hatry & Morley, 2008, 9.

11. Stevens, 2008, 12–13.

12. Ridzi, Sylvia, & Singh, 2014.

13. Ridzi, Sylvia, Qiao, & Craig, 2016.

14. Singh, Sylvia, & Ridzi, 2015.

15. See for instance Hatry & Morley (2008) and CELEBRATING OUR BRIGHTEST STARS.

(n.d.). Retrieved April 4, 2017, from http://gradelevelreading.net/our-network/pacesetter-honors.

16. Boyer, 1990.

17. See for instance the work of Furco (2010).

18. (n.d.). Retrieved April 4, 2017, from http://adultliteracy.xprize.org/.

19. (n.d.). Retrieved April 4, 2017, from http://adultliteracy.xprize.org/.

20. (n.d.). Retrieved April 4, 2017, from http://www.readtosucceedbuffalo.org/results.

21. FSG Social Impact Advisors. 2010. "Shared Measurement System for Literacy Coalitions" Conference Presentation Slides from the National Community Literacy Coalition Conference, March 16, 2010.

22. (Carlson et al., 2011) see also Believe 2 Become. (n.d.). Retrieved April 4, 2017, from https://believe2become.org/.

23. (n.d.). Retrieved April 4, 2017, from https://believe2become.org/programs/project-lift/.

24. Chaná Edmond-Verley and Mel Atkins II. 2016: 2.

25. Chaná Edmond-Verley and Mel Atkins II. 2016: 5.

26. About the GROW-Rochester Program Screening Children Early for Developmental Challenges. (2016). Retrieved April 4, 2017, from https://www.childrensinsti tute.net/programs/grow-rochester/about.

27. ROC the Future Report Card. (2016). Retrieved April 4, 2017, from http://www.actrochester.org/roc-the-future.

28. Ridzi, 2017.

29. (n.d.). Retrieved April 4, 2017, from https://clearimpact.com/results-score card-and-collective-impact-in-the-united-states/.

30. Oakland Literacy Coalition. (n.d.). Retrieved April 4, 2017, from http://www .oaklandreads.org.

31. This quote comes from a written document provided by a research participant.

32. In this case, the school districts then changed their kindergarten readiness tool and the community was back to 57 percent on the new tool and had to work hard to

raise that number on the new measure to 78 percent through a concerted effort. Data come from a written document provided by a research participant.

33. Data was provided to authors upon request.

34. The Campaign for Grade-Level Reading Midpoint Snapshots. (2016). Retrieved April 4, 2017, from http://gradelevelreading.net/wp-content/uploads/2016/04/MidpointSnapshots_Apr12.pdf.

35. (n.d.). Retrieved April 4, 2017, from http://www.strivetogether.org/sites/default/files/StriveTogether_Theory_of_Action_v3_06.2016.pdf.

36. Beard, 2013.

37. Data provided by the interviewee noted above and verified online. Online source withheld to preserve confidentiality.

38. Foster-Fishman, Berkowitz, Lounsbury, Jacobson, & Allen, 2001.

39. Butterfoss et al., 1993.

40. Butterfoss, 2007.

41. Goodman et al., 1996, 53.

42. Special thanks for feedback on portions of this section to Monica Sylvia. Portions presented as "Got Coalition? A National Study of the Differences Between Literacy and Non-Literacy Coalition Communities." Frank Ridzi and Monica R. Sylvia National Conference on Family Literacy. Louisville, Kentucky, April 27–30, 2013.

43. Goodman et al., 1996, 53.

44. Feinberg et al., 2004 in Kegler et al., 2010, 2.

45. Cramer et al., 2006.

46. Clark et al., 2010.

47. Ridzi, Sylvia & Singh, 2011.

48. Goodman et al., 1996.

49. Goodman et al., 1996, 55.

50. Hatry & Morley, 2008, 9.

51. This sample includes the entire online listing of known literacy coalitions across the United States. It is available online at the following location. http://literacypowerline.com/literacy-coalitions/.

52. If this is the case it may be a moot point since we would want to emulate these communities anyway and one of the things they are doing is having coalitions.

53. Kania & Kramer, 2011; Kaye, 2001, 269.

54. Butterfoss, 2007, 71.

55. Kania & Kramer, 2011, 38.

56. Butterfoss 2007, 71.

57. Aldrich et al., 2009, 147.

58. Jagpal & Laskowski, 2013, 18.

59. We adopt this term from our colleague David Laird, personal communication.

60. Keith, 1993.

61. Keith, 1993.

62. Keith, 1993.

63. Keith, 1993.

64. Social capital variables were accessed from data acquired from Rupasingha and Goetz (2008). Positive relationships also persisted with: religious organizations,

business associations, political organizations, labor organizations, golf organizations and sports clubs, and managers and promoters. Negative relationships were statistically significant with: civic organizations, professional organizations, bowling centers, and physical fitness facilities.

65. It should be noted here that this analysis used the raw values of the social capital values rather than the per 10,000 in the population as used in the other analyses. In this analysis the population density was controlled for as was the metro status.

66. Portes, 1998, 19.

67. According to Putnam, bonding tends to be exclusive while bridging helps groups reach across silos. As Putnam puts it, "Strong ties with intimate friends may ensure chicken soup when you're sick, but weak ties with distant acquaintances are more likely to produce leads for a new job." Putnam (2000, 363).

68. Putnam, 1993, 1.

69. Easterling, 2008.

70. Special Thanks for assistance in this section goes to Lindsay Nash, who helped to prepare part of this research on coalition funding. A preliminary analysis was presented at the 2013 Annual Meeting of the Society for the Study of Social Problems (SSSP) New York, NY entitled "Re-Imagining Community Assets through Collaboration—Are Literacy Coalitions an Effective Way to Compete for Federal Grants?" Authors: Frank Ridzi and Lindsay Nash.

71. A statistically significant finding at the .01 level.

72. These findings were also statistically significant at the .01 level.

73. These findings were also statistically significant at the .01 level.

74. Butterfoss et al., 1993.

75. Kramer, 2009; Benz et al., 2010, 3.

76. This is the full population mean but the difference was also statistically significant at the .01 level.

77. This is the full population but this difference was also statistically significant at the .01 level.

78. Charting A Course For Change: Advancing Education, Income And Health Through Collective Impact. (2012, June). Retrieved April 4, 2017, from http://unway.3cdn.net/ea3f8667b2a4bad0e2_0gm6yxly7.pdf.

79. Charting A Course For Change: Advancing Education, Income And Health Through Collective Impact. (2012, June). Retrieved April 4, 2017, from http://unway.3cdn.net/ea3f8667b2a4bad0e2_0gm6yxly7.pdf.

80. This is the full population but the difference was statistically significant at the .01 level.

81. To double check this relationship, we also re-ran the analysis and found that this relationship predicting 2009 graduations holds up if we were to control for 1990, or 2000 graduation rates (as we did with 1980). Hence, we find that, regardless of where a community starts off in terms of high school graduates, having a coalition is significantly correlated with better high school graduation percentages later. On an intuitive level, this makes sense since an estimated 91 percent of literacy coalitions that provide direct services focus on serving adults, although this percentage has likely decreased since the addition of Campaign for Grade-Level Reading coalitions began its work.

In order to further examine this relationship, we examined whether this relationship also existed in the case of college graduates. This mainly helps us to investigate the possibility that something else that we are not aware of is making all types of education increase, even those not focused on by coalitions. While many coalitions serve adults, they do so in the areas of adult education, not higher education. They tend to offer adult basic education, English as a Second Language, and GED-training programs. These programs tend to lead up to and focus on earning a high school equivalency diploma. Hence, we would not expect to find the same relationship between coalitions and college graduates unless there was some uncontrolled or lurking variable that we somehow failed to include in our statistical model. Running the same pre- and post-analysis with control variables for college graduates we find that, controlling for their 1980 starting point, coalitions are not significantly correlated with later 2009 college education (four-year degrees and higher). In fact, what does remain significant is the percent with a college education starting out in 1980. Hence, we see a situation in which more high school graduates in 1980 predict more high school graduates in 2009 and more college graduates in 1980 predict more college graduates in 2009. This reinforces the idea that more highly educated parents have higher educated children. However, as we would expect, coalitions do not have an effect on this relationship for colleges (an area where coalitions do not focus).

82. Hall, 1999; Putnam, 2000; Glaeser et al., 2002 in Iyer et al., 2005, 1025–1026.

83. Iyer et al., 2005, 1025–1026.

84. Putnam, 2000, 296.

85. Putnam, 2000, 299. This also goes well beyond education as Putnam shows: States that score high on Social Capital Index—join organizations, volunteer, vote, socialize (and trust others) are where kids tend to be better off—teens tend not to drop out of school (296 and 297)—and a host of other things such as be born unhealthy become involved in violent crime, commit suicide or homicide or become teen parents (Putnam, 2000, 296).

86. Putnam (2000, 488 note #9) the social capital index is also negatively correlated with the state high school dropout rate (1990–1995).

87. Putnam, 2000, 297.

88. Putnam, 2000, 301.

## Chapter Four

# Measuring Impact and Moving Toward Best Practices

Best practices are hard to come by when looking at large-scale efforts at community change. We need only look at some of the heavyweights in the field to know that increasing the education level of the populace is a daunting task, and resources alone certainly do not guarantee success. In its long chain of evolution, the Bill & Melinda Gates Foundation has successively emphasized small high schools, raising teacher quality, and a variety of ways to assess teacher quality.[1] In the words of the Gates Foundation itself, many of the efforts it has made in the way of education (not unlike their encounters with other areas of investment internationally) have been lackluster. As the Gates Foundation explained in its 2009 annual letter:

> Many of the small schools that we invested in did not improve students' achievement in any significant way. These tended to be the schools that did not take radical steps to change the culture, such as allowing the principal to pick the team of teachers or change the curriculum. We had less success trying to change an existing school than helping to create a new school. Even so, many schools had higher attendance and graduation rates than their peers. While we were pleased with these improvements, we are trying to raise college-ready graduation rates, and in most cases, we fell short.[2]

While this is certainly disheartening, it by no means is an indication that interventions cannot make a difference. It is just an admission that long-term, intractable social problems that have taken decades to evolve may take similarly long periods of time to solve. As Bill Gates shared in an interview, "It would be great if our education stuff worked, but that we won't know for probably a decade."[3]

Far from an afterthought, developing best practices has often been among the foremost goals of collective impact and school reformers alike. As Newark,

New Jersey's Democratic mayor (Cory Booker), teamed up with the state's Republican governor (Chris Christie) and Facebook's inventor (Mark Zuckerberg), they pledged a total of $200 million raised by Zuckerberg with matching funding from private individuals and foundations. "Their stated goal was not to repair education in Newark but to develop a model for saving it in all of urban America."[4] In this sense, Newark, as with most collective impact and school reform approaches, has a dual goal of making life better for local individuals and forging a new trail for the rest of the nation to follow.

In many ways, the collective impact community coalition phenomenon described in the preceding chapters is part of this broader cross-sector education reform movement. Coalitions set out to create change in their home communities, but central to the vision of their purveyors is the hope that coalitions will develop a blueprint that will cure similar ills across the nation. Most major initiatives, as we see in the words of Bill Gates, are aspirational. Groups like Strive and the Campaign for Grade-Level Reading hope to see changes over time. But will we, as a society, be ready to recognize and measure these successes with any useful degree of specificity? Will we be able to dissect them and learn precisely what aspects of these initiatives worked, and how well?

The GLR Campaign is trying to do just that. As Ron Fairchild reports,

From the beginning, the GLR Campaign has been very clear about results, giving communities the opportunity to mobilize around making measurable progress by 2020 and recognizing promising trends and visible momentum. The evidence is beginning to show that change is happening as the community goals are made achievable and actionable. At the beginning of 2017, nearly 200 of the 303 GLR Campaign communities reported moving the needle on at least one of the following measures for low-income children: school readiness, school attendance, summer learning, and/or grade-level reading. While most of the credit for this progress goes to the commitment, energy, and action of GLR Network states and communities, their ability to make this progress also reflects in important measure the inspiration and assistance they have received from the GLR Support Center. By focusing on results and building a network characterized by communities that are learning from and with each other, GLR Campaign is also making the case that it's possible to make more progress by working together. The majority of communities in the GLR Network that are making progress are actively engaged with other peer communities in their state and/or region that face similar challenges. GLR Network members consistently report deriving value and realizing benefits from being part of this type of peer learning community and connecting to something beyond their individual communities.

In the previous chapter we explored what mechanisms are in place for measuring success, and we have paid close attention to their weaknesses and shortcomings. In this chapter we put aside our misgivings about the weaknesses of extant data and instead embrace the reality that there are very few, if any, things in this world for which perfect data exist. We further endeavor to leverage the advantages that we do have. Unlike the nascent efforts of Gates, Zuckerberg, and others, collective impact community coalitions have been around for decades. If we are to start learning lessons about what works best within the coalition paradigm, there is no need to wait another decade.

This chapter is devoted to both harvesting lessons learned and offering a cautionary tale. We do our best to harvest what can be known given existing data structures and case studies. Yet at the same time we offer a cautionary tale that the data we have will leave us less than fully satisfied. Better knowledge will not be available to probe the programs being launched today once they have matured in ten years if we do not invest more heavily in data infrastructures today.

In the following pages we first use a sample of communities that participated in our national survey to look at coalitions on the key indicators of the coalition virtuous cycle. Based on this, we see that not all coalition communities are part of such cycles that outperform the nation. Using these same communities, we spend the rest of the chapter using quantitative and qualitative information that is available to explore promising areas where best practices for coalitions might be emerging.

## LOOKING AT COALITIONS ACROSS THE NATION

If we examine the coalitions in our national sample, we see considerable variation in terms of community indicators. For instance, as seen in figure 4.1, the vast majority outperform the national average when it comes to percent of adults with high school degree and college degree, but some do not.

On the right side of the chart we see high performers that outperform the national average in terms of having a higher percentage of population age twenty-five or older with a high school education or higher. These same counties also tend to outperform the national average by having a higher percent of population over age twenty-five with four years of college education or more.

As we move to the left, the performance generally declines such that both the percent with a college education and the percent with high school are less exceptional and closer to the national averages. At the far left, we see coalition counties that are worse than the national average both when it comes to college and high school graduation. If we were to add community resources (i.e., per capita revenue and assets) we would see that coalition communities with better outcomes in terms of raising resources for their nonprofit efforts also tend to have better educational indicators. In general, as revenues and assets increase, so do educational outcomes.

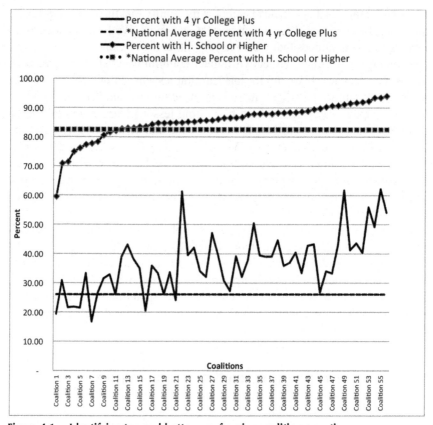

**Figure 4.1.    Identifying top and bottom performing coalition counties.**
*Source:* Data collected by the authors in collaboration with the Literacy Funders Network, 2012.

Such a relationship suggests the importance of asking what is it about some coalition communities that makes them perform better across all measures and what is it about others that makes them perform worse? While we are unequipped to answer such questions given the data available, it is helpful to turn to the nascent implementation science that has been developing around coalitions for some clues.

## WHAT DOES COALITION THEORY SAY ABOUT ACHIEVING POSITIVE OUTCOMES?

Theories of coalition building have focused on such things as factors that enable or encumber a community's capacity to bring about community change through collaboration. They include empowerment theory (Fawcett et al. 1995), phases of coalition formation, maintenance and institutionalization (Ridzi, Carmody, and Byrnes 2011), and the importance of collective action to bring about lasting social change (Kania and Kramer 2011). As with many of the other approaches, much of the research that forms the basis for Butterfoss's community coalition action theory focuses on coalition functioning and intermediate measures of effectiveness, such as satisfaction of coalition members, participation, and action plan quality and implementation (Butterfoss 2007, 89; Butterfoss and Kegler 2002). Though this evidence and more recent case studies are informative, they "are difficult to generalize from, and they focus less often on associations among constructs" (Butterfoss 2007, 89). In this chapter we aim to begin filling this gaping hole with national data by taking a closer look at the relationship between constructs that were theorized from case studies. In the following pages we explore some of the developing understandings and how the present data serve to deepen our understanding.

## Community Change Is Related to Policy or Systems Change

Much of the growing literature on coalitions suggests that what sets them apart from other forms of intervention is that they are capable of marshaling the community resources needed to bring about changes in policy or local systems. The thinking is that only through such changes can we see true improvement at the scale of the community level, as opposed to seeing change only in the lives of those who participate in certain programming that, while encouraging, is not statistically large enough to appear in community-level data. In our national survey, we asked coalition communities the following questions: "Does your coalition work to bring about policy or system change?" and "Has your coalition been responsible (in whole or part) for bringing about policy or systems changes in your community to improve literacy?" Overall, about 64 percent of all coalitions set out to achieve policy change, reporting that their coalition does "work to bring about policy or system change." Percentages seeking to bring about such change (as opposed to not) were higher among all coalition age groups.

When looking at reported outcomes, older coalitions were more likely to feel that they had indeed succeeded in this effort and had been responsible for helping to bring about policy or systems change. Overall, the majority (52 percent) felt they were able to bring about policy change and more than 67 percent of those seeking such change felt they were able to achieve it. As figure 4.2 shows, success at policy or systems change seems to be associated with both age of the coalition and intentionally seeking out such change.

These findings are meaningful because Gates and others say they hope for success that will be evident over time. Here we see the type of increased

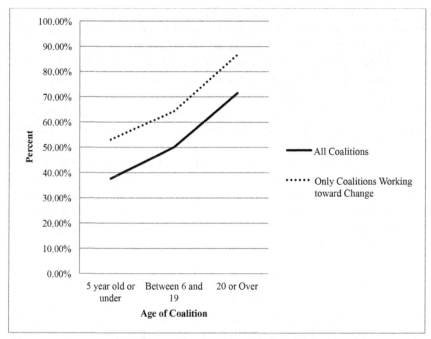

**Figure 4.2.** Percent of coalitions that have been responsible (in whole or part) for bringing about policy or systems change (by age of coalition).

*Source:* Data collected by the authors in collaboration with the Literacy Funders Network, 2012.

impact correlated with longevity that such kindred efforts hope to attain. Coalitions have been hypothesized to help bring about "changes in community policies, practices, and environment" as an intermediate outcome on the way to more significant impacts such as community resources and capacity to address problems and ultimately social outcomes, such as health or education levels (Butterfoss 2007, 75). Since policy or system change is only an intermediate level outcome, we then looked to see if it was associated with better community performance on community education level. Looking at the top twenty performing coalition counties we find that 56 percent reported success in bringing about policy or system change as opposed to only 33 percent of the twenty lowest performing coalition counties. Furthermore, when looking at coalition communities that had policy change we found their educational attainment was better than their counterparts who had implemented coalitions without achieving policy change, and both types of coalition communities were better off than non-coalition counties. Coalition counties that reported achieving policy or system change had on average only 13.22 percent of their population age twenty-five or older with less than high school (as opposed to 15.53 percent for all coalitions and 17.6 percent for communities with no coalition).[5]

A similar story was found in terms of revenues and assets. Again, coalition communities that had achieved policy or systems change were able to obtain better community level resources than those that had not, and both types of coalition communities outperformed non-coalition communities. When it came to per capita revenues raised by community nonprofits, coalition counties that had attained policy or system change reported $9,417 on average as compared with $7,819 among all coalition counties and only $2,730 among non-coalition counties. In the area of assets per capita accumulated by community nonprofits, coalition counties that had attained policy or system change reported $26,137 on average as compared with $18,435 among all coalition counties and only $6,031 among non-coalition counties.[6] These relationships suggest that working to achieve policy or systems change within one's community is indeed a meaningful goal for coalitions seeking to have impact at the community scale. Again, while we cannot ascertain whether such changes actually caused the community's positive outcomes, the two seem to be related to each other. In the following section we continue to probe this issue by examining what types of coalition practices are related to successes in the area of policy and systems change.

## Defining Coalition "Practices" Linked with Policy or Systems Change

As explored in the preceding chapters, coalitions are remarkably diverse. Nevertheless, they share many common practices that allow us to recognize them as more or less related to each other and appropriately called coalitions. In this section we explore whether some of these reported coalition practices are more likely than others to be associated with the policy or systems change that has been linked with coalition success. Specifically, we rely on the work of Butterfoss (2007, 72–73), who has laid out a series of propositions based on multiple case studies of community health coalitions. She suggests that a series of practices are associated with successful coalition outcomes but did not have a national data set with which to test her hypotheses. We attempt to do so here by using our sample of literacy coalitions. In the following pages we operationalize these practices and then test Butterfoss's theory by looking to see if those communities that carry out more of the practices she identified are more likely to have success with policy or institution change. We then follow through to see if carrying out more of these practices is related to positive community outcomes. In both cases, we find support in favor of her theory.

## The Butterfoss Scale

Butterfoss developed what is perhaps the most comprehensive logic model that exists with respect to coalition composition and functioning. In her model, a lead agency or convener group pulls together a coalition member-ship that carries out three key functions: operation and process, leadership and staffing, and structures. Carrying out these functions prompts three synergistic practices: pooling of resources, member engagement, and assessment and planning. These synergies lead to implementation strategies, which in turn lead to community change outcomes (such as increases in resources and capacity) and eventually changes in community level indicators or outcomes.

In order to put Butterfoss's theory to the test we created the Butterfoss Scale to measure the level to which communities carry out each of the components of the Butterfoss model. A higher score on the scale indicates greater conformity to the Butterfoss model. The scale was constructed by asking coalitions to identify all services they currently provide, or have provided in the past. More specifically, Butterfoss argues that technical assistance and financial or material support are critical functions of the convening or lead organization. Those coalitions that reported that they provide technical assistance and resource supply/distribution were thus awarded credit for each of these practices, respectively (scale items 1 and 2). When it comes to operations and processes, Butterfoss asserts that "open and frequent communication among staff and members helps to create a positive climate, ensures that benefits outweigh costs, and makes collaborative synergy more likely."[7] Coalitions that reported "communication" as one of their services were coded as carrying out this function (scale item 3). In terms of leadership and staffing, Butterfoss stresses the importance of "paid staff who have the interpersonal and organizational skills to facilitate the collaborative process, improve coalition functioning, and make collaborative synergy more likely." [8] Those that reported that they have paid staff were coded as meeting this staffing criteria (scale item 4).

Butterfoss asserts that "formalized rules, roles, structures, and procedures make collaborative synergy more likely." [9] For this structural dimension, we coded coalitions that reported having a 501(c)(3) tax exempt charity status as approximating this tenet, since this status requires such formalized rules, roles, and structures (scale item 5). In the realm of synergy and pooled resources, Butterfoss explicates how this "prompts effective assessment, planning, and implementation of strategies." [10] Coalitions that reported providing "community planning/strategic planning" and "evaluation/accreditation" were thus coded as complying with this vision (scale items 6 and 7). Finally, with respect to implementation, Butterfoss argues that "coalitions are more likely to create change in community policies, practices, and environment

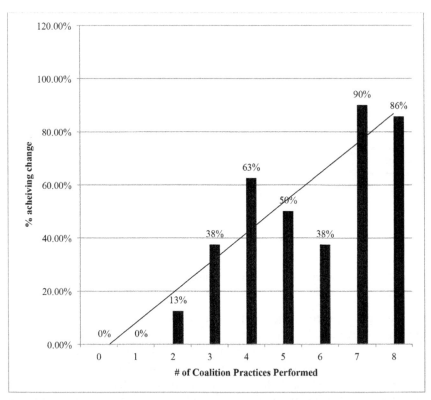

**Figure 4.3.**   **Percent achieving policy or systems changes in their community by number of coalition practices performed.**
*Source:* Data collected by the authors in collaboration with the Literacy Funders Network, 2012.

when they direct intervention at multiple levels."[11] To gauge efforts in this regard, coalitions were coded as consistent with Butterfoss's vision when they reported that they intentionally "work to bringing about policy or system change" (scale item 8).

The creation of this scale allows us to gauge how closely a coalition adheres to the model as articulated by Butterfoss. A coalition receives a score from 0 to 8, with a higher number meaning it carries out more of the practices that Butterfoss identified. In figure 4.3 we compare each possible score on the Butterfoss Scale (0 through 8) with the percentage of coalitions so rated that achieved policy or systems changes aimed at improving literacy in their community (in whole or in part due to their work).

As figure 4.3 shows, more closely corresponding to the Butterfoss model of coalition practices is associated with having a higher likelihood of achieving policy or systems change aimed at improving community literacy. When further analyzed to predict likelihood of achieving change,

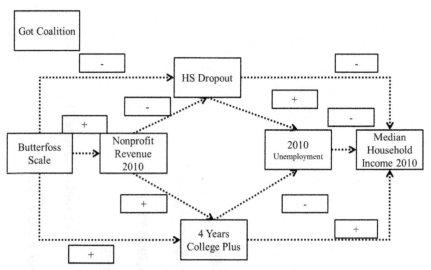

**Figure 4.4.  Exploratory path analysis controlling for population per square mile in 2000.**
*Source:* Data collected by the authors in collaboration with the Literacy Funders Network, 2012.

the number of practices performed is statistically related to the predicted outcome of change.[12]

Based on this we begin to see a relationship between coalition practice and community change outcomes. In the above path analysis-style model, we take this relationship a few steps further using the national data we have available from the U.S. Census, the IRS, and our survey. In this analysis we attempt to map out a very rough sense of the relationship in the present data between the newly developed Butterfoss scale and more long-term community social outcomes.[13] This is more of a theoretical exercise than proof of these relationships so we try to summarize our findings by adding in a plus sign when the relationship was positive and a negative sign when it was negative. We would need more and better data to build a model such as this with confidence. Our results are shown in figure 4.4.

Evident by the statistically significant relationships shown in this model, we can begin to flesh out the rudimentary relationships that, until this point, have only been hypothesized and speculated about by coalition scholars. We can see that a higher score on the Butterfoss scale (i.e., closer adherence to the coalition practices articulated in Butterfoss's community coalition action theory model), is positively related with nonprofit revenue in the community. It is also positively related with higher rates of college attainment and lower rates of high school dropouts (we can also see that nonprofit revenue is related in a logical fashion with these educational outcomes as well). These educational attainments are, in turn, statistically related with appropriate drops in unemployment and increases in median household income. In this way, even though we do not know if coalitions are causing these desirable community outcomes, we can say with some degree of confidence that coalition adherence to model practices is potentially related to the types of community outcomes we desire. These findings beckon an increased hope in the potential of an implementation science for coalition creation and implementation. In the next section we use statistical techniques to analyze our present limited data in the hopes of identifying potential best practices that future research may uncover with respect to coalitions.

## MOVING TOWARD COALITION BEST PRACTICES

Though overall, it appears that engaging in more activities common to coalitions is associated with better community outcomes, it stands to reason that certain activities provide better payoff for certain types of community outcomes. At the present time we are unable to identify what practices are indeed "best practices" for coalitions. However, we can certainly use the data at hand to predict what types of practices will be associated with positive community outcomes after further study. In the following pages we highlight what the present data can tell us about what are promising practices in each of the areas of coalition implementation. To ascertain promising practices in the areas of when, what, who, where, and how, we use statistical procedures in which the choice of predictive variables is carried out by an automatic procedure.[14] In essence, we are using statistical procedures to automate "data mining" to see which variables within a given set of variables, if any, are associated with positive community outcomes (as defined by increased revenues, assets, and high school graduation).

To mine the data for promising practices we created a different model for each set of variables (according to themes such as activities, membership, or funding). Then, instead of using identity as a literacy coalition (or not) as an independent variable (as done in chapter 3) we used only the coalition activities and characteristics reported by each community to predict community outcomes. In other words, we did not compare by coalition or not, but by what coalition activities a community did or did not undertake and used this to determine which coalition characteristics predict better outcomes. We first looked at coalition longevity and its relationship to desirable community outcomes. The results of the analysis suggest that the longer a coalition is in existence, the better off a community would be. Each year of coalition existence, in this analysis, was associated with an additional $267.44 in revenue per capita raised by the local nonprofit community and an additional $649.50 per capita in assets. Thus, two years of a coalition's existence has an estimated benefit of $534.88 and $1,299.00 in terms of assets. Similarly, when we look at high school dropouts, each year of coalition existence is associated with a .178 decline in the percent of adults age twenty-five and older who do not have a high school diploma. While this may not sound meaningful, in a county with 500,000 adults, this amounts to approximately 890 more high school graduates per year. Again, while we cannot attribute such gains to coalitions with any certainty, these findings suggest that future research may find a link between coalition longevity and the improved well-being of coalition communities.

In general, literature on the creation of coalitions, whether it be from the community empowerment approach (Fawcett et al., 1995), the community coalition action theory model (Butterfoss 2007, Kegler et al. 2010), a competencies approach (Foster-Fishman et al. 2001) or the Institutional Entrepreneurship model (Ridzi, Carmody and Byrnes 2011) tends to follow three basic steps. They roughly translate into: gathering members of the community around a cause, creating some form of institutional structure to carry out actions, and carrying out permanent changes that have community-wide, macro-level impact. To date, these models have been developed based on case studies of communities that have gone through a coalition formation process. The national survey data collected for this project, however, helps to reaffirm this understanding of a coalition life course in several ways when we look at coalition characteristics in comparison to the age of the coalition (see figure 4.5).

First, in terms of coalition membership, individual coalitions have shared that they begin with as broad a spectrum of partners as possible in their first few years of life. Over time, however, after this wider group has provided input and direction, a core group of members continues the coalition's work. We see this same pattern in the national survey such that coalitions in their first few years of life (zero to five) have an average of over eighty member organizations while these numbers level off at around sixty for coalitions mid-life course (between six and nineteen years old) and around fifty for coalitions over twenty years old. Literature has pointed out that coalitions typically emerge and continue to operate under the umbrella of a lead agency rather than as an independent nonprofit.[15] However, offering evidence that coalitions typically outgrow this structure, our data reveal that the percent of coalitions that have filed with the federal government to be an independent nonprofit (501(c)(3) status) jumps substantially from around 60 percent in their early years to over 80 percent after six years and to 100 percent once they have existed for twenty years or more. Similarly, while literature suggests that coalitions usually have some paid staff and that the degree of formalization ranges from very formal with strict adherence to bylaws and

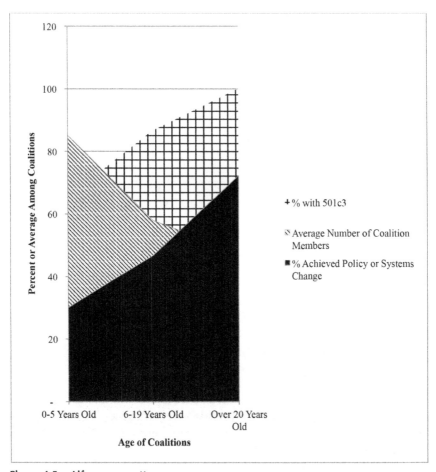

**Figure 4.5.   Life course patterns.**
*Source:* Data compiled by authors in collaboration with the Literacy Funders Network.

contractual relationships to rather informal, our research shows that this, too, tends to vary with the coalition's maturity.[16] Over time we see that staffing becomes more formalized, with about 60 percent of the youngest coalitions having paid staff and 80 percent of the oldest ones paying their staff. Similarly, across these age groups the percent with a paid executive director jumps from 60 percent among the youngest to 90 percent among the oldest.

In addition to internal structure, coalition resources and activities tend to vary over the life course. Only approximately 40 percent of the youngest and middle-aged coalitions provide direct services, while nearly 70 percent of the oldest ones do. Accompanying this is a growth of annual budgets from approximately $164,076 in the early years to $229,857 in middle age and, finally, $588,813 among the most mature coalitions. In addition, it seems

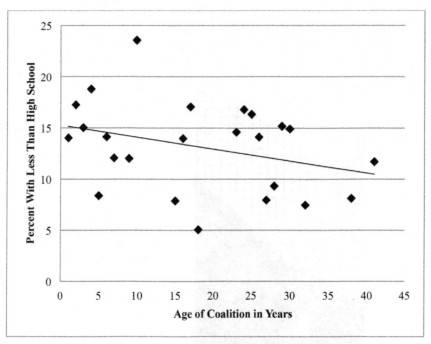

**Figure 4.6.  Percent with less than high school by age of coalition.**
*Source:* Data collected by the authors in collaboration with the Literacy Funders Network, 2012.

while about 70 percent of coalitions at all ages tend to work toward policy or systems change, the rate at which coalitions report success at reaching this goal tends to increase considerably across age groups from 42 percent to 57 percent and eventually 91 percent.

In addition, examining community level outcomes such as percent of people with less than high school education reveals that better outcomes are correlated with older coalitions (see figure 4.6).

Older coalitions also seem to be correlated with higher nonprofit per capita revenue and assets. Given these co-occurring patterns (which at this stage are just that since we do not know if there is any causal relationship), it seems that coalition longevity is an important component to consider.

## COMMUNICATION AND ADVOCACY ARE THE HALLMARK ACTIVITIES OF SUCCESSFUL COALITION COMMUNITIES

While the preceding chapters describe a wide host of activities conducted by coalitions, this analysis elevates two in particular: communication and advocacy. Communication as a coalition function was perhaps the most universally associated with positive community outcomes. Counties that had coalitions performing a communication function had an average revenue advantage and an advantage in terms of educational outcomes. These coalitions were associated with a 3.81 percent lower rate of high school dropouts. This relationship may be due to improved service delivery coordination as a result of improved communication pathways.

Though advocacy was not associated with educational outcomes, it was strongly correlated with increased resources with coalition counties that carry out an advocacy function averaging $8,333 more in nonprofit revenues per capita than counties that did not. This relationship also held true for assets with advocacy counties averaging $21,379 more per capita. For revenue, training and curriculum development was also related, with an average increase of $7,970 per capita for those communities that performed this form of coalition work. It is possible that communities that engage in this type of work are more successful in rounding up resources for the nonprofit community.

## Nonprofit Literacy Providers as Coalition Anchors

While coalitions are defined in large part by their diversity, and the literature has suggested that greater diversity leads to greater success,[17] it seems from this analysis that one core constituency is indispensable to this mix: nonprofit literacy providers. Having such literacy providers as part of the membership was positively associated with approximately $96 in revenues and $231 in assets per capita and, with respect to educational outcomes, nonprofit literacy providers as part of the coalition predicted a 0.09 percent decline in people not completing high school.

The next most important group to ensure is part of the coalition membership is schools. Counting schools among a coalition's membership predicted an $88 advantage in revenue and a $366 advantage in assets for the nonprofit community per capita. Finally, the involvement of colleges in the coalition seemed to help raise revenue by approximately $122 per capita.

While this analysis highlights the value of having certain coalition members, it by no means should diminish the importance of the other members. As the literature has suggested, "diversity is essential to coalitions. Members should include a broad range of stakeholders who are invested in or affected by the coalition's issues."[18] Each community, the previous chapters tell us, tends to build its coalition from the willing partners it has that are ready to come to the table. What this analysis suggests is that when nonprofit literacy providers, schools, for-profit businesses, libraries, and colleges come to the table, the community has a greater likelihood of success.

## Coalitions Can Be Effective on the City, County, and State Level

Just as coalition membership and activities vary, so does the geographic scale at which coalitions form. Though the county level is the most frequently occurring, it is slightly less than the majority. Cities are by far the least frequently occurring. However, what this analysis reveals is that city-level coalitions are just as associated with positive outcomes, if not more so. City-level coalitions have an estimated advantage of $10,481 in revenues and $23,621 in assets per capita.

County-level coalitions are associated with 3.321 percent lower high school dropout rates among their population age twenty-five and older. State-level coalitions, on the other hand, are associated with $3,372 higher revenues, and $14,844 higher assets per capita than counties without state coalitions.

State coalitions seek to provide a value-added component to their local partners. Their ability to reach out and make connections to statewide networks for funding, training, and nonprofit management enables them to make links that local coalitions may not easily make for themselves. By virtue of their location in state capitals, these coalitions keep abreast of legislative initiatives and advocate for changes that busy local coalitions may not have time to monitor or impact.

State coalitions have similar problems to local coalitions in terms of seeking funding for their backbone functions. Most are funded primarily through private donations. However, more recently, newer state coalitions have aligned with existing networks that are already part of a funded system. Examples include Educate Texas, funded through the Communities Foundation of Texas and the Iowa Council on Foundations has taken on the state coalition role. The history of state coalitions adds another dimension to the story.

In state or national discussions, community coalitions were small voices, even though they boasted large local memberships. As the first literacy coalitions grew, they desired a voice at the state level with the goal to change legislation, increase funding, and raise awareness. In this instance the whole is bigger than the sum of the parts; the concept of state coalitions took shape and increased representation not just from a larger geographic network but, in the same way franchises reduce costs for their members, so it is with state networks. Just as individual providers were isolated and needed a local coalition to support their work and increase their voice at the local level, state coalitions felt a need to link with national networks and coalitions, including Literacy USA. Many of the state coalitions developed from nonprofits, state libraries, state adult education agencies, and from state-level national affiliate organizations.

Rather than suggest that one geographic model is best, this analysis suggests that each approach is associated with certain improved levels of higher community well-being when compared with communities that lack coalitions. Further research is certainly needed to explicate the reason for the variations in outcomes observed here.

## Paid Staff Members Are Key

When seeking to establish a working structure for coalitions, there are many aspects to consider, including whether to pursue a 501(c)(3) and whether to become a part of local government. This analysis suggests that there is one decision, however, that should not be overlooked. Having paid staff was positively associated with all outcomes. On average, paid staff was associated with $6,797 in revenues per capita, $13,060 in assets per capita, and a 4.071 percent lower rate of high school dropouts. As seen in one Iowa coalition, the evolution toward more staff can be more circuitous than linear and can include both expansions and contractions.

> [Our] organization operated exclusively with volunteers until 2007 when a state Empowerment grant was used to hire a part-time executive director. That funding was cut in half in 2008, so the board changed to contract with a part-time parent educator to develop a program to teach parents effective ways to enjoy books with their young children. This position has been maintained with a combination of donated funds and grants. By 2014 [we] arranged enough funding to hire a part-time executive director again. In 2015 the board made the position full time in order to support our growing programs and expansion countywide. (Iowa)

Having an advisory committee was also positively associated with a $5,084 advantage in revenues, and a $9,381 advantage in assets per capita.

## Backbone Structures Are Interchangeable

There has been much focus in recent literature on what collective impact scholars have called a backbone structure[19] or what coalition literature has referred to as an engine organization.[20] The backbone structure is the central nucleus or bedrock of a coalition. It may be the initial convener of the coalition or the entity that houses the coalition's staff, or the organization that provided the majority of the funding for the coalition. In this analysis, we attempted to identify the ideal type of backbone structures that exist among our data. Our analysis found that these structures are all more or less associated with successful outcomes.

This is perhaps seen most strongly in the stand-alone model in which a coalition has its own 501(c)(3) and has emerged as a nonprofit in its own right. This model was associated with positive outcomes across the board. A network model in which there is more diffuse general ownership across multiple organizations was also strongly associated with all outcomes except high school graduations. A foundation-centric model in which foundation staff comprise much of centralized coalition organization was, like the network model, associated with positive outcomes in all areas other than high school graduation. There is growing interest in the concept of backbone organizations since they fulfill a key center around which coalition members can gather. This analysis suggests that perhaps, at least in mature coalitions, pursuing 501(c)(3) status is the most efficacious means to community success and impact. The lesson perhaps is that while there can be a number of different backbone structures for a successful coalition, a paid staff member, strong multi-faceted funding streams, and diverse representation from multiple community partners are essential for longevity.

## WHAT TO LOOK FOR WHEN
## EXAMINING SUCCESSFUL COMMUNITIES

While future research is needed, the field is certainly far from starting from scratch. We know from the preceding pages that coalitions undertake a host of key activities that we suspect are connected to greater community outcomes. However, the qualitative research done in the course of researching this book has also yielded other nuanced lessons from the field. Below we probe what seems both to be true about the evolving field of collective impact community coalitions as well as lessons about leadership patterns.

As evident in the preceding chapters, coalitions tend to begin with a catalytic event. Whether the realization of a major community problem, a needs assessment, or some other provocation, this event is the birth of what may later become known as a community literacy coalition. But what do we know about the actual people who have been the day-to-day engines behind coalition launch and evolution? Below we examine some themes in coalition leadership on a range of scales, including both local and national levels.

## THE ROLE OF LEADERSHIP IN COALITIONS

Throughout the development and evolution of coalitions, many and varied leaders and champions have emerged. Some were board chairs, some executive directors, and others were community champions, volunteers, and celebrities. Some are young, some old, some unlikely candidates, some with great experience, some with none, some coming with an already developed reputation, and some others completely unknown. Successful coalition leaders shared common traits, including passion, confidence, curiosity, integrity, strong values, vision, positive attitude, and a sense of humor.

Before there was a staff at most coalitions there was a tireless individual leading a team of volunteers committed to jump-starting the coalition. New leaders emerge over time as organizations mature, as priorities are redefined, and as political and community issues align with the vision of the coalition.

To write about leadership related to coalition development is a challenge because there is so much to include. Below we reflect on key leadership roles that have emerged in the coalition movement.

## CHAMPIONS

Most leaders are there for the long haul, but champions can inspire in a single instance, as these examples illustrate. In a packed auditorium at a Dallas Reads event, Darth Vader's menacing voice had a message: The ability to destroy a planet is insignificant compared with the power of literacy. James Earl Jones, the voice of Darth Vader, is a national spokesperson for literacy who has raised his powerful voice to support both coalitions and national literacy organizations. *Wheel of Fortune* co-host Vanna White served as Verizon's Literacy Champion for California.[21] Verizon also partnered with the NFL to feature star athletes, including New York Giants star Tiki Barber. This was all part of Verizon's Literacy Champion program, a campaign to raise awareness in coordination with Verizon Reads literacy coalitions. The purpose was to reach out to athletes and celebrities "to give literacy a familiar face, bring attention to a critical issue, and raise awareness and funds for the cause of literacy." "I was inspired by reading to my two young children," White shared.[22] "By partnering with Verizon, I am able to help spread the message that literacy is important to both individual success and the success of our communities."[23] In another instance, TV personality Steve Allen championed the work of community coalitions as he addressed the issue of poor school performance across the country and the need for coordinated community response.

Sean Astin, who rose to fame as Samwise in *Lord of the Rings,* spoke of coalitions and collaboration and shared his perspective on the power of literacy.

I play many roles—parent, actor, literacy advocate—but my most important role is reading to my child," Astin said. "This is why I am the National Center for

Family Literacy's Verizon Literacy Champion. My role in this endeavor is to encourage parents to create good reading habits in their home; to model how to enjoy good books, to read with their children, and to make reading a fun activity. [24]

Another champion was Erik Weihenmayer, the "only blind athlete to summit
the seven highest peaks on each of the world's continents."[25] His mission is
"to improve literacy for blind and low-vision schoolchildren."[26] Weihenmayer
shared his story with blind and low-vision schoolchildren before his speeches to
coalitions across the country. "I'm very excited to meet the kids," he said "As
a former teacher, I have a special passion for the issue of literacy, particularly
for young students who are blind or have low vision." Weihenmayer is the
volunteer spokesperson for the National Campaign. "Through literacy, I have
reached the summit of my dreams, and Verizon's campaign is helping to ensure
that every blind and low-vision child will have that same opportunity."[27]

Some champions do much more than the important task of raising awareness and funds. Singer and actress Dolly Parton developed an impressive
reading program, Imagination Library, adopted by hundreds of coalitions and
literacy organizations across the country. "When I was growing up in the hills
of East Tennessee, I knew my dreams would come true," she said. "I know
there are children in your community with their own dreams. They dream of
becoming a doctor or an inventor or a minister. Who knows? Maybe there is a
little girl whose dream is to be a writer and singer. The seeds of these dreams
are often found in books and the seeds you help plant in your community can
grow across the world."[28]

## BOARD CHAIRS

Board chairs usually have a short term, but some have a powerful impact on
the coalition they serve. Their role in building the backbone is key to success. Without a strong board chair, coalitions have floundered. Even more
so than most nonprofits, coalition board chairs must foster inclusiveness
because of the very nature of the culture of coalitions. Generating trust,
inclusiveness, and a forum for open dialogue is essential. Ensuring that
board members are valued and appreciated helps them to fulfill their roles
of oversight, policy, and resource development. The board is a partner with
the management team, which looks very different in small coalitions with
only one or two staff members than it does in coalitions with many staff
members. The smaller the coalition, the more it needs a working board to
support the executive director. The larger the coalition, the larger role the
board plays in policy making and oversight.

The chair of the one Literacy Coalition remembered the early challenges of the role.

> I would say that as a novice in the literacy arena in [the 2000s], I was pleasantly surprised that so many participants came to the task force meetings and eagerly contributed thoughts and writings about the status of literacy in the community. I really began as an absolute novice and needed the expertise and energy of those in the community who could help put a collaborative together. This community gathered together a host of resources for the effort in spite of the naysayers who thought some leaders might not get behind building a coalition and might consider it a particularly political criticism of the community. (Oklahoma)

The leader who jump-starts a coalition is often the most impactful individual the coalition ever encounters.

## EXECUTIVE DIRECTORS

Healthy, strong coalitions have engaged both supportive board chairs and strong executive directors. Looking at successful coalitions over time it is interesting to note that the greatest success often comes when the relationship between the board and the executive director is the most vibrant and collaborative. A coalition director must be a people person who can work at every level of the organization with staff, volunteers, community partners, funders, and board members. Executive directors are in it for the long haul and work with any number of board chairs over time. Many directors recall the early days of the coalition, when they were the only staff member. They were the receptionist, office clerk, cleaner, book hauler, and performed many other jobs to get the coalition under way. The directors of some of the biggest coalitions have more than twenty staff members and dozens of volunteers in complex departments managing the many coalition functions.

The executive director in one coalition reflected:

> Maybe I didn't quite appreciate what was happening back then, but I found myself in the middle of something new and exciting, that, after months of meetings, the people who I had been working with over the past year had expressed their commitment to formalizing their relationships . . . This meant that we had come to know each other and to trust each other in a way that would result in a common vision, and that we would coordinate literacy services in [this] County to maximize resources and to invest in each other's well-being and professional growth, with the ultimate goal of enhancing access to quality literacy services for all. (California)

This experience underscores the importance of trust relationships as key to success. The trust between the executive director and the board chair, the trust between the providers and partners and the executive director, and the trust of the community to support the coalition with such a critical task are critical.

Selecting the right executive director has been fraught with problems in several coalitions. The board chair of the one coalition notes:

> Our first executive director was a real challenge. We really did not know enough about being employers. We would advise new coalitions to seek good advice from other nonprofit organizations about how to be a good employer and what to look for in a director.

This raises a very good point: It is not just about selecting the right candidate, but also appropriately training and supporting that candidate.

As the early coalitions matured and charismatic founding executive directors retired, most coalitions that had implemented a process of succession planning had no trouble replacing their directors. However, where no planning was in place, the transition faced problems. Not only succession planning, but systems have to be in place and organizational history and policies clear so that the director doesn't retire and leave with essential information that only he/she knows.

In one coalition where a very strong, passionate staff worked tirelessly to support their network of provider organizations, the executive director retired and the board hired a new director. It was clear from the start that things were not right. Finally, the board learned that the director dropped by the office to make sure the staff was busy working before he headed off to the golf course every day. He did a great job presenting the work of the staff at board meetings and it took six months before the board realized what was happening. In that six months, the organization went from a smooth running, high-powered, successful coalition to one where the demoralized staff began to quit. The whole organization eventually closed. This is an extreme case, of course, but the lesson is that the board has a serious responsibility in ensuring the effective oversight of the coalition, especially in times of transition.

## COMMUNITY LEADERS

Community leaders may include any number of key partners—the head of the local workforce development board, the United Way director or the Junior League chair, the library director, or the school superintendent. These community leaders see the value added of the coalition and serve as spokespersons, gate openers, dialogue facilitators, and issue elevators.

Political leaders from mayors to county executives have been instrumental in providing the impetus for success. In Houston, every mayor from Kathy Whitmire in 1987 to Sylvester Turner in 2017 embraced the work of the Mayor's Coalition for Literacy. Mayor George Hartwell in Grand Rapids, Mayor James Hahn in Los Angeles, and Mayor James Kenney have all supported their cities' literacy coalitions. Where mayors stepped up to the plate, coalitions enjoyed the prestige of the powerful support of city hall and, in many cases, the funding to go along with that support. The lesson here is that where mayoral support transcends specific administrations, literacy is seen to be a city or countywide priority over time.

One example of local county council leadership in coalition development began with the creation of a Coalition for Adult English Literacy. A council member was concerned at the lack of English literacy skills among his constituents. In 2002, he created a task force of community leaders to explore the issue and especially noted the concern of business leaders who relied on a workforce that could communicate in English. A study was commissioned by the County Council and they contracted with a local college. The study identified a powerful array of individual ESL providers offering services in the county, including government, community, and faith-based providers. However, it showed that they were working in isolation and in funding silos; there was a serious lack of coordination of services across the county. In fact, the study revealed over 2,000 people on the program waiting list. By 2008 the coalition was fiscally independent and under the leadership of the full-time executive director and the county council designated a continuing role for the coalition to review and award all council funding for adult English literacy programs. The symbiotic relationship between the council and the coalition happened not just because a serious literacy service gap was identified, but because a working relationship based on trust and respect grew over time. This backbone role of leadership has proven time and again to be a mainstay of long-term success.

## NATIONAL LEADERSHIP

A description of coalition leadership cannot be complete without a salute to First Lady Barbara Bush. Very few people are both national champions and local literacy leaders, as she is. With a national platform of literacy, Bush championed many literacy coalitions across the country, but especially her hometown coalition, the Houston READ Commission, later renamed the Houston Center for Literacy. She used her bully pulpit to raise awareness of the issues, helped include literacy in the president's agenda, and talked from the heart to bring communities together to support the local literacy coalition wherever she spoke. Whenever Bush attended a coalition event, she insisted on meeting the students and their families. Amid sharing books with children under Houston's reading tree and saluting adult learners as her heroes as they sang "Wind Beneath My Wings" to her, Bush challenged and took on tough tasks including working with the president to support literacy legislation and taking on public opinion. The Barbara Bush Foundation for Family Literacy continues to raise substantial levels of funding focused on annual literacy celebrations in several states and supports new research and initiatives like the XPrize for Literacy.

U.S. Senator Edward Kennedy championed coalitions and expanded the understanding of the role of intermediary organizations in a number of national dialogues. As the federal Workforce Investment Act came up for reauthorization in 2009, his staff met with coalition leaders and helped introduce language that included coalitions in funding opportunities. Kennedy promoted the message of collective impact and the need for local stakeholders to work together for improved literacy, coordination of effort, and integrated vocational training. When the senator's chief of staff, Jane Oates, became undersecretary at the U.S. Department of Labor, the growing understanding that literacy and workforce development were inextricably linked together provided yet another platform to include coalitions in career pathway dialogue and funding opportunities.

A discussion about local leadership must acknowledge two national organizations that have played a major role with their local affiliates since the beginning of coalition development in the 1980s: the United Way and the Junior League.

In Oklahoma City, San Antonio, Birmingham, and many other cities, dedicated Junior League volunteers have driven coalition development. Oklahoma City is a good example. Beginning in 2004, the Junior League adopted a ten-year literacy focus and in 2006, helped establish the Literacy Coalition for Oklahoma City. At the end of 2008, all new Junior League community projects included a literacy component.[29]

United Ways have supported and funded dozens of literacy coalitions, and in recent years, with the growth of the CGLR coalitions, they have been even more engaged in the work. In Syracuse and Cleveland, the coalitions were housed in United Way facilities for many years. In Sacramento, Atlanta, and New York City, United Way launched CGLR coalitions.

At the national level, the United Way was instrumental in the formation of the National Alliance of Urban Literacy Coalitions (NAULC), which became Literacy USA. A partner in California notes, "at Literacy USA I learned that I was not alone, that there were other coalitions like mine, living my experiences, and this was a very reassuring thing, to have people who did what I did, who felt what I felt, and who spoke the language that I could only speak to them." Literacy USA provided the first opportunity for coalitions to collaborate, advocate, and commiserate and included nonprofits as well as businesses. Business leaders on the corporate advisory board included Time Warner, IBM, Verizon, Half Price Books, BCI, Nevada Power, Toys R Us, Philip Morris, and Pitney Bowes. There has been a trend that local coalitions have looked to state coalitions for support and, in turn, both local and state coalitions have looked to national coalitions. This kind of collaborative leadership has strengthened the entire field.

## PARTNERS AND SERVICE PROVIDERS

One key component of leadership is the voice of the partners and service providers that make up the coalition. These include the organizations and individuals who represent the learners at the heart of the work, the families and the neighborhoods that are most impacted. When coalitions get off track and begin to "do to" not "do with" the communities they serve, it is often the local representatives who ask the powerful questions, listen carefully, question trust, and challenge assumptions. Provider leadership keeps the coalition on track, ensuring that partner voices are heard, that resources are maximized, and goals are being accomplished.

Different leaders and leadership skills are needed at different stages in coalition development. The successful coalitions are those that not only do the job of convening partners and providers but impact and influence the systems around them. Leadership is about commitment and investment in the work. The 2015 *Stanford Social Innovation Review* article "The Dawn of System Leadership" defined the roles of shared and collaborative leadership.

> As system leaders emerge, situations previously suffering from polarization and inertia become more open, and what were previously seen as intractable problems become perceived as opportunities for innovation. Short-term reactive problem solving becomes more balanced with long-term value creation. And organizational self-interest becomes re-contextualized, as people discover that their and their organization's success depends on creating well-being within the larger systems of which they are a part.[30]

As coalition boards and advisory councils have grown, local leadership has helped shift the focus of the work from problem solving to changing the future together. The article goes on:

Ineffective leaders try to make change happen. System leaders focus on creating the conditions that can produce change and that can eventually cause change to be self-sustaining. As we continue to unpack the prerequisites to success in complex collaborative efforts, we appreciate more and more this subtle shift in strategic focus and the distinctive powers of those who learn how to create the space for change.[31]

Because the very nature of coalitions requires constant change, growth, and reinvention, leadership must be poised for change, too. Coalitions require ongoing improvement, assessment and tracking of progress; evaluation of where the coalition has come from and where it is going; measurement of impact and achievement. All these elements support the goal of improving literacy and creating healthy successful communities.

Leadership, especially in a coalition setting, requires understanding that the coalition is both for and of its members. Often it is a delicate balance that is much more complex than in a simple nonprofit. There is potential for misunderstanding, conflict, and controversy. The most effective coalition leaders recognize problems early and anticipate the need for speedy resolution of issues. Coalition leaders must be skilled listeners, negotiators, and communicators and have a calm, respectful, and reasoned approach to flexible solution building.

In addition to other key members of coalitions, the role of funders cannot be overlooked. In the first part or this chapter we focused on potential emerging best practices for coalitions to help their communities. Now we turn our lens to potential emerging best practices for funders and purveyors to encourage and cultivate coalitions themselves. We begin by looking to see if any patterns exist in terms of community well-being with respect to funder involvement. We then turn to the purveyor role played by funders of various sorts and examine whether some appear to be emerging as potential sites of best practices.

## TOWARD BEST PRACTICES FOR FUNDERS

In the previous section we focused on potential emerging best practices among literacy coalitions. Here we turn our attention to exploring where best practices may also be emerging among funders. To do so, we first look to see whether there is any evidence that might lead us to believe that whether a funder funds coalitions makes a difference for the community. Finding that communities in which funders support coalitions are better off, we then look to examine what specific types of funder activities might be making a difference.

If we return to the initial reason that funders offer for engaging in catalytic philanthropy in the area of literacy, we see a fairly consistent emphasis on completion of high school credentials. When we examine these indicators of community well-being on the national level by pairing our survey respondents with U.S. Census data, we find some interesting patterns that suggest further research is warranted.

First, counties that have literacy funders outperform the national average when it comes to the percent of adult population with less than a high school degree. Counties with funders that use a coalition strategy, however, outperform both groups (i.e., whereas the national average is 18 percent, counties with literacy funders have 1 percent lower dropout rates among their adult populations, and those with literacy funders that use coalitions have a 3 percent lower rate).

While these patterns by no means prove that catalytic philanthropy is more effective than other philanthropic tools, or than doing nothing, they do move the conversation forward. Such patterns warrant further scrutiny and suggest that a variety of intervening factors might be at play. The following chart helps us to begin to explore these factors by contrasting how funders that fund coalitions differ from those who don't when it comes to specific funding requests (see figure 4.7).

First and foremost, there is a noticeable difference in that literacy funders who fund literacy coalitions are 37 percent more likely to fund community convening such as to collaboratively apply for grants or address areas of community need. This logically makes sense since this is a key strategy for literacy coalition and collective impact work. Another notable difference is that the same funders are 26 percent more likely to fund advocacy and 23 percent more likely to fund community planning and strategic planning. These too are core collective impact approaches. Also of note are that funders who fund coalitions are more likely to fund program development, software and technology support and the developing of collaborative project teams, which all have been used as strategies for coalitions as well. In addition, they are more likely to fund staff development, which is a mainstay of many coalitions as they seek to improve the quality of the field by building professionalism.

There are also some other interesting patterns that may not otherwise have come to mind. For instance, literacy funders that fund coalitions are 39 percent more likely to also fund libraries. In many coalitions across the country libraries are key partners and hubs of programming. Interestingly, funders that fund literacy coalitions tend to be more likely to also support nonprofits that focus on literacy. While all funders in the survey are identified as funding in the area of literacy, only 70 percent of those that don't fund coalitions provide support to nonprofits whose primary focus is in the area of literacy. In contrast, 90 percent of funders who funded coalitions also support nonprofits that primarily focus on literacy.

In sum, funders who fund coalitions are much more likely to fund convening, program development and program development when they also fund

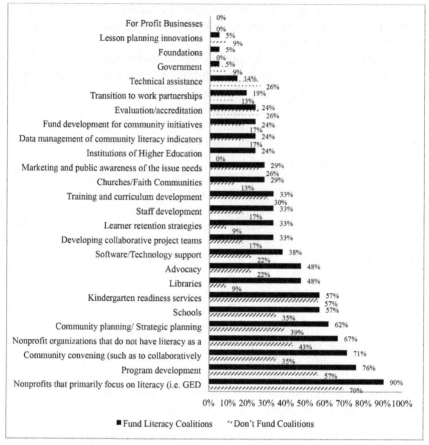

**Figure 4.7.   How literacy funders who fund coalitions fund differently than those that don't.**

*Source:* Data collected by the authors in collaboration with the Literacy Funders Network, 2012.

coalitions but there are also some other patterns worth exploring in future research. For instance, as has been a theme in the previous chapters, funders often get involved by assuming the role of purveyors who work to have initiatives scaled up. We turn to exploring this next.

## TOWARD BEST PRACTICES FOR PURVEYORS AND NATIONAL INITIATIVES

So far in this chapter we have focused on best practices for literacy coalitions in their communities, and how funders can most effectively lend their support. Here we turn our attention to examining potential emerging best practices among national purveyors of collective impact. We have referred to these throughout the preceding pages when we talked about how local coalitions draw support and direction from national efforts such as the Campaign for Grade-Level Reading and the Strive Network. We have also looked at a community's ability to join such national initiatives as a potential indicator of that community's social capital. In this section, we turn our attention to exploring where best practices among purveyors may be uncovered with future research. In order to do this, we first look at initiatives across the nation to examine whether any are having a level of success which would make us want to look further in order to learn from their experiences. Finding that many of these national initiatives are associated with communities that are, on average, outperforming the nation in terms of improvements in recent graduations, we then turn to a closer look at these networks of communities. Our goal is to characterize the major trends in the ways that they have served as purveyors for communities across the nation. In doing so, we hope to direct future research toward the types of activities that may be associated with effective practices for cultivating the growth of impactful collective impact efforts in multiple locations.

## PURVEYORS AND THE SCALING
## UP OF INITIATIVES NATIONALLY

As noted in a primer for program replication by Geri Summerville and Becca Raley of Public Private Ventures (a group that seeks to identify innovative programs, evaluate them, and reproduce them in new locations): "despite general agreement among policy makers and philanthropists about the value of replication, successful efforts to bring social programs to scale have been limited, and rarely is replication advanced through systematic public policy initiatives."[32] A research paper jointly produced by The Conservation Company and Public/Private Ventures found that replication heretofore tends to be driven less by domestic policy or governmental infrastructure. Rather, it involves local social entrepreneurs who are typically the creators of the program themselves and who "champion" it by seeking out financial backers and marketing approaches.[33] Furthermore it revealed reality to be contrary to what Schorr has identified as the simplistic view of "many social reformers and most public and philanthropic funders today" who "see the problem of identifying "what works" as a technical matter of sorting the *proven* from the *unproven*, the *evidence-based* from the rest" and then scaling those up.[34] Instead, the study found that "more often than not, the programs replicated did not have in hand research evidence that proved their effectiveness."[35] Furthermore, it was not even a case of lack of any evaluation research, since sometimes programs with evidence of impact were not replicated. The key factors in facilitating program replication were matches with local need or problem, widespread recognition of the program through aggressive marketing or media attention, and the champion's ability to fundraise and deploy marketing savvy.[36] The developing field of collective impact community coalitions is no different.

When it comes to promising practices, scaling up the collective impact approach is similar to much of the nonprofit field. As with other efforts, coalition approaches do not necessarily need to have been proven in a scientifically rigorous randomized control group experiment type of way. We have devoted considerable attention previously to why this is not feasible. Rather, coalition approaches that have proven themselves in other, more qualitative ways, have been scaled up across the nation. In this sense an evidence base can include such things as building civic muscle, social capital, and a spirit of collaboration.[37] In addition, perhaps much of what we have explored as the virtuous cycle of coalitions has already been evident within the field, though in an anecdotal sense rather than in a quantitative national analysis as we presented in the last chapter. Furthermore, as the literature suggests, we should not discount the importance of the collective impact coalition approach resonating with local community needs and problems that appear too large for a single agency or program or even government to deal with on their own.

While the coalition approach is, at its heart, a local phenomenon, when we look at the broader development of the field we cannot help but notice striking similarities across communities. This isomorphism, or striking parallels, highlights that this countrywide revolution of civic engagement is mediated by national actors that serve a key role as institutional entrepreneurs. Such a role appears in the business and social science literature as a key factor in the transformation of social institutions.[38] In this sense and in institutional theory, we see institutions not as a single organization, but as a field of related organizations. Thus education, marriage, the government sector and other broad areas of related activity can be considered institutions. They have standard practices governed by norms and expectations. While every marriage or every city hall or business office is unique, we see striking patterns of similarity. There are expectations about what a marriage does and doesn't include, for instance, and these expectations have certainly changed over time. In the same way, the collective impact coalition approach can be seen as one of challenging institutions, and in the case of literacy coalitions, we can see a challenge to the institution of education, which includes not just schools but also family literacy practices, after school, summer school, adult education, and job training. We also see the notion that coalitions are part of a social movement, though admittedly more grasstips than grassroots as we explored in the introductory chapter. We see recognition of this sense of revolutionary change in efforts such as the UN-sponsored Right to Literacy campaign, which has attempted to challenge existing institutions by recasting literacy as a basic human right like voting. We also see this sense of monumental change in the words of one veteran literacy purveyor urging communities to act:

> Literacy is a problem but we have not been able to institutionalize change. The women's rights and war on poverty and equal rights movements have been able to institutionalize change, but we have not been able to.

Once viewed through this lens, the collective impact coalition approach can be seen as one of many forms of social movements that have sought to bring about wide sweeping change to national and even international conventions that have, thus far, been unable to prevent the many travesties of youth and adult illiteracy. It's important to note that many hundreds of thousands of lives have been changed by the efforts of literacy coalitions and their partner organizations. The problem is not only that there are more in need than can be served but also that new individuals with limited skills continue to drop out or graduate from high school without the requisite levels of education, so the pool in need is constantly being replenished.

In order to achieve this vision of institutional change, the collective impact coalition movement has sought to rise to scale and bring about change in not just one community, but in many. In the following pages we explore some of the key purveyors of coalitions that we have discussed over the last few chapters and take a look at the patterns that have been emerging among them as they seek to scale up the collective impact approach. Viewing them as institutional entrepreneurs we acknowledge that they play creative and entrepreneurial roles in working to transform the current institution of education. Examining their work reveals that patterns are emerging when it comes to who they are, whether they use funding, the scale of the communities they focus on, and the nature of the initiative.

## WHERE MIGHT WE LOOK FOR EMERGING BEST PRACTICES AMONG PURVEYORS?

One thing that has become clear in this research is that coalitions, like any organization or institution, go through phases. At some periods of time the organization is well resourced and "firing on all cylinders." At other points in time, such as after the loss of a major funder, a coalition may be scrambling just to stay intact. In this section, we seek to take a brief snapshot of communities that are on the move and in the process of "moving the needle" in recent years. The hope is that this will spur further research into what components are at play in their communities that are contributing to such success. To do this one could simply look at graduation rate changes nationally and go to those communities to see what they are doing. This, however, would be quite time consuming and lacks a clear hypothesis.

Since the focus of this chapter is on sketching out a pathway toward best practices, we hypothesize that communities with collective impact coalitions such as described in previous chapters will be more likely to have experienced recent improvements. The hope is that by examining whether this is true, and where this is true, future research on community impact can be expedited. It will help us to focus in greater detail on communities with coalitions that are finding success to discern if such success has anything to do with their initiative and if so, what specific actions. To be clear, this is not an effort to determine which of the national initiatives examined are effective. Rather this is an effort to discern which initiatives are ready to be harvested at this moment in time to examine what we can learn from them about best practices.

To carry out this analysis we paired each county in the nation with the initiatives being implemented within it (see table 2.1). We then matched this with the changes in high school graduation rates calculated from the Robert Wood Johnson Foundation (RWJF) dataset that includes county-level graduation rates between 2010 and 2014. Below we present the overall averages by program. The results supported our research hypothesis that counties with education related collective impact initiatives did on average have greater improvement in graduation rates than did counties without such initiatives. This does not mean that communities with collective impact initiatives were outperforming those without such initiatives, since the RWJ foundation cautions against comparing communities against others given that many calculate graduation rates differently. In fact, a further examination reveals that it is likely that these initiatives were often implemented in communities that had lower graduation rates precisely because of these lower graduation rates. Furthermore, even after experiencing faster than average growth it is likely that many of these communities identified for initiatives are still not performing as high as the national average for graduation rates. Indeed caution is advised against reading too much into faster growth rates since those who start out with lower rates have plenty of space for growth as compared with those who start out higher. Nevertheless, the findings do reveal that not all communities have grown at the same pace.

In the first chart below (see figure 4.8), we see that the majority of initiatives (65 percent, or fifteen out of twenty-three) had an average graduation

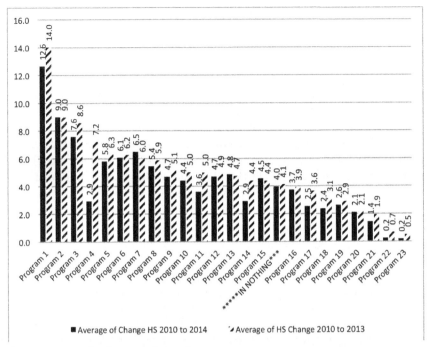

**Figure 4.8.   Graduation rate change by program.**

*Source:* Data collected by the authors in collaboration with the Literacy Funders Network and the National Results and Equity Collaborative, 2015.

rate increase that was higher than the average graduation change for counties with none of the initiatives included in this study. The average change for communities with no programming was an increase of 4.1 percent in graduation rates between 2010 and 2013 and an increase of 4 percent in graduation rates between 2010 and 2014.

In order to avoid misinterpretation of the results, we do not identify each of the twenty-three programs. Some may be only newly forming, in a phase of expansion to new communities, or focusing on much earlier in the education pipeline (i.e., kindergarten readiness). As a result, there may be a long gestation period before those communities could be expected to see growth in average high school graduation rates. Others may have recently seen growth in graduation rates and have leveled off. Blinding the programs avoids creating the misperception that such initiatives are ineffective.

If this chart were re-sorted based on 2010–2014 data, we would see that only twelve of twenty-three (52 percent) of initiatives had an average graduation rate increase that was higher than the average graduation change for counties with none of the initiatives included in this study. This could be due to weaknesses in the data. While 2014 is more recent, data were not available for many communities for that year. Again, caution should be used not to misinterpret these findings as an evaluation of any of these programs for a wide variety of reasons. In addition to what has been mentioned, they are furthermore implemented at different geographical units (such as school district, city, county, or state), offer different components (some offer funding and some do not, for instance), and are scaled up to different degrees (for instance, ELEV8 is in seven locations and the CGLR is in 168).

Nevertheless, we believe that this form of analysis is helpful because, if we wish to search for developing best practices, we believe they are most likely to be found, and most likely clearly illustrated, within communities that have been able to "turn the curve" or "move the needle" with respect to improving graduation rates. This analysis helps us to identify where collective impact approaches are most likely mature enough to have evidence-based best practices in place that can be linked with measurable community improvement. If we zoom in to view what is happening over time within some of the key initiatives that we have identified as making measurable progress, we see that, on average, we are able to identify that the curves are turning for the better.

## EXAMINING NATIONAL COLLECTIVE IMPACT APPROACHES TO IDENTIFY PROMISING PRACTICES

In figure 4.9 we identify several national initiatives from our data to illustrate that, for each of these we can observe that they are "turning the curve" in a positive way. Looking at their beginning starting points in 2010, every one of these national initiatives included communities that, on average, had high school graduation rates that were well below the national average. However, for each of these national initiatives we can see that, over this brief amount of time, they have made considerable positive progress toward bridging the gap between their graduation rates and the national average. Based on this overall trend of improvement, in the following pages we look to distill themes that are emerging across both these initiatives and other national initiatives whose memberships, on average, are also improving high school graduation levels at a rate that is faster than the national average.

## KEY THEMES FOR PURVEYORS

In order to begin learning from national initiatives that are correlated with positive community growth in high school graduations we examined each

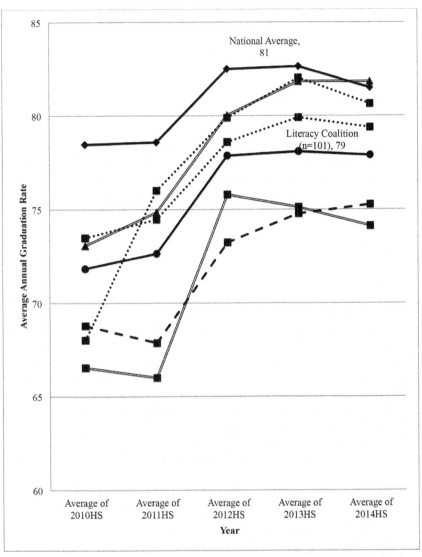

**Figure 4.9. Curves of initiatives with highest average growth in graduation rates from 2010–2014.**

*Source:* Data collected by the authors in collaboration with the Literacy Funders Network and the National Results and Equity Collaborative, 2015.

initiative's activities and approach. Below we offer general reflections based on this analysis that are meant to offer a starting place for future research into emergent best practices. These include the roles of purveyors in catalyzing action, offering specialized support, fostering rigor, and elevating the cause.

## Catalyze Action

The first major theme is that many of these national initiatives were success-ful in catalyzing or sparking action among communities that previously did not have a collective impact effort in place. While certainly some of these initiatives also absorbed existing collective impact efforts into their approach, for the majority of communities involved in a purveyor network, they are part of only one of these networks.

In this sense then, these national initiatives deserve credit for catalyzing collective impact effort where it previously did not exist. How do they do so? Some have offered grant funding such as planning and implementation grants. While such grants are certainly competitive, some initiatives have been able to spark collective impact without offering funding by simply creat-ing a national competition.

When looking at all of these national initiatives on the whole, we see that the majority, 61 percent offer some form of funding but the remaining 39 percent do not. Interestingly, funding is more likely among the 28 percent of these initiatives that are sponsored by the federal government. For these gov-ernment funded initiatives 80 percent carry funding with them. Among the 72 percent of national initiatives launch by nonprofit organizations, including funders, only approximately 54 percent carry funding with them. Interest-ingly, we see that government led efforts are more likely to be associated with a network's communities seeing an average improvement that is better than the national average. This is not to say that those run by nonprofit purveyors do not see success, since many of them also observe improving graduation rates beyond the national average among their networks.

For these purveyors, fostering a healthy sense of competition in which communities that do a good job receive recognition or have access to specific technical and other supports are important levers that have been deployed. Some examples that future research might do well to look into include the federal Promise and Choice programs that offer funding for planning and implementation and the Campaign for Grade-Level Reading, which has or-chestrated a national competition that does not offer funding but rather offers recognition to communities that see the most progress.

Federal programs clearly within the realm of collective impact include the twin programs of Promise Neighborhoods (funded by the U.S. Department of Education) and Choice Neighborhoods (funded by the U.S. Department of Housing and Urban Development). Promise Neighborhoods[39] was in part inspired by the work of the Harlem Children's Zone and an effort to scale up such community collaborations across the nation. Although sponsored by the federal government, there are three ways to participate: as an unfunded partner (PROM-U), as the recipient of a planning grant (PROM-P), or by receiving an implementation grant (PROM-I). As with other collective impact approaches, the goal is not just to help communities develop cradle-to-career pipelines but to do so by "integrating programs and breaking down agency "silos" so that solutions are implemented effectively and efficiently across agencies."[40] This same goal is embedded in HUD's Choice Neighborhoods program to such an extent that DOE and HUD representatives often appeared at conferences and workshops together to encourage collaboration across their programs.

As with Promise, Choice[41] offered both planning grants (CHOICE-P, Choice Neighborhood Planning) and implementation grants (CHOICE I, Choice Neighborhood Implementation). Similarly focused on the broader community, Choice required the creation of transformation plans that focused on the renovation and replacement of public and assisted housing in struggling neighborhoods. Similar to other initiatives such as the CGLR and Promise this plan was to be the organization's marching orders once it secured funding. While officially a housing program, improving education and involving educational stakeholders is a central component to the collective impact approach described here:

> Local leaders, residents, and stakeholders, such as public housing authorities, cities, schools, police, business owners, nonprofits, and private developers, come together to create and implement a plan that transforms distressed HUD housing and addresses the challenges in the surrounding neighborhood. The program is designed to catalyze critical improvements in neighborhood assets, including vacant property, housing, services, and schools.[42]

On the national level, Choice Neighborhoods is a White House Neighborhood Revitalization Initiative (NRI), "an interagency partnership between HUD and the Departments of Education, Health and Human Services, Justice, and Treasury to support locally driven solutions for transforming distressed neighborhoods."[43]

The Campaign for Grade-Level Reading is underwritten by the Annie E. Casey Foundation and a host of collaborators in partnership with the National Civic League (NCL). The NCL has helped with outreach to local elected officials to encourage them to implement policy and environmental changes to bolster local efforts. Furthermore, as the conveyor of the All-America City

(AAC) Award, the NCL has leveraged this distinction to encourage communities to take action. This award, sometimes referred to as the "Nobel Prize for
constructive citizenship" is one of the oldest and most prestigious community
awards designed to recognize "exemplary grassroots community problem
solving and is awarded to communities of all sizes that collaboratively tackle
challenges and achieve results."[44] In 2012 the AAC award was dedicated to
Campaign for Grade-Level Reading communities that put forth the best plans
for community change. The 2016 award was dedicated to "communities developing innovative solutions to ensure all children are healthy and supported
to succeed in school and life."[45] In 2017 the award was once again dedicated
to CGLR communities, but this time to ones that have achieved success on
the CGLR measures (school readiness, summer learning loss, chronic absence, and third-grade reading).

## Offer Specialized Support

A second major theme that emerges among networks whose membership
have seen improvement is that of offering substantial ongoing support to
communities that seek to launch and sustain a collective impact effort. This
type of support seems to come in a diverse array of formats, including learning networks, conferences, professional development opportunities, and
training for specific programming.

Perhaps most prominent is learning networks. In general, these are long-
term, peer-to-peer mediums that are designed for ongoing consultation, sharing
of ideas, and offering of opportunities for communities to replicate what each
other is doing. Sometimes these are virtual communities and are conducted via
online webinar or phone. Other times the groups meet in person on a routine basis. Connected to this is the practice of offering periodic conferences in which
communities convene in one physical location to present on their progress, offer detail on their ongoing efforts, and share what they have learned from their
experiences. Sometimes attendance is mandatory but not always.

Many of these collective impact initiatives are program agnostic in that
they focus on cross-sector collaboration and collective impact themes without
specifying any specific programs to be run. Others are more prescriptive in
that they have a specific and detailed design of activities and practices related
to direct service delivery. For this latter variety support networks often include concrete training on how to deliver these programs and how to measure
them for impact.

Some examples of networks that have helped collective impact occur
through national initiatives include the Promise Neighborhoods and Campaign for Grade-Level Reading examples listed above as well as Ready

By 21. Examples of such networks that focus on specific programming that might prove fruitful to study include Elev8, Full-Service Community Schools, and Next Generation.

Ready by 21 (RB21)[46] is an initiative that does not fund its participants. It is billed as "a set of innovative strategies developed by the Forum for Youth Investment that helps communities improve the odds that all children and youth will be ready for college, work, and life."[47] Working with national partners in the areas of education, government, nonprofits, business, research, and philanthropy, RB21 seeks to "provide tools, training, and technical assistance to increase the collective impact of community and state efforts."[48] Like many of the other national initiatives profiled here, RB21 seeks to help communities avoid reinventing the wheel or spinning their wheels due to indecision. It provides clear standards, model programs, and expert support as it aims to build a holistic pipeline from youth through successful adulthood.

One subgroup of the community schools approach is Elev8. Launched in 2007 by The Atlantic Philanthropies, a limited life foundation, Elev8 is a community schools program aimed at middle school students. With the goal of being ready for high school by the end of eighth grade, participants engage in such programming as extended learning time, health services, and family support initiatives.[49]

Elev8 schools:

- Extend learning opportunities for students beyond the classroom and traditional school year
- Provide high-quality school-based health services to children and their families
- Encourage parents to be actively involved in their children's education
- Offer family supports and resources designed to promote economic stability, good health, and continuing education.[50]

While Elev8 is different from other community schools approaches in that it is funded, it is not the only one. Full Service Community Schools (FSCS)[51] is a good example of a collective impact approach that is funded by the federal government (the U.S. Department of Education) and that is parallel to an unfunded network led by non-governmental entities. Similar to the concept of community schools, FSCS offer social service, health, and other services designed to create a school-centered community. As with other collective impact approaches, coordination among local education agencies, nonprofit organizations, and community-based organizations is central to this approach.

The Wallace Foundation-funded Next Generation After School System Building Initiative (NGEN),[52] also an NLC initiative, offers competitive grants to cities to strengthen after school systems that serve children and youth. In collective impact fashion, this typically involves coordinating local after school opportunities offered by schools, city departments, and nonprofits and working to improve data collection and sharing.[53] One of the first gatherings of literacy coalitions nationally was hosted by the Wallace Foundation. They had a series of meetings in the late 1990s when they invited communities to gather to discuss strategies for coalition development.

## Foster Rigor

A third theme that appears among national purveyors of collective impact is an emphasis on improving the rigor with which communities both take action and measure their progress. This is in some ways endemic to the collective impact approach, but purveyors have played a role in ensuring that communities aspire to these standards. For instance, some require that very specific shared indicators are measured. Others require that specific infrastructures are in place such as a measurement system or a process for gaining ongoing community member input. Often, at the least, purveyors require a community plan which lays out the need that the collective impact effort is trying to address and articulates the strategies that the community will take, the goals it hopes to reach, and the ways it plans to measure success. While simply having a plan may seem rudimentary, without the nudging of national purveyors many communities would not have these intentions as well articulated, able to be distributed, and available to public scrutiny and community pressure to succeed. Furthermore, without the standards of rigor introduced by national purveyors, local communities would be much more susceptible to finding their efforts stalled as they reached impasses and disagreements over minor details and major goals alike. By imposing a larger framework, the decision-making at the community level is simplified drastically such that a community needs only decide to comply with the standards or not rather then select their own standards from a seemingly endless and overwhelming array of possibilities. Here, rigor provides a simplified version of reality that communities can adopt, and often adapt, with efficiency so that they can spend the majority of their time working to implement community change rather than becoming stymied in planning that change.

Furthermore, by offering the advantage of a peer group, purveyors improve rigor by promoting comparison across communities. This pushes each community to seek impressive and meaningful change that will not look feeble in comparison to the efforts of peer communities. Finally, related to this rigor, purveyors often endorse specific data platforms or are able to provide discounts to communities due to economies of scale. As reflected on in the preceding pages, such efforts push the entire field toward shared standards of measurement and the use of evidence-based practices for attaining measurable community goals. In addition to the government programs listed above, which often seek highly rigorous evaluation standards, and the Campaign for Grade-Level Reading, which has made available specific results based accountability tools, some promising examples of rigor for future research include the Strive network and the United Way's EDI.

The Strive network is run by the Knowledge Works Foundation and subsidized by the Ford Foundation, Annie E. Casey, and Living Cities.[54] Despite not offering funding to its network of members, membership in Strive requires strict adherence to a clearly delineated theory of change and concrete evidence of forward motion. In this sense, Strive is perhaps one of the scaling up paradigms most focused on fidelity to the model and adherence to common benchmarks of progress. In keeping with the franchise model, as of 2014 the Strive Network began charging an annual membership fee for its Cradle to Career Network members.

Nationally, the United Way, which has embraced collective impact as one of its public goals, also funds efforts that help to scale up the collective impact community coalition approach. The United Way's unfunded work includes the Ready by 21 Southeast Challenge, which helps communities implement RB21. The United Way offers funding for its Early Development Instrument (EDI).[55] The EDI, used by United Ways across the country (and also popular in Canada and Australia), is an assessment tool that measures children's strengths and vulnerabilities by the time they reach kindergarten. By administering this to kindergarteners, educators, school administrators, and local leaders can detect which neighborhoods are producing children with the most vulnerabilities. Accordingly, they can work together to adjust their programming to strengthen the birth-to-school pipeline for future cohorts of children.

### Elevate the Cause

A fourth theme that emerges among national purveyors whose membership is associated with positive progress involves elevating the cause. Because of their national reach, purveyor networks are in a unique position to raise the profile of the entire network's efforts when it comes to awareness, credibility, and urgency. In terms of awareness, national purveyors, because of their economies of scale and broader audience are able to invest in awareness campaigns and ancillary materials that would be impractical for a single community. Creating brochures, public service announcements, web content, and branding are all costly activities that make a lot more sense to invest in when they will be used again and again by a large number of communities across the nation. Whether those communities contribute funding to the effort or not, the per community cost of these efforts is greatly diminished and it becomes a wiser investment.

National initiatives can also afford to bring in big names such as movie stars and political celebrities who would not agree to come to one small city or even a series of cities, but will agree to endorse a major national initiative.

Having such national endorsements from celebrities, including at times celebrity researchers, enhances not only public awareness of the issue that the collective impact effort is trying to address but also the credibility of the approach that is being taken. Being able to point to related research on community issues and evidence of best practices is critical for collective impact efforts. However, because they are designed as community collaboratives, often with limited resources, coalitions lack the capacity to do this type of research or gather evidence of research from the broader field on their own. Here, being connected with a purveyor network enables local communities to present a well-reasoned and well-documented approach to their potential partners, funders, and collaborators. When reaching out to a new prospect, communities have shared that pointing to a national website, or sharing a promotional video about the effort has worked wonders with respect to convincing others to join the effort.

Many people in each community have their own passions about specific community needs and indeed there are often plenty of causes competing with each other for the attention of local elected officials, foundation leaders, community leaders, and residents. National purveyor initiatives help to create a sense of urgency around their goals in particular that elevates them above the "noise." Purveyors tend to do this not only through the presentation of key alarming research but also through their imposition of artificial timelines, such as for grants or competitions. These timelines help to push local efforts forward because it makes a community's deliberations simpler. If a community would like to be part of this collective impact movement then a clear timeline is implied and a deadline forces people to resist putting this effort on the back burner while dealing with other more pressing issues. Without such deadlines, communities might quite feasibly acknowledge a need to act but never get around to actually taking that action.

Finally, because these purveyor groups are on the national stage, they are the best positioned to support policy advocacy and lobbying for policy change at the national and subnational levels. Local policy advocacy is much enhanced when it is tied into a larger and more comprehensive effort that includes appealing to policy change on the national level as well.

Many of the aforementioned examples are exemplary when it comes to elevating the issue or cause. In addition, however, we could add to this list the Let's Move! initiative and the National Neighborhood Indicators Partnership.

Launched in 2010 as part of First Lady Michelle Obama's Let's Move! Initiative, Let's Move Cities, Towns, and Counties (LMCTC) is an anti-childhood obesity campaign carried out in partnership with the U.S. Department of Health and Human Services, the U.S. Department of Agriculture, and the National Association of Counties. Somewhat different from funded efforts (such as Race to the Top, Promise Neighborhoods, Choice Neighborhoods, and Full Service Community schools), the LMCTC is more of an awareness campaign paired with a series of resources, including technical assistance from experts, peer learning, and structured gathering of success stories and best practices. While Let's Move is not explicitly a literacy campaign, the campaign points out that, "there have been some studies showing that obese children are not learning as well as those who are not obese. Further, physical fitness has been shown to be associated with higher achievement."[56]

The National Neighborhood Indicators Partnership (NNIP)[57] is a collaboration between the Urban Institute and local partners to gather and disseminate neighborhood-level data systems that can support creation of strong communities and informed policies. Partners work to democratize information, encouraging the use of data by city and community leaders to improve struggling neighborhoods.

## PURVEYORS AS A WHOLE

Taken together, we begin to see the outlines of a social movement when we look at this host of national efforts to nurture and support the growth of local collective impact community coalitions. We also begin to notice trends, such as what types of strategies are most popular among purveyors of coalitions. We see a heavy emphasis on developing peer learning networks and helping communities gain access to literature and research relevant to solving problems that are common among communities. We also see that in many cases communities are encouraged to compete against one another for a top honor or in some cases for planning or implementation grants. Advocacy is sometimes mentioned but in almost all cases there was a sense that there is great importance in letting communities know that they are not alone and that they can learn from one another.

Any attempt to summarize these diverse national efforts is contingent on the fact that many are continuing to evolve. Furthermore, their proclivity toward leveraging each other's efforts and piggy backing on one another in true collective impact fashion can make it difficult to discern where one initiative ends and another begins. So, rather than a definitive list, we have shared snapshot of emergent popular tactics for fostering the scaling up of collective impact approaches. While previous research emphasizes that replication occurs "when a program prototype has gained recognition as being successful, thus worthy of expansion to additional sites" this is not always the case.[58] Success as defined by a rigorous evaluation does not always take place prior to "scaling up." In some cases proven success is of secondary concern to fostering a powerful concept or encouraging local innovation. In many senses, this is what we are seeing in the case of collective impact community coalitions. The promising practices when it comes to scaling up coalitions that have emerged to date are less about proven outcomes. As we have explored in previous chapters, measuring such outcomes for coalitions can be a difficult task. Rather, promising practices of scaling up of collective impact community coalitions have more to do with the ways in which national entities have found ways to inspire local collaboration.

Overall, much more research is needed to ascertain the overall efficacy of scaling up collective impact approaches. Perhaps the biggest challenges pertain to measuring and a lack of adequate data. First and foremost is the issue of graduation rates as a measure. In 2015, National Public Radio (NPR) enlisted the help of reporters to identify the mechanisms by which states and districts tried to improve their graduation rates between 2011 and 2014. They included "stepping in early to keep kids on track; lowering the bar by offering alternate and easier routes when students falter; and gaming the system by moving likely dropouts off the books, transferring or misclassifying them."[59] NPR's article quoted Daria Hall of The Education Trust, who said, "I think we have to take it with a big grain of salt. It's a lot better than it used to be; we used to have no confidence in graduation rates."[60] This is merely a reminder that our measures are far from perfect. Even if they were, the present state of research is also limited by challenges that include unit of analysis (we have county-level data but many initiatives are at the city or school level), and time (these initiatives started at different times in different communities). Future research should try to collect data on starting point and anticipate the gestation period before such initiatives would likely have an impact on graduation rates. Finally, future research should seek greater specificity of what collective impact means and how it is being implemented.

## MORE QUESTIONS THAN ANSWERS

While the present chapter offers considerable insight into potential best practices that may emerge from future study of coalitions, we are, regrettably, left with more questions than answers. National-level data suggest that we can glimpse patterns of coalition structure, activity, membership, and long-term planning that are strong bets for long-term community well-being. These data also suggest that communities will be better off the longer a coalition exists within them. However, we still do not know for sure if these patterns are directly related in any way to coalition formation, or, if they are related, the direction of causality. What we can say with greatest certainty is that coalitions need to find better ways of measuring the value they add in the lives of individuals, organizations, and community attitudes and in linking these social contributions to community-level indicators. Such efforts already are underway in many communities, but they are costly. Nevertheless, they remain our best hope for arriving at definitive outcome-based best practices for coalitions. We will continue this look into future needs in the concluding chapter.

## NOTES

1. Ravitch, D. (2014, June). When Will Bill Gates Admit He Was Wrong—Again? Retrieved April 4, 2017, from http://dianeravitch.net/2014/06/03/when-will-bill-gates-admit-he-was-wrong-again/.

2. Strauss, V. (2015, January 3). That surprising thing Bill Gates said. Retrieved April 4, 2017, from https://www.washingtonpost.com/blogs/answer-sheet/wp/2015/01/03/that-surprising-thing-bill-gates-said/?tid=sm_fb.

3. Strauss, V. (2015, January 3). That surprising thing Bill Gates said. Retrieved April 4, 2017, from https://www.washingtonpost.com/blogs/answer-sheet/wp/2015/01/03/that-surprising-thing-bill-gates-said/?tid=sm_fb.

4. Kotlowitzaug, A. (2015, August 19). Sunday Book Review: 'The Prize,' by Dale Russakoff. Retrieved April 4, 2017, from http://www.nytimes.com/2015/08/23/books/review/the-prize-by-dale-russakoff.html?_r=0.

5. All of these educational differences were statistically significant at the .01 level or better.

6. All of these educational differences were statistically significant at the .05 level or better.

7. Butterfoss, 2007, 74.

8. Butterfoss, 2007, 74.

9. Butterfoss, 2007, 74.

10. Butterfoss, 2007, 74.

11. Butterfoss, 2007, 77.

12. At the .01 level of significance.

13. We use statistical regression models with standardized coefficients (controlling for population per square mile to rule out urban and rural dynamics).

14. Stepwise linear regression.

15. Butterfoss, 2007, 279.

16. Butterfoss, 2007, 72.

17. Butterfoss (2007, 73) argues more diverse members leads to success.

18. Butterfoss, 2007, 177.

19. Turner, S., Merchant, K., Kania, J., & Martin, E. (2012, July 18). Understanding the Value of Backbone Organizations in Collective Impact: Part 2 An in-depth review of what it takes to be a backbone organization, and how to evaluate and support its work. Retrieved April 4, 2017, from http://www.ssireview.org/blog/entry/understanding_the_value_of_backbone_organizations_in_collective_impact_2.

20. Butterfoss, 2007, xix.

21. (n.d.). Retrieved April 4, 2017, from http://www.prnewswire.com/news-releases/vanna-white-named-verizons-literacy-champion-for-california-75307502.html.

22. (n.d.). Retrieved April 4, 2017, from http://www.prnewswire.com/news-releases/vanna-white-named-verizons-literacy-champion-for-california-75307502.html.

23. (n.d.). Retrieved April 4, 2017, from http://www.prnewswire.com/news-releases/vanna-white-named-verizons-literacy-champion-for-california-75307502.html.

24. "Lord of the Rings" Star Sean Astin Debuts as Verizon Literacy Champion Benefiting National Center for Family Literacy at a Reception in L.A. on Oct. 22. (2003, October 13). Retrieved April 4, 2017, from http://www.businesswire.com/news/home/20031013005526/en/Lord-Rings-Star-Sean-Astin-Debuts-Verizon.

25. Legendary Blind Athlete Erik Weihenmayer in Dallas July 31. (n.d.). Retrieved April 4, 2017, from http://www.afb.org/Section.asp?SectionID=44&TopicID=192&SubTopicID=34&am.

26. Legendary Blind Athlete Erik Weihenmayer in Dallas July 31. (n.d.). Retrieved April 4, 2017, from http://www.afb.org/Section.asp?SectionID=44&TopicID=192&SubTopicID=34&am.

27. Legendary Blind Athlete Erik Weihenmayer in Dallas July 31. (n.d.). Retrieved April 4, 2017, from http://www.afb.org/Section.asp?SectionID=44&TopicID=192&SubTopicID=34&am.

28. (n.d.). Retrieved April 4, 2017, from http://usa.imaginationlibrary.com/.

29. (n.d.). Retrieved April 4, 2017, from https://www.jloc.org/community/signature-projects/oklahoma-city-metro-literacy-coalition/.

30. (n.d.). Retrieved April 4, 2017, from http://ssir.org/articles/entry/the_dawn_of_system_leadership#sthash.4FpJitLr.dpuf.

31. (n.d.). Retrieved April 4, 2017, from http://ssir.org/articles/entry/the_dawn_of_system_leadership#sthash.4FpJitLr.dpuf.

32. Geri Summerville and Becca Raley 2009. *Laying a Solid Foundation: Strategies for Effective Program Replication*. Philadelphia, PA: Public/Private Ventures. Page 2.

33. The Conservation Company and Public/Private Ventures. 1994. Building From Strength: Replication As a Strategy for Expanding Social Programs That Work.

34. Schorr 2009:6 emphasis in original. Schorr, Lisbeth. (2009). "Realizing President Obama's Promise to Scale Up What Works to Fight Urban Poverty." Center for the Study of Social Policy. Washington, D.C.

35. The Conservation Company and Public/Private Ventures. 1994. Building From Strength: Replication As a Strategy for Expanding Social Programs That Work. Page 1.

36. The Conservation Company and Public/Private Ventures. 1994. Building From Strength: Replication As a Strategy for Expanding Social Programs That Work. Page 1.

37. David M. Laird of the Central Carolina Community Foundation coined the term "civic muscle" in a personal communication.

38. Pacheco, York, Dean, & Sarasvathy, 2010.

39. FUNDED; Government; Planning & Implementation Grants; City/Town/ County. (n.d.). Retrieved April 4, 2017, from http://www2.ed.gov/programs/promise neighborhoods/index.html.

40. FUNDED; Government; Planning & Implementation Grants; City/Town/ County. (n.d.). Retrieved April 4, 2017, from http://www2.ed.gov/programs/promise neighborhoods/index.html.

41. FUNDED; Government; Planning & Implementation Grants/ Support; City. (n.d.). Retrieved April 4, 2017, from http://portal.hud.gov/hudportal/HUD?src=/pro gram_offices/public_indian_housing/programs/ph/cn.

42. FUNDED; Government; Planning & Implementation Grants/ Support; City. (n.d.). Retrieved April 4, 2017, from http://portal.hud.gov/hudportal/HUD?src=/pro gram_offices/public_indian_housing/programs/ph/cn.

43. FUNDED; Government; Planning & Implementation Grants/ Support; City. (n.d.). Retrieved April 4, 2017, from http://portal.hud.gov/hudportal/HUD?src=/pro gram_offices/public_indian_housing/programs/ph/cn.

44. (n.d.). Retrieved April 4, 2017, from http://www.nationalcivicleague.org/ aboutaac/.

45. (n.d.). Retrieved April 4, 2017, from http://www.nationalcivicleague.org/ncl -announces-2016-all-america-city-finalists/.

46. UNFUNDED; NPO; Collaboration/ Support/ Information Sharing; City/ County/ State. (n.d.). Retrieved April 4, 2017, from http://www.readyby21.org/what -ready-21.

47. UNFUNDED; NPO; Collaboration/ Support/ Information Sharing; City/ County/ State. (n.d.). Retrieved April 4, 2017, from http://www.readyby21.org/what -ready-21.

48. (n.d.). Retrieved April 4, 2017, from http://www.readyby21.org/what-ready-21.

49. FUNDED; NPO; Direct Service Delivery/Collaboration/Advocacy/Research; City. (n.d.). Retrieved April 4, 2017, from http://www.elev8kids.org/.

50. (n.d.). Retrieved April 4, 2017, from http://www.atlanticphilanthropies.org/ subtheme/community-schools.

51. FUNDED; Government; Planning & Implementation Grants/ Support; City. (n.d.). Retrieved April 4, 2017, from http://www2.ed.gov/programs/community schools/index.html.

52. NGEN (NLC)—FUNDED; NPO; Implementation Grants/ Support; City. (n.d.). Retrieved April 4, 2017, from http://www.nlc.org/find-city-solutions/institute -for-youth-education-and-families/afterschool/afterschool-archives/next-generation -afterschool-system-building-initiative.

53. (n.d.). Retrieved April 4, 2017, from http://www.nlc.org/article/five-ways -cities-can-promote-afterschool-and-summer-meal-programs/.

54. (n.d.). Retrieved April 4, 2017, from http://www.strivetogether.org/cradle -career-network.

55. FUNDED; NPO; Collaboration/ Support/ Information Sharing; City/ County. (n.d.). Retrieved April 4, 2017, from http://www.liveunitedsem.org/pages/edi-about.

56. (n.d.). Retrieved April 4, 2017, from http://www.letsmove.gov/health-prob lems-and-childhood-obesity.

57. UNFUNDED; NPO; Collaborative/ Support/ Advocacy/ Research; City/Town/ County. (n.d.). Retrieved April 4, 2017, from http://www.neighborhoodindicators.org/.

58. See for instance page 3 of The Conservation Company and Public/Private Ventures. (1994). Building From Strength: Replication As a Strategy for Expanding Social Programs That Work. Retrieved April 4, 2017, from http://ppv.issuelab .org/resource/building_from_strength_replication_as_a_strategy_for_expanding_so cial_programs_that_work.

59. (n.d.). Retrieved April 4, 2017, from http://apps.npr.org/grad-rates/.

60. (n.d.). Retrieved April 4, 2017, from http://apps.npr.org/grad-rates/.

# Conclusion

Working together is nothing new in the grand scope of human existence. However, coming together to form a cross-sector, community-wide collaborative structure aimed at addressing a common problem is a phenomenon that has grown in recent decades and is worth noting and examining in detail. The preceding chapters have sought to do just that, probe collective impact community coalitions as a social artifact with both a developing history and a promising future. In specific, we have examined community coalitions in the context of literacy coalitions, just one of the many venues in which the coalition approach has thrived.

Though distinct from community health coalitions, neighborhood development coalitions and anti-crime coalitions, literacy coalitions are also quite similar to these efforts. They conform to the growing consensus around a definition of coalitions as multi-sector, collaborative engines of social capital building that are aimed at solving some of today's most intractable social problems. In the case of literacy coalitions, this need arises from the fact that we are in an era of global economic upheaval in which education is perhaps the only way forward to a prosperous and self-fulfilled life. Concurrent with this challenge, many communities across the nation are feeling underprepared for the jobs of the future given stubbornly low high school graduation rates—despite the fact that the nation has achieved an all-time high for graduation rates.[1] This paradox seems possible because of the growing unequal distribution of wealth and poverty such that some communities thrive while others just miles away languish. As occurs with other coalitions, we see a broadening of purpose to face the entwined challenges of education, poverty, health, and other related fields. Also, as with coalitions addressing other community needs, literacy coalitions offer a potential solution, or at the very least, a way forward toward a solution. We have seen in the preceding chapters that, judging from the evidence of the past and present, coalitions are growing, scalable, and most importantly, associated with positive community outcomes. All these factors suggest that coalitions not only have a noteworthy past and a cutting-edge present, but also a promising future.

## A NOTEWORTHY PAST

Coalitions have grown immensely in popularity over the last few decades. In the pattern of institutional entrepreneurship, community leaders across the nation have risen up to take ownership of shared social problems and to rally others around the cause. These leaders are sometimes elected, but most often self-appointed, called by a personal desire to strive toward a better future for their community. These coalitions come in all shapes and sizes, some dominated by local government, literacy providers, librarians, and others by funders, yet they are strikingly similar in their efforts to forge community institutions that will keep literacy in the spotlight of the community and orchestrate communal efforts so that they work together in more intelligent and strategic ways. There are a multitude of functions that such organizations can and have offered, ranging from direct services to community members to the more common functions of fostering communication and coordination among nonprofits, schools, funders, governments, and the broader community.

Though diverse, coalitions are correlated with positive community outcomes in terms of bringing in material resources for education-related work, having better funded and managed nonprofits, and higher percentage of high school graduates. Though these are encouraging findings for coalition proponents, we also see in preceding chapters that not all coalitions are created equally. There is considerable variation in their community-level outcomes and it is this reality that makes it possible to work toward distilling best practices for coalitions. Based on the preceding chapter, we can say that coalition theories developed in other venues such as community health coalitions are applicable to the subpopulation of literacy coalitions. Furthermore, statistical analysis builds our confidence that the components of such theory can help us to better understand what types of activities within coalitions are associated with desirable community outcomes. These analyses are at best exploratory, but they point us in clear directions for future research and offer concrete input to the nascent implementation science of coalition building. These are critical needs at a time when collective impact structures are trending and in search of a paradigm for assessing their efficacy.

## A CUTTING-EDGE PRESENT

Coalitions are all "the rage" these days.[2] They provide a means to connect the charitable field of catalytic philanthropy with community theories of collective impact and empowerment and an age of government by network.[3] To fully understand their significance, we must look beyond literacy coalitions alone and see the coalition approach as a paradigm shift that de-emphasizes the silos of the past, in which each organization did its work as an insular unit without much interaction beyond its own walls, and champions cross-sector collaboration. In their recent book, *The Metropolitan Revolution*, Jennifer Bradley and Bruce Katz examine the many ways in which community leaders are learning that the best way to lead is often through networks.[4] Whether the community need is reshaping a city's economy, helping its immigrants climb the employment ladder, or fixing its broken political system, communities are finding that the quality of community networks is critical. As Bradley and Katz assert, "There is a growing body of research suggesting that, as a system or problem becomes more complex, arriving at a solution requires multiple minds from multiple sectors or perspectives."[5] Much like more recent literature on institutional entrepreneurship that has disavowed a hero mentality as misleading and even destructive, Bradley and Katz argue, "This search for the lone superhero, or one lone team of superhero buddies, is misguided. Metropolitan areas are so big, complicated, and diverse that they don't need heroes. They need heroic networks."[6] Here we see a striking parallel with the growing popularity of the collective impact approach that argues that we don't need silver bullets, but silver buckshot.[7]

When we take a step back from these approaches, we see that they are all variants of the collective impact community coalition model. Though they may have different community members (ranging from local government to foundations to social justice advocates) serving as catalysts, and though their specific membership and character are highly reflective of their specific task at hand, they are more alike than different. In fact, the narratives offered in *The Metropolitan Revolution* seem strikingly parallel to the ones outlined in chapter 1 about the birth of literacy coalitions. For instance, in the case of Northeast Ohio, as detailed by Bradley and Katz, the trajectory of their economic development network could just as easily be one of the over 100 literacy coalitions across the nation if we just switched the name of the community and swapped "literacy" for the word "economic." It began with widespread meetings of community residents in 2005–2006 in which they focused on community assets, challenges, and priorities. Convening in a series of broad community meetings with the same focus on assets, challenges, and priorities was a unifying theme among coalitions. In Northeast Ohio, this led to a commitment on the part of community members that seems like a page right out of coalition membership recruitment:

> In testimony to the network's efforts, more than 90 individuals and organizations, including U.S. senators, local chambers of commerce, local governments, universities, hospitals, and business groups, agreed to be partners in this sweeping agenda and orient their activities around those four goals.[8]

Again, just as with coalitions, the Northeast Ohio network experienced fits and starts in which their agenda met with roadblocks, stalled, then experienced spurts of rebirth. Five years after they started, an independent review found that they had had little impact on the community.

Just when it seemed that the network approach was a failure, as with coalitions, what kept them going was a belief that by bringing together a multiplicity of diverse people they would strengthen or build up what David Laird calls "civic muscle."[9] The hoped for result was a critical mass of people, situated in a wide diversity of professional locations, who would begin, metaphorically, to row in the same direction, toward shared goals and an inclusive approach that could unite them all. Networking, like coalitions, was viewed as a tool for strengthening the region.

As with coalitions, local philanthropic foundations stepped up to foster this vision. In the tradition of catalytic philanthropy, they spent money ($425,000 across four years) "to facilitate meetings, organize grant application reviews, conduct relevant research, and generally do what it takes to hold dozens of partners together."[10] As one of the key members involved explained, this was a means to an end that had an economic return on investment, not unlike those hoped for by literacy funders who invest in coalitions: "The Fund put $25,000 in to buy the donuts . . . and we got a $30 million return on investment."[11] In this respect, when it comes to activities and outcomes, the journey followed in Northeast Ohio reads like a logic model for literacy coalitions. They use meetings to link a wide diversity of community stakeholders who would not normally come into contact with each other (in their case representatives from sectors as varied as fine arts, environment, economy, anti-poverty, and health). Local funders provided the start-up capital for these community members to work together; they commissioned research, conducted public outreach, and developed shared goals and priorities. The result, not unlike what we see in chapter 3, was successful competition for highly competitive state and national grant monies that would benefit the region as a whole. As with literacy coalitions, however, these increased resources are both an outcome and a means to an even greater end. Whereas chapter 3 details literacy coalitions seeking increases in graduation rates, the Northeast Ohio network's ultimate successes will be measured in jobs created and payroll increases.

In stark contrast to the indifference and cynicism that has been asserted about contemporary civic life[12], these efforts share optimism and a hope for the future. They embody what the Task Force on Civic Education of the American Political Science Association points out as the necessary civic engagement of communities within a democracy:

> American democracy, perhaps uniquely, depends on the civic work of ordinary people who, located in diverse, plural communities, work on behalf of their communities and seek eagerly for common goods, both heroic and mundane.[13]

However, the ties with democracy do not stop with the importance of civic work; the cross-sector thinking epitomized by coalitions has even spread into the field of public administration and governance. In their jointly issued report and later book, Harvard's Kennedy School of Government and Deloitte Research, under the authorship of William Eggers and Stephen Goldsmith, have asserted that "Government by Network" has become an imperative of future democratic governing.

The tenets of Governing by Network, as the authors articulate them, parallel the hallmark features of collective impact coalitions:

> The era of hierarchical government bureaucracy, the predominant organizational model used to deliver public services and fulfill public policy goals for a century now, is coming to an end. Emerging in its place is a fundamentally different model—one that we call governing by network—in which government executives redefine their core responsibilities from managing people and programs to coordinating resources for producing public value. Government agencies, bureaus, divisions, units, and offices are becoming less important as direct service providers, and more important as levers of public value. This new model is characterized by the web of multi-organizational, multi-governmental, and multi-sectoral relationships that increasingly constitute modern governance.[14]

In the example of literacy coalitions, we see not only further evidence of this multi-sector networking trend, but also a proven sustainability model for this new paradigm. We furthermore see a shared optimism and a hope for the future.

## A PROMISING FUTURE

As the often-cited Task Force on Civic Education declares, though they require considerable time, coalitions are a key step on the way to social change:

> Persistent civic engagement—the slow and patient building of first coalitions and then majorities—can generate social change. This is the history of women's

suffrage and, while not yet finished, it is the history of increasing protection of civil liberties.[15]

Indeed, some in the area of literacy coalition building have pushed forth under the inspiration of civil liberties and the women's suffrage movements, holding a conference and launching an international campaign for the right to literacy. While this approach honors the venerable history of coalitions of all sorts (including political ones) in this nation, the present day also offers considerable new opportunities for collective action.

As explored in the preceding pages, coalitions are a key area of collaboration around data. It is hard to comprehend the many factors that go into community-level indicators such as census numbers. It is furthermore difficult to digest and process how what we do in our everyday lives can have an impact on such numbers for the better. Given the social capital they build up as part of their creation and persistence, coalitions are uniquely situated to help communities not only focus on setting and moving toward measurable community goals, but also to thrive in the new era of big data. Everyone from global marketers and police stations[16] to mayors focusing on public health,[17] to schools[18] seems to be focusing on the emergence of big data and how we might use it to improve the lives of citizens. Indeed, this is the entire concept behind the Data Smart City Solutions project at Harvard.[19]

While there is considerable debate about just what big data is and how big the data need to be before they meet the criteria, in general we have a situation in which larger and larger amounts of data are being collected routinely. This certainly presents challenges to present capacity when it comes to collecting, storing, and making sense of such data, but it also offers quite a bit of promise. In particular, much of the data collected are relational and could be linked to each other across presently existing silos or institutional boundaries. So, for instance, school district data could be shared with county social services and with nonprofit service providers. If done carefully with full protections in place for confidentiality and avoidance of data misuse, these data could yield a new world when it comes to being able to "see" how our actions in one part of the community ripple through to impact outcomes that are only visible in another part of community life. Communities that collect data on early childhood caregiving quality could link those data with kindergarten readiness scores collected in schools and then work to improve the relationship and handoffs between the two. Or adult education providers could follow through with their former clients to track how well they do in the job market or how well their children do in school.

Some communities have already begun to embrace this paradigm and have found that the challenge with such community-level data sharing projects is not so much the technology, but the trust among organizations.[20] In this respect, the advantage of the future will go not to those communities that have the best technology; such things are readily mobile and will travel to wherever there is a market for them. Rather, the advantage will reside in communities where the trust and track record of working together are strongest.

## WILL COALITIONS STAND THE TEST OF TIME?

Given the rise of coalitions in popularity, it is only natural to wonder whether collective impact is an approach that will stand the test of time by continuing to remain popular in the years to come. Indeed, some of the largest proponents of collective impact community coalitions have wondered about their place in history.[21] In the following pages we reflect on the preceding chapters in order to discern the emerging themes that seem most likely to affect the future of coalitions. We do this by first taking a hard look at one possible future, the demise of coalitions. To explore this possibility, we examine a series of cases in which coalition efforts have failed to persist. Referring to this as the "coalition graveyard" we seek to learn from their experiences by reflecting on just what went wrong. Following from this we emerge with a set of themes that we see as pivotal issues that will decide the fate of coalitions as a social phenomenon moving forward. These include the ability of communities to create models that meet their diverse needs and allow them to mature over time, the extent to which they embrace a model that infuses literacy through existing infrastructure rather than seeking to create their own infrastructure, ability to broaden the base of constituents through such innovations as super coalitions, the future levels and types of funding, and the degree to which standardization of the coalition field takes place.

### The Coalition Graveyard

To explore the future any social movement it is often helpful to review concrete cases where it has met with failure in order to foresee potential troubles on the horizon. Collective impact community coalitions are no different. In the following pages we seek to discern lessons from coalition efforts that have gone by the wayside in what we term the "coalition graveyard." The coalition graveyard includes coalitions in Ohio, California, Connecticut, Texas, Indiana, and New Orleans. In one case in Ohio, for example, the mayor led the way for the city to unite around a mayoral coalition, and for many years it was highly active. The city budget included a line item to cover the operating expenses of the coalition and only required an annual application and yearly progress report for renewal. The coalition expected the funding and appreciated it as the lifeline that sustained operations, but the year the staff forgot to apply, the funding stopped and the coalition struggled to attract other funders. After several months the coalition closed operations.

A similar story took place in California where a local corporation provided a seed grant for the literacy coalition and the staff spent the grant on services but did not seek to raise any additional funding. In Connecticut, a coalition developed with the support of the city, the local workforce board, and the city library. The groundwork, local research, and needs assessment were highly acclaimed. A community plan was crafted over many months, but the coalition was challenged in the implementation of its work. The community needed to see concrete action, which did not materialize.

Texas holds another example of a coalition's demise. A national corporation had moved in and launched a national awareness campaign for literacy. Almost overnight, this Texas coalition had the wealthiest coalition in the nation. Stars of stage, screen, and sports became spokespersons for the coalition's efforts. It was housed in a rent-free facility provided by a local foundation. It had a state-of-the-art video conferencing center, a remarkable marketing program, and the potential for unprecedented achievement in the literacy coalition field. But two things heralded its failure. First the coalition became alienated from the partners that it was created to serve. Second, after years in this Texas community, the major corporation moved its headquarters to another state. While these two challenges ended the coalition, there is more to the story. Two new initiatives developed to take the coalition's place. One coalition was formed to bring the literacy providers together again, and another emerged as a local StriveTogether partner. Hence, the work continued, but in a radically different form.

In one California community a very small networking coalition was embraced by the local newspaper and found a home at the corporate giant's downtown headquarters. Later, the paper also embraced a complementary literacy program with a strong parental component and eventually housed both programs in offices with higher visibility and on a higher, more prestigious, floor in the office. The coalition created an annual event that spotlighted literacy with a distinctive movie star flair. As the coalition grew, the mayor explored the city's need for a stronger workforce and gave the task of developing a workforce development arm for the coalition to the deputy mayor. City leadership rallied around the effort, and the Chamber of Commerce, the workforce board, and the United Way played leading roles in developing a plan of action. The United Way published a powerful document highlighting the needs of un- and underemployed job seekers and their families. Much work was completed, but over time and a change of mayor, the initiative lost momentum. Then a change of coalition director and reductions in both funding and in levels of fundraising followed. The coalition board determined that a merger with a workforce development nonprofit would give the work new life in a more secure home. That change proved to be the death knell for the coalition.

In one Louisiana community a single coalition has twice escaped death. In the late 1980s the leaders of the city's literacy providers came together to build a networking coalition in which a monthly luncheon meet and greet and two community awareness events each year filled their need to collaborate and to support each other's mission and vision. Then an interesting series of events occurred. One local university received a grant for an academic project and at another university leaders determined that there should be an equal level of support for their university.

They agreed that low literacy was symptomatic of the deeper issues of poverty and racism and determined to take a stand to address the problem. A U.S. Department of Housing and Urban Development grant was secured for the university to administer, and a literacy center was born. Most of the funding was spent on a beautiful state-of-the-art library for the university. After some controversy about the appropriate use of the funding, a new director was hired to run literacy programs, but community concerns about that funding led to the development of a new literacy coalition. A community needs assessment and action plan were put in place for a new coalition to replace the existing one and a ceremony was held to mark the death of the former coalition.

The new coalition was founded and did a considerable amount of work, especially in workforce development and community literacy, with the support of a large team of AmeriCorps members and continued funding from local religious funders. After six successful years, a natural disaster hit. The coalition disappeared as the floodwaters retreated, along with the providers and most of their students. Today a new, very small, networking coalition is in place that looks remarkably like a reincarnation of the original small networking coalition.

The demise of a coalition in one Indiana community also provides insights. In this community local foundations collaborated to increase literacy and educational attainment. The result was a coalition supported by a major national corporate foundation. It was a coalition of community foundations, literacy organizations, education, workforce development, and business leaders that provided regional coordination of literacy opportunities to raise the educational attainment levels in this part of Indiana. The coalition was a $15 million dollar initiative to improve educational attainment and pilot best practices with a strong evaluation component and replication strategies. There was no shortage of funding which continued to support the coalition over eight years. But this coalition's demise reveals that even well-endowed efforts are not guaranteed a future.

The lifespan of a coalition might be five years or fifty years. If there is a thread that links all the lessons learned together, it would be that coalitions should not take long-term stability for granted. While it is difficult to pinpoint the actual causes of each coalition's demise, some themes that have emerged in the course of this research are that conflicts among partners can be lethal. These can undermine even the best of intentions. While we tend to see coalitions as an exercise in good will, they nevertheless take place within existing community backdrops that include rivalries and other inter-organizational tensions. Personality conflicts and conflicts of interest are all a part of this challenge and can make or break a coalition. If these cannot be overcome, the coalition model can fail to find fertile ground for growth and prosperity. Leadership from among community members is also crucial. A coalition board of directors that fails to become cohesive and set a clear vision for a way forward can be just as deadly as an executive director who fails to assume a collaborative leadership role.

In addition to such personnel landmines, losing sight of the importance of diversifying funding streams and continuing to conduct outreach for future sources of funding can lead to a coalition's sudden demise, even in cases where collective impact efforts seem to have abundant resources and ample programming. Funders, as we have explored, can be fickle and are susceptible to trends in globalization that may lead them to uproot and move to another community. Yet another potential pitfall for coalitions is becoming disconnected from the constituents that are the reason for their existence in the first place. Such disconnects can lead to an internal revolt and a coalition's loss of credibility and reason to exist.

Coalitions seldom remain static over time. With new knowledge, economic changes, investment adaptations, and leadership transitions, coalitions grow and partnerships and plans evolve in a constant metamorphosis. Often this occurs on a forward-moving trajectory but sometimes it might seem like one step forward and two steps backward as development is impacted by both internal and external factors for successful growth.

As it happens, while some coalitions have met their demise, others have come perilously close and offer an example of tenacity and reinvention. Communities try to get it right the first time with a model that will work for all the component parts, but sometimes it takes several tries to create a successful model. A coalition in a community in Michigan is a case in point. The group had met with consultants from FSG as the original planning was developing and was committed to the goals of collective impact. As the 2012 *Stanford Social Innovation Review* article "Channeling Change: Making Collective Impact Work" makes clear, one of the keys to maintaining success is maintaining the strength and effectiveness of the coalition's backbone organization.[22] In this community over time, as with some other coalitions, the backbone organization was challenged to maintain forward momentum, and the community took steps to address this. As one coalition partner explained:

> We [the coalition] determined either we needed to take a new direction or we needed to dissolve the initiative. This committee met for two years and determined that the initiative should be housed under an organization that was large enough to bring it structure and also a neutral entity that was not providing literacy services directly. [A national] foundation pledged a three-year commitment of funding, and the committee proceeded to interview various organizations, primarily colleges. The challenging realization came that significant change would need to occur and to have staff from the new entity oversee it, more funding would be required. At this point we were close to dissolving, all getting discouraged.

Being prepared to address these challenges was a strength of the leadership that proved to be critical. The educational leadership, local government, and both business and private funders played an important and intentional role in the reinvention of the coalition. Many of the original leaders and the organizations they represented understood that their goals remained the same, but their infrastructure needed to change. Eventually, a national funder awarded a grant and a new board was configured with strategic representation built into it.

This coalition is an example of the way a backbone organization may need to change over time to ensure that it continues guiding vision and strategy, working to support partner activities, and positioning itself to establish shared measurement practices, advance policy, and access funding. The community needed to see the changes that were happening and rally behind the new face of the initiative. Over time this Michigan coalition took shape and began to impact the growth and development of the programs it supported. It maintained direct services as many coalitions do to fill gaps identified in planning. These services included both tutoring programs for children and adults as well as services to employers for vocational and workforce education.

This story illustrates that coalition persistence is perhaps less a factor of having the right formula and more a matter of having grit. Recent attention has pointed to grit as a desirable quality that helps youth persist to achieve goals.[23] The same could be said of coalitions.

## A Diversity of Models That Allow for Maturation over Time

The first key theme that will be critical to whether coalitions stand the test of time is their ability to continue to appear in a diverse set of configurations that are custom tailored to each individual community's needs, and allow each community to mature over time. When we revisit what a literacy coalition is, we are reminded that, "A coalition is at once a distinct organization and a collective of many organizations and stakeholders. It is both the lead organization and its membership. The coalition's work is to act on behalf of the collective. Primary tasks for literacy coalitions are to facilitate change and track improvement in literacy in the community as a whole."[24] Hence, to be effective, a coalition must both heed its members and lead its members. This requires ample flexibility and ability to be responsive first and foremost. With respect to responding to community literacy needs, this is also a moving target as communities are impacted by the economy, immigration, resources, and leadership changes. Such a changing landscape is not new to the coalition movement, however. The federal adult education system in place in the 1980s did not work as effectively as it might have and only a tiny percentage of those needing services were enrolled in programs. Service delivery was fragmented and uncoordinated. The coalition movement was born because this situation created a vacuum. By the decade starting in 2010, the original literacy coalitions were infusing the tenets of collective impact and system change and collaborating and metamorphosing into more sophisticated, structured systems under the leadership of a new generation of creative directors utilizing the goals of adaptive leadership. As the leaders changed so did the coalitions.

As with any venture, the stronger the foundation and scaffolding, the longer the life of the coalition. The stages of planning, including assessing community needs, planning with leadership, designing the plan, raising seed funding, creating the coalition, selecting the first projects, and implementing the plan are the basics for the first phase. However, in the lifespan of a literacy coalition there are many models, from simple networking where independent providers come together monthly to network to the fully integrated community collaboration model (see figure 5.1).

What is perhaps surprising is that some coalitions have survived without much change over time. Some have filled a need in the community by simply managing a student and volunteer hotline, training volunteers, and coordinating a number of awareness and book distribution events each year. One literacy coalition in Indiana does this and is very successful in tackling a few things and doing them very well. In some cases, coalitions have transformed through many phases reinventing themselves in the constant drive to meet changing community and stakeholder needs. One coalition in New York has done this and in its current iteration is meeting the community need for increased and improved professional development for its partners. In some communities in recent years, instead of one overarching coalition, other

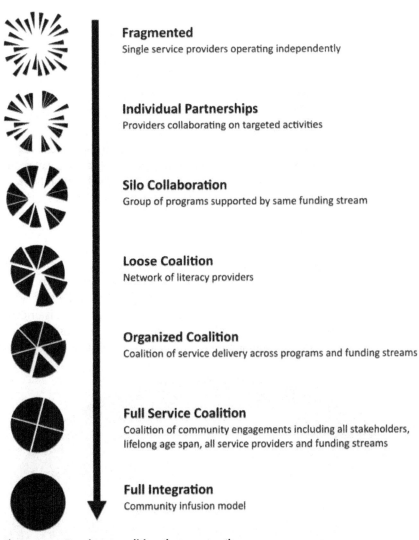

**Fragmented**
Single service providers operating independently

**Individual Partnerships**
Providers collaborating on targeted activities

**Silo Collaboration**
Group of programs supported by same funding stream

**Loose Coalition**
Network of literacy providers

**Organized Coalition**
Coalition of service delivery across programs and funding streams

**Full Service Coalition**
Coalition of community engagements including all stakeholders, lifelong age span, all service providers and funding streams

**Full Integration**
Community infusion model

**Figure 5.1.  Dominant coalition themes over time.**
Graphic courtesy of the authors.

complementary coalitions have grown around the original coalition to fill in the gaps and better address issues. At a literacy coalition in Texas the focus has reverted to adult education and a separate initiative has grown up to provide support for children's education.

In the early stages of development coalitions often tackle one issue or project at a time. The problem of low literacy is daunting and choosing a starting point with a clear and achievable goal makes the work more manageable.

More mature coalitions that have developed in structure and strength have the community support, staffing, and funding to take on broader and more ambitious goals. The coalition movement's founding goals were based on its work across five development areas: building the community, strengthening the family, ensuring people's right to self-determination, improving the workforce, and transforming the literacy system.[25]

These were also the principles that formed the basis of the U.S. Right to Literacy Campaign for the UNESCO Decade of Literacy (2003–2012) that coalitions used to build awareness and visibility. In the lifespan of coalition development, the guiding principle of coalitions was that learners matter and that change happens one learner at a time. Learners are at the heart of the work supported by the network of service providers and which, in turn, is supported by the stakeholder community and its coalitions. The result is a literacy-specific model similar to Bronfenbrenner's ecological systems model (see figure 5.2).[26]

Coalition longevity depends on measurable success and visibility. To sustain itself over time a coalition must be seen to provide value-added services that raise education levels in the short term that in turn help people step out of poverty and increase individual and community prosperity over the long term. Measuring value to the community and return on investment has historically been hard to track, but a growing number of coalitions have demonstrated their success in ways whereby communities and funders saw their worth.

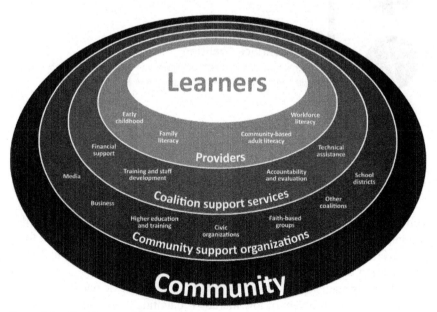

**Figure 5.2. The Literacy Coalition Ecosystem.**
Graphic courtesy of the authors.

As coalitions matured, many embraced FSG and its model of collective impact. This provided a tool through which coalitions could reassess their work and their role in the communities they served. Such tools were unavailable to the coalitions of the 1980s and 1990s, and many had to change to meet the demands of the new century. In Ohio, an early coalition provided basic services for only adult education providers, creating a gap that was filled by the emergence of the StriveTogether program. The early coalitions that focused only on adult education and did not grow to incorporate family literacy found themselves facing competition from newly emerging coalitions that were "twinkle to wrinkle," "lifelong learning," or "cradle to career" networks.

Mature coalitions striving for sustainable longevity embraced newly emerging models and practices. One such model was the Campaign for Grade-Level Reading, which took a new and different approach. It looked at defining a point in time in a child's education at which future success or failure could be determined and where interventions could be provided to ensure success. "In the U.S. about 67 percent of children nationwide and more than 80 percent of those from low-income families are not proficient readers by the end of third grade," Ralph Smith reports from the CGLR.[27] With support from the Annie E. Casey Foundation, the program's managing director, Ralph Smith described the need to "rebuild what is now a chaotic system of early care and early grade education by using grade-level reading proficiency as a unifying goal; promoting quality teaching for every child in every setting every day; supporting community solutions to address lack of school readiness, chronic absence, and summer learning loss; and helping parents succeed in their critical roles as first teachers, most-important brain builder, and best advocates." Local coalitions developed Community Solution Action Plans that were supported not only by the GLR Campaign but by the National Civic League, National League of Cities, United Way Worldwide, and other founding partners. The 2012 All-America City Awards, which focused exclusively on grade-level reading, provided high visibility for the issue and added the element of competition into the mix.[28]

In the lifespan evolution, existing coalitions like one in New York embraced the new models maintaining one central coalition but in some cities new coalitions emerged with complementary goals. In one city in Texas, for instance, the original adult education coalition had not grown to include the broader spectrum of lifelong learning. Consequently, an interesting metamorphosis occurred in the community, creating two different initiatives. The mayor embraced each initiative and saw each component coalition collaborate under the broad leadership of a P–16 canopy. Its goals—supporting literacy providers, sharing the issues with the community at large, and advocating for change—enabled it to collaborate with other partners. Add to the mix a Promise Neighborhood program and the community enjoyed a plethora of new and old partnerships to redefine the way the city tackled the issue of low literacy.

In this coalition and in many other cities and counties, change did not come easily. Sometimes there was controversy when new coalitions emerged. Turf and trust issues loomed high as new groups vied for the support of the city or the county government and as funders were conflicted about who and what to support. Coalitions unable to adapt and create new partnerships were hard pressed to stay afloat. In this narrative, we are reminded that the coalition approach is an ongoing process, one of rebirth as well as reinvention.

## Infusion Rather than Re-Creation

A second major theme that promises to shape the future of coalitions is whether they embrace a model that infuses literacy through existing infrastructure rather than seeking to create their own infrastructures. While coalitions have certainly proved intent upon raising funding and increasing the amount of resources in their home communities, we have also learned that such funding is often intermittent, undependable, and insufficient to replace the vast investments that communities have already made in their local infrastructure through government, nonprofits, and philanthropy. Rather than replace these infrastructures, coalitions seem to be most in their element when they are simply tweaking these structures to ensure that priority themes such as literacy are reinforced throughout them. The collective impact approach emphasizes coordinated activities and infusion is a prominent way in which coalitions have been able to achieve this objective.

To date, we have seen evidence of this approach gaining in popularity. Integral to the development of coalitions was the incorporation of the concept of community literacy. This involved collaborative dialogue, issue debate, and a collaborative planning process that united communities around the vision of 100 percent Literacy through 100 percent Community Engagement. Under this paradigm, everyone can own the issue. Everyone benefits when literacy levels are raised. Community literacy includes many community stakeholders. "It facilitates literacy infusion, the practice of including literacy throughout all community initiatives. Incorporating literacy into diverse community efforts promotes a general awareness and understanding of all its complexities and addresses issues on a communitywide scale."[29] Community ownership elevates the issue, too, and helps promote the fact that high levels of literacy reduce poverty and increase economic prosperity. One key way that the literacy movement has helped to broaden its base has been through infusion, which helps to spread the movement across unlikely partners.

Literacy infusion began to be included in the planning process for mature coalitions in the late 1990s. Assessing multiple levels of partnerships offered coalitions a means to breaking down silos within their own membership:

> Literacy infusion promotes literacy through a collective approach. Traditionally, separate agencies practice a "silo" approach whereby each works to achieve goals, with particular funding streams, measurements, and in isolation. Through the concept of literacy infusion, improved literacy becomes a common goal of all organizations. Each agency recognizes its role not only to fulfill its unique specific mission, but also to contribute to the shared vision and to the development of community economic prosperity. The implementation of literacy infusion is both bottom up and top down, both a grassroots and "grass tips" effort. All sectors can be included in community literacy initiatives.[30]

As the concept of literacy infusion emerged, coalition development changed. Instead of networking with only existing literacy providers, coalitions increased partnerships with other social service nonprofits, school districts, and agencies to more fully integrate literacy services and funding. For instance, in one coalition in Indiana, partnerships were forged with the school system, and in another in Alabama, the corrections program with the county prison system created access to services for the incarcerated. These partnerships resulted in a less fragmented approach and more coordinated services through infusion and by using in-place infrastructures rather than building something completely new.

The infusion model has helped coordinate and build community buy-in throughout the nation where it has been applied. Literacy has become less the goal and more the tool toward a goal that did not belong in any one social issue area, but in all. "Before this approach, most communities addressed social issues, including literacy, in isolation. They compartmentalized both their problems and their attempts to solve them in separate boxes. The infusion model has broken literacy out of the service delivery system box and put it into every box (see figure 5.3)."[31]

Hence, the infusion approach became a hallmark of literacy coalition work that also helped to broaden the base of constituents involved. The emergence of super coalitions is another forward-looking trend that also helps to broaden the base of collective impact efforts.

## Super Coalitions and Broadening the Base

A third theme that will likely shape the future of coalitions and whether they stand the test of time will be their ability to broaden the base of stakeholders in order to improve the likelihood of their success. Many of the problems that

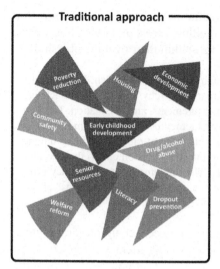 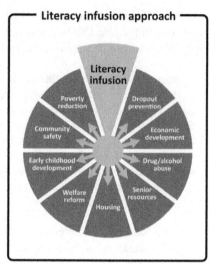

**Figure 5.3. Literacy Infusion.**
Graphic courtesy of the authors.

coalitions face, such as literacy, are what many have referred to as "wicked problems" and as such are not bound to one particular field or focus area. Rather, solving them will require reaching out across multiple fields and institutions. One trend that has emerged to address this is the super coalition. What is a super coalition? At the local level it is the kind of coalition that embraces the entire spectrum of lifelong learning and represents all the multiple networks that could partner for community change: educational partnerships, health networks, workforce development, financial literacy organizations, housing, social services, transportation, and others. The early coalitions represented individual providers but not usually multiple networks of providers across the lifespan. In a number of communities with multiple coalitions (an early learning network, an adult education partnership, a collaboration of school districts, a workforce development alliance, and others) one organization, a super coalition, has emerged to bring all together to align efforts.

Such coalitions can be powerful change agents recognizing opportunities, identifying approaches, tracking progress, and making change happen. Where they maintain integrity, progress toward goals, and servant leadership, they are highly effective. In another Michigan example, as the coalition took on the challenge of low educational performance, it embraced the philosophy of community capitalism (as discussed in a previous chapter). The community has a super coalition orchestrating the many parts of the whole and tracking progress over time. It points to racial disparities in high school graduation as a key goal for community change, but at the same time it also takes into consideration other related factors such as domestic violence, hence taking a more holistic perspective on "at-risk," "vulnerable," and "disadvantaged." Hence, such super coalitions broaden their base of constituents by including not only those who are concerned with literacy and education, but also those concerned with racial disparities, and those who are concerned with domestic violence. In this way, we can see the potential for the blending of multiple existing coalitions that focus on distinct community needs such that they begin to reinforce one another by setting shared community goals.

While the super coalition approach may be distinguished by its breadth, some may consider coalitions with remarkable depth to be another variant of the super coalition approach. In a different super coalition model, a community in Texas focused on adult and family literacy from its start-up in the 1980s. As a coalition, it partnered with other collaborative efforts over time including a variety that focused on early childhood, adult education, and research. Each had its own independent plans and goals, but there was not an overarching lifelong learning plan for the whole city. A new entity was needed to galvanize, coordinate, and help integrate the full spectrum of lifelong learning. What emerged was a new entity, incorporated as a foundation, to fill this role.

The new foundation has taken on the important catalytic role of leadership in the community's ever-evolving literacy movement. The foundation developed to fill the gap to ensure lifelong learning coordination. It undertook a citywide analysis, community mapping, and needs assessment, bringing together all the lifelong learning components from early learning through workforce development. The analysis and planning resulted in a city-wide plan, endorsed by all the key city players and each of the coalitions. Signing onto the plan in a highly visible ceremony provided the opportunity for city leaders, organizations, organizers, and school districts to demonstrate collaboration. The foundation also took on several back office roles supporting funding, centralized volunteerism, specific services, and place-based projects. This promoted coordination between and among the various entities to implement change and transform competition into collaboration.

A key part of this process was to engage other foundations and the business community. City leaders and residents signed a Literacy Promise pledge to put an end to low literacy levels in the city. Holding together a collaboration of many moving parts, maintaining coordination, and ensuring that all voices are heard and the needs of collaborators are addressed requires building leadership and trust. This has been the initial success of the foundation and the initial implementation of the plan.

Will the super coalition model successfully resolve educational issues and bring the U.S. up to the higher educational levels enjoyed by many other developed countries? The answer is perhaps—the same possibility that existed for those early coalitions in the 1980s. For all the much-needed sophistication of collective impact, the danger of these large coalitions may be that they can lose track of their partner voices and cease to fully represent the community they serve. Is there a "too big to fail" caution in coalition development? The Dodd-Frank reform became federal law in 2010 to ensure that taxpayers would not have to step in to bail out the big banks. When all educational support services are linked under one lead agency, is there a danger of creating too much bureaucracy and insufficient support or measurable outcomes? Can nonprofit coalitions suffer from the same disease and demise as a for profit? Just as Ma Bell (the Bell System of telephone companies) grew and grew, can coalitions grow too big for their britches? Further, if the needle does not move and strategies do not bring promised success, failure to adapt and tweak will diminish likelihood of achieving expected performance outcomes. But the emergence of super coalitions and the lessons learned offer a promising development for future coalitions to consider.

## The Future of Funding

A fourth theme we have identified that is likely to impact the future of coalitions is the tendency to follow funding. This has been a theme throughout the preceding pages as funds, or even a hint of funds, have spurred new coalitions to form and old ones to recalibrate. This trend is likely to continue, but perhaps in a different form. Alternative approaches to funding are already emerging. One coalition in Texas figured out that if funding followed each student so that they did not drop out but transferred into alternative programs (often vocationally aligned), this arrangement would provide resources to the coalition as an intermediary and would be a strong incentive to deter dropping out. Students would be "dropping in" to a program more suited to meet their needs. In Ohio, a coalition helped negotiate a partnership between a school district and a provider whereby students who had dropped out were enrolled into a part-time alternative program of credit recovery and vocational exploration and preparation. The school district provided the funding.

From a coalition in Arizona's experience we have learned that an effective strategy to fund coalition work is to align key strategies and associated professional development with existing publicly funded systems. Where school districts and human service providers can see the value-added role and expertise of the coalition, a win-win situation for the partners can be a win for children and families. Child care, adult education, and workforce development are the mainstays of the safety net. The budgets for Temporary Assistance for Needy Families (TANF), and other human service programs include billions of dollars. For many of these funding streams, literacy is an eligible activity. When workforce investment, education, and other funding streams are linked, creative blending and braiding make for solution building focused on literacy as a recognized link to self-sufficiency and poverty reduction.

As coalitions have developed, there have been efforts to fund the adult and family literacy work of coalitions with federal adult education funds. The New York State Department of Education has promoted the concept of Literacy Zones and implemented the model in both existing and new coalitions. The department and the New York State Board of Regents planned to close the achievement gap by meeting the needs of the community from birth through adults. Communities came together to assess needs, build a plan, and set up Welcome Centers in their Literacy Zone under the guidance of their stakeholder coalitions.

Across the country, the network of state literacy coalitions also played an important role over time in funding, although they have never been as strong as local coalition partners would have liked. Where they have been successful, they have assisted with direct cash grants, pro bono training, and centralized data collection and analysis that has taken some of the burden off the local coalitions. The Ohio Literacy Network, with financial support from the state's department of education, helped create adult education coalitions in nine Ohio cities. These partnerships included both federally funded programs and nonprofit providers and recognized the importance of collaboration across program types and funding streams. In Arkansas and Illinois, coalitions developed a model of funding that operated in parallel to the publicly funded system to provide a mechanism to encourage nonprofits and coalitions. The Arkansas plan was to develop a state literacy coalition as an intermediary and flow funding to the nonprofit literacy providers and coalitions through that mechanism. The Illinois Secretary of State's Office also identified funding for literacy in nonprofits and libraries. In both instances, although they provided support that would otherwise have excluded the nonprofit system, the level of funding per students was lower than that provided through Adult Education System funding. Hence, while this does help address the issue of funding for coalitions, it can also be criticized for maintaining nonprofit partners as an underclass and setting the system up as less effective.

## Moving Toward a More Standardized Field

A fifth and final theme that will likely determine the future of coalitions is the extent to which the field of coalition building becomes standardized. In

2005, Literacy Powerline and ProLiteracy developed guidelines for coalition success in an effort to create standards of practice. More recently the standards developed by Strive and the Campaign for Grade-Level Reading are helping to better define goals and track changes. These efforts to develop and measure transformational solutions give serious consideration to creating well-regulated, well-managed coalition structure and beg the question: Are coalitions better with or without strict bureaucratic scaffolding?

In *Bureaucracy,* by Ludwig von Mises he described bureaucracy as "management bound to comply with detailed rules and regulations fixed by the authority of a superior body."[32] Such adherence to a higher authority is perhaps most likely in the case of defining success. For a for-profit organization, "success" is not whether the organization closely follows certain rules and procedures, but whether it is profitable. For a nonprofit success is related to measurable success described by its mission and the community change brought on by that success.[33] One piece of advice that has emerged from communities is the importance of focusing on the end goal and not the details. As one community member shared, certain data are much more political than others and they can be seen as a political "third rail" of data collaboration such that, like the electrified third rail of a subway train tracks, they will stop you dead in your tracks if you touch them. As a result, one community found success convening a data action team that focused from the onset on the skills desired rather than on the specific test. From that shared vision of skills, the group eventually agreed upon specific tests.

As Ralph Smith, managing director of the GLR Campaign, shared at an NCFL conference session, the sustained effect of a coalition should have a chain of outcomes that include both leading and lagging indicators. In his words "Steve Covey reminds us that it is helpful to distinguish leading and lagging indicators. Since grade-level reading is a lagging indicator, we need to see movement on the leads—school readiness, school attendance, summer learning. Our logic model holds that if these local coalitions can move the needle on the leads, we will see movement on the lagging."

While there is much hope that coalitions will see concrete evidence of this impact, there is also pushback within the nonprofit field against the hyper-focus on outcome measurement. As Lisbeth Schorr recently wrote in the *Stanford Social Innovation Review*:

> Evaluation guru Thomas Schwandt also urges caution in how we approach documenting effectiveness. In the 2015 book, *Credible Evidence in Evaluation and Applied Research* (S. Donaldson, C. Christie & M. Mark, Eds.), he wrote, ". . . the field of evaluation seems captivated by discussions of methods needed to produce evidence of impact . . . [distracting] us from carefully attending to a

variety of important issues related to evaluative evidence and its use." He suggests that "the term evidence base must be interpreted with caution: To claim that evidence may figure importantly in our decisions is one thing; to claim it is foundation for our actions is another. We would be well advised to talk about evidence-informed decision making instead."[34]

The issue of evidence is particularly tricky in instances such as coalitions that are part of larger initiatives, in which models and approaches are being scaled up nationally. As Angus Deaton, a Princeton University professor who won the 2015 Nobel Prize in Economics, pointed out, even with a randomized control trial experiment finding that an "intervention worked is no guarantee that it will work again, or in another context."[35]

As Schorr continues in response to Deaton's observation,

To get better results in this complex world, we must be willing to shake the intuition that certainty should be our highest priority. We must draw on, generate, and apply a broader range of evidence to take account of at least five factors that we have largely neglected in the past:

1.  The complexities of the most promising interventions
2.  The practice-based evidence that spotlights the realities and subtleties of implementation that account for success
3.  The importance of fitting interventions and strategies to the strengths, needs, resources, and values of particular populations and localities
4.  The heavy context-dependence of many of the most promising interventions
5.  The systematic learning and documentation that could inform future action

One way to accomplish this goal is for all those involved in intentional social change—including philanthropies, public policy makers, and nonprofit organizations—to go about the business of knowledge development in a way that would enable us reliably to achieve greater results at scale in tomorrow's world by making sure that all public and philanthropic funding is evidence-informed.[36]

Indeed, in the preceding chapters we believe we have presented ample examples of the "complexities" of coalition building. Furthermore, we have tried to bring out the "subtleties of implementation" and the "context dependency" of the collective impact community coalition movement across the nation. In the end, we hope to have moved the field forward much as Schorr has suggested by contributing to the "business of knowledge development" that will help to increase the likelihood that "public and philanthropic funding is evidence-informed." However, research alone is not enough. Schorr concludes, "Of course, solving big problems takes political will, not just more and better knowledge."[37]

## MOVING FORWARD: CHANGING METAPHORS FROM SILVER BUCKSHOT TO REVISING THE TRAFFIC GRID

As we look toward the future of collective impact community coalitions it is helpful to re-examine the metaphors that have helped to define this work. In perhaps the most famous metaphor, John Kania has referred to collective impact as a shift from looking for silver bullet programs that will solve our social problems in a single salvo to a silver buckshot approach.[38] The advantage of buckshot is that all the many well-intentioned and often effective programs that we already offer within our communities are oriented in the same direction. The hope is that, with everyone pushing in the same direction, so will our communities move in that direction. But what buckshot gains in collective force, it loses in precision. While a silver bullet fired from a rifle can aim directly at the bull's-eye of a target, buckshot is content to scatter in the general vicinity of the bull's-eye. Indeed, this is sometimes how coalition work can feel in the trenches. It can seem like endless meetings with people working to collaborate on low-risk things like book drives and coordinated literacy celebrations. In the inertial tendencies of daily life, coalition work can feel much more mundane and disconnected from the lofty visions of catalytic philanthropy and collective impact. Long exposure to this type of muddling through without seeing tangible results can create fatigue and even an eventual rejection of the coalition approach.

As Ralph Smith, managing director of the GLR Campaign, has pointed out, coalition work is more like a relay than a sprint. But a relay involves more than just dividing up the work; without precise coordination, success will be elusive.

Fielding the faster runners does not guarantee the gold. Especially if the race is a relay. Just ask the U.S. Olympic team. Since the Seoul Games of 1988, especially in the 4x100 relay, U.S. teams have failed to medal on several occasions. Why? Muffing the handoff or dropping the baton. Like relay teams, social services are a hand-off enterprise—the "warm hand-off." No one organization, program or service is sufficient to solve the important problems in a family or community. Yet, we continue to exalt organizational effectiveness while paying little or no attention to the cross-training needed to prevent the functional equivalent of the dropped baton—children and families falling through the cracks and off the cliff. As with the proverbial "silver bullet," philanthropy needs to close the gap between what it says and what it does. Philanthropy needs to encourage, support and fund efforts and organizations willing to work on the hand-off. And, in many respects, this could become a major contribution of what we know now as backbone organization.

In *We Make the Road by Walking*,[39] we learned of the first efforts to improve literacy in the United States. Now that road has been paved and is easier to follow, but there is always room for improvement in the infrastructure. Telling coalition leaders that they are like a bicycle might help them run the organization, but will leave them lacking direction. It would be like training a business in organizations and management without focusing on profit, or like starting a nonprofit without a clearly defined social problem it will address. We need more than a vision to improve literacy; we need a vision of how to improve literacy.

Throughout the research for this book, it has occurred to us that the creation of successful coalitions means creating successful coalition communities. The success lies not in the coalition, but in the community change that it facilitates. A well-organized literacy constituency forces the creation of a new and improved infrastructure to foster a more literate citizenry. This rings true when we think of policy change and community infrastructure change as being at the heart of coalition success. Not only does the vision of a roadway infrastructure seem apropos when describing the goals of a coalition, but it also helps to put the long and winding road of coalition ups and downs into perspective.

We need only think of the New York City roadway infrastructure for an example of how this metaphor speaks to the experience of coalitions. Initially, the streets had emerged organically with a dizzying maze of twists and turns that reflected the local topography and the ways in which the community had grown over time. The proposal for a grid system was a new approach, much like coalitions are a new approach to the existing maze of literacy provision and services. Beyond this there are additional similarities. First, in both cases there have been naysayers and those who doubt the wisdom of such a move. As Christopher Gray of the *New York Times* writes, "To many, the inflexible grid of the Commissioners' Plan of 1811, which made Manhattan's streets an iron fist of right angles, was the worst planning mistake ever made in the city."[40] But these pioneers were driven to make change anyway with a clear goal articulated in terms of the common good: "a free and abundant circulation of air" in order to combat disease and a sense of practicality since "straight-sided and right-angled houses are the most cheap to build."[41] As with many who enter the coalition field, they were not the first. Rather the proponents of Manhattan's grid system were inspired by the growing popularity of grids in newer cities. In many ways, this is not so different from today, when legacy cities with heavily subdivided school systems and arcane and defensively proprietary data practices long to have the single countywide school districts and open data sharing practices of newer communities.

As with coalitions, it was easy to focus on what was wrong with the new street grid. To some it seemed like a financially driven decision made in self-interest, and there are some who see coalitions as a way to shoehorn into funding in a way that creates winners and losers. Others critiqued the lack of deference to the existing structures and the destruction of winding roadways and scenic vistas. As we have seen with coalitions, they too leave what one literacy veteran described as "dead bodies" in their wake as coalition efforts displace pre-existing structures and the balance of power, prestige, and funding may shift from extant leaders to the coalition.

But for all the detractors, Manhattan's grid system has stood the test of time. Though some have seen the grid as boring and monotonous, much like the day-to-day work of coalition building, it is the restructuring of the streets that allows people a "straight-line view of the sunsets and sunrises."[42] But beyond the aesthetics, the grid system may be, at least in part, to thank for the city's ongoing vibrancy. Imagine a New York City without such a grid system to evenly distribute mega traffic loads daily, enable orderly trash pickup, and the precise and rapid response of emergency vehicles. Furthermore, what would it be like to locate businesses without such an orderly system, or the wide avenues that attract retail and commercial use? New York has continued to thrive not only because of its commerce but also, as one critic asserts, "New York survives because of the high quality of its public services" and these services are efficient in large part due to this grid system.[43]

Coalitions, like the grid system, are not an easy undertaking. They involve years and perhaps decades in the making. They have detractors and proponents and involve just as much mundane and boring work as they do exciting visions. In the end, however, they are both about structural systems change with the goal of the common good. While we may never have a definitive conclusion as to whether the grid system's benefits outweighed its costs, hopefully we can do better in the case of coalitions. As Frances Dunn Butterfoss, one of the giants in the field of community health coalitions shares in her online video on the Coalitions Work website, coalitions are a good strategy because "we think they work."[44] Hopefully, the preceding chapters help us to move beyond simply a hunch.

# NOTES

1. U.S. High School Graduation Rate Hits New Record High: Achievement gap continues to narrow for underserved students. (2015, December 15). Retrieved April 9, 2017, from https://www.ed.gov/news/press-releases/us-high-school-graduation -rate-hits-new-record-high-0.
2. Kaye, 2001, 269.
3. Goldsmith & Eggers, 2004.
4. Bradley & Katz, 2013.
5. Bradley & Katz, 2013, 1.

6. Bradley & Katz, 2013, 1.

7. Silver buckshot metaphor was first seen in John Kania's 2012 presentation at the All America Cities/Campaign for Grade-Level Reading conference in Denver, Colorado.

8. Bradley & Katz, 2013, 7.

9. David M. Laird of the Central Carolina Community Foundation coined this term in a personal communication.

10. Bradley & Katz, 2013, 7.

11. Bradley & Katz, 2013, 7–8.

12. Carter & Elshtain, 1997, 745.

13. Carter & Elshtain, 1997, 745.

14. Goldsmith & Eggers, 2004.

15. Carter & Elshtain, 1997, 745.

16. (2013, April 25). Retrieved April 5, 2017, from http://www.futuregov.asia/articles/2013/apr/25/integrating-governing-and-managing-big-data/.

17. (2012, November). Retrieved April 5, 2017, from http://citizenibm.com/2012/11/using-big-data-to-improve-public-health-in-louisville.html.

18. (n.d.). Retrieved April 5, 2017, from http://www.brookings.edu/research/papers/2012/09/04-education-technology-west.

19. (n.d.). Retrieved April 5, 2017, from http://datasmart.ash.harvard.edu/.

20. Carlson et al., 2011.

21. Butterfoss, 2007, 120.

22. Hanleybrown, Kania, & Kramer, 2012.

23. Davis-Laack, P. (2014, August 25). Grit: The Secret Ingredient to Success: The importance of having passion and perseverance to achieve your goals. Retrieved April 5, 2017, from https://www.psychologytoday.com/blog/pressure-proof/201408/grit-the-secret-ingredient-success.

24. Hatley and Morley, Guide to Performance Management for Community Literacy Coalitions, NIFL, 2008.

25. Written by Margaret Doughty and adapted for the Literacy Cooperative, www.theliteracycooperative.org.

26. Bronfenbrenner, 1979.

27. Smith, R. (2017). From the Managing Director. Retrieved April 9, 2017, from http://gradelevelreading.net/about-us/from-the-managing-director.

28. Smith, R. (2017). From the Managing Director. Retrieved April 9, 2017, from http://gradelevelreading.net/about-us/from-the-managing-director.

29. (n.d.). Retrieved April 5, 2017, from www.theliteracycooperative.org Written by Margaret Doughty and adapted for the Literacy Cooperative.

30. (n.d.). Retrieved April 5, 2017, from www.theliteracycooperative.org Written by Margaret Doughty and adapted for the Literacy Cooperative.

31. (n.d.). Retrieved April 5, 2017, from www.theliteracycooperative.org Written by Margaret Doughty and adapted for the Literacy Cooperative.

32. Von Mises. (1944). Bureaucracy. Retrieved April 5, 2017, from https://mises.org/system/tdf/Bureaucracy_3.pdf?file=1&type=document, page 45.

33. Von Mises. (1944). Bureaucracy. Retrieved April 5, 2017, from https://mises .org/system/tdf/Bureaucracy_3.pdf?file=1&type=document.

34. Schorr, L. B. (2016, January 8). Reconsidering Evidence: What It Means and How We Use It. Retrieved April 5, 2017, from http://ssir.org/articles/entry/reconsider ing_evidence_what_it_means_and_how_we_use_it.

35. Schorr, L. B. (2016, January 8). Reconsidering Evidence: What It Means and How We Use It. Retrieved April 5, 2017, from http://ssir.org/articles/entry/reconsider ing_evidence_what_it_means_and_how_we_use_it.

36. Schorr, L. B. (2016, January 8). Reconsidering Evidence: What It Means and How We Use It. Retrieved April 5, 2017, from http://ssir.org/articles/entry/reconsider ing_evidence_what_it_means_and_how_we_use_it.

37. Schorr, L. B. (2016, January 8). Reconsidering Evidence: What It Means and How We Use It. Retrieved April 5, 2017, from http://ssir.org/articles/entry/reconsider ing_evidence_what_it_means_and_how_we_use_it.

38. Kania, Hanleybrown, & Juster, 2014.

39. Freire, Paulo & Miles Horton (1990). We Make the Road By Walking. Temple University Press.

40. Gray, C. (2005, October 23). Are Manhattan's Right Angles Wrong? Retrieved April 5, 2017, from http://www.nytimes.com/2005/10/23/realestate/are-manhattans -right-angles-wrong.html.

41. Gray, C. (2005, October 23). Are Manhattan's Right Angles Wrong? Retrieved April 5, 2017, from http://www.nytimes.com/2005/10/23/realestate/are-manhattans -right-angles-wrong.html.

42. Gray, C. (2005, October 23). Are Manhattan's Right Angles Wrong? Retrieved April 5, 2017, from http://www.nytimes.com/2005/10/23/realestate/are-manhattans -right-angles-wrong.html.

43. Gray, C. (2005, October 23). Are Manhattan's Right Angles Wrong? Retrieved April 5, 2017, from http://www.nytimes.com/2005/10/23/realestate/are-manhattans -right-angles-wrong.html.

44. (n.d.). Retrieved April 5, 2017, from http://coalitionswork.com/services/.

# Bibliography

"About Educate Texas." Educate Texas. http://www.edtx.org/about/overview.

"About The Council." San Antonio Commission on Literacy. http://literacysandiego.org/about-the-council.

AL.com, and The Birmingham News. "New Seeds of Trust." *AL.com* (blog), April 27, 2007. http://blog.al.com/bn/2007/04/can_we_trust_one_another.html.

Aldrich, Leslie, Daniel Silva, Danelle Marable, Erica Sandman, and Melissa Abraham. "Using Community-Based Participatory Evaluation (CBPE) Methods as a Tool to Sustain a Community Health Coalition." *The Foundation Review,* 1, no. 1 (2009): 46–147.

Amenta, Edwin, Neal Caren, Elizabeth Chiarello, and Yang Su. "The Political Consequences of Social Movements." *The Annual Review of Sociology* 36 (April 9, 2010): 287–307. doi:10.1146/annurev-soc-070308–120029.

Aminstad Digital Resources. "Social and Economic Issues of the 1980s and 1990s." Aminstad Digital Resource. 2009. http://www.amistadresource.org/the_future_in_the_present/social_and_economic_issues.html.

Angang, Hu, Hu Linlin, and Chang Zhixiao. "China's Economic Growth and Poverty Reduction (1978–2002)." In *Internationl Monetary Fund.* Proceedings of International Monetary Fund Seminars. 2003. https://www.imf.org/external/np/apd/seminars/2003/newdelhi/angang.pdf.

Ashoka Innovators for the Public. "Ashoka Honors North America's Top Social Entrepreneurs with Lifetime Election to Global Fellowship." News release, February 18, 2008. Ashoka Innovators for the Public. https://www.ashoka.org/node/4545.

"Assassination—The History of Dr. Martin Luther King Jr." Assassination—The History of Dr. Martin Luther King Jr. http://nhdexample1.weebly.com/assassination.html.

Baldwin, Yvonne Honeycutt. 2006. Cora Wilson Stewart and Kentucky's Moonlight Schools: Fighting for Literacy in America. The University Press of Kentucky.

Beard, Peter. "Charting a Course for Change through Collective Impact." United Way (blog), November 5, 2013. https://www.unitedway.org/blog/charting-a-course-for -change. Accessed December 29, 2016

Beder, Hal. Adult Literacy: Issues for Policy and Practice. Malabar, FL: R.E. Krieger Pub., 1991.

Best, Joel. Threatened Children: Rhetoric and Concern About Child-Victims. Chicago: University of Chicago Press, 1990.

Bourdieu, P. "The Forms of Capital." In Handbook of Theory and Research for the Sociology of Education, edited by JG Richardson, 241–58. New York: Greenwood.

Bradley, Jennifer, and Bruce Katz. The Metropolitan Revolution: How Cities and Metros Are Fixing Our Broken Politics and Fragile Economy. Brookings Institution Press, 2013.

Brandt, Rose M. "Steering Committee Nominee Personal Statement." https://philalit eracyalliance.files.wordpress.com/2012/03/rose-brandt.pdf.

Bronfenbrenner, Urie. "Developmental Ecology Through Space and Time: A Future Perspective." In Examining Lives in Context: Perspectives on the Ecology of Human Development, edited by P. Moen, G.H. Elder, Jr., and K. Lüscher, 619–47. Washington, D.C: American Psychological Association.

Bronfenbrenner, Urie. "Ecology of the Family as a Context for Human Development: Research Perspectives." *Ecology of the Family as a Context for Human Development: Research Perspectives* 22, no. 6 (1986): 723–42. doi:10.1037//0012–1649.22.6.723.

Brooks, David. "The Virtues of Virtue." The New York Times, August 7, 2005. http:// www.nytimes.com/2005/08/07/opinion/the-virtues-of-virtue.html?_r=0.

Brooks, F. Erlk, and Robert J. Robinson. "Richard Arrington Jr." Encyclopedia of Alabama. 2014. http://www.encyclopediaofalabama.org/article/h-3244.

Bush, George. "Address Accepting the Presidential Nomination at the Republican National Convention in New Orleans." Speech, New Orleans, August 18, 1988. The American Presidency Project. http://www.presidency.ucsb.edu/ws/?pid=25955

Business Roundtable. "Momentum for America." Business Roundtable. http://busi nessroundtable.org/growth.

Butterfoss, F. D. 2007. Coalitions and Partnerships in Community Health. San Francisco, CA: Jossey-Bass.

Carlson, Neil E., Edwin Hernández, Chaná Edmond-Verley, Gustavo Rotondaro, Eleibny Feliz-Santana, and Susan Heynig. "Developing a Master Data Sharing Agreement: Seeking Student-Level Evidence to Support a Collaborative Community Effort in Education." *The Foundation Review* 3, no. 4 (2011): 15–33

Carter, Lief H., and Jean Bethke Elshtain. "Task Force on Civic Education Statement of." *PS: Political Science and Politics*, December 30, 1997, 745.

Chaná Edmond-Verley and Mel Atkins II. 2016. Disruptive Strategies for Change Making: The Grand Rapids Story of Reducing Chronic Absenteeism. September 2016. Believe 2 Become (B2B). https://believe2become.org/documents/disruptive -change-strategies-for-change-making.pdf Accessed online December 29, 2016.

Christeson, William, Sandra Bishop-Josef, Natasha O'Dell-Archer, Chris Beakey, and Kara Clifford. *I'm The Guy You Pay Later*. Report. Fight Crime: Inverst In Kids. 1–8.

Committee for Economic Development. "Business Leaders Outline Critical Need for Early Childhood Education at CED Report Event in Detroit PNC and Kelly Services CEOs Voice Commitment." News release. https://www.ced.org/pdf/CE DUnfinishedBusinessPPDetroitFinal6–26–12.pdf.

Connerly, Charles E. "The Most Segregated City in America City Planning and Civil Rights in Birmingham, 1920–1980." *The University of Virginia Press*, 2005.

Crutchfield, Leslie, and Heather McLeod Grant. *Forces for Good: The Six Practices of High-Impact Nonprofits*. 2007

"CyberGrants | Employee Engagement. Grants Management." CyberGrants. http://www.verizonreads.net/.

"Data-Smart City Solutions." Data-Smart City Solutions. http://datasmart.ash.harvard.edu/.

Davis-Laack, Paula. "Grit: The Secret Ingredient to Success: The Importance of Having Passion and Perseverance to Achieve Your Goals." Psycology Today (blog), August 25, 2014. https://www.psychologytoday.com/blog/pressure-proof/201408/grit-the-secret-ingredient-success.

DeVol, Ross, Perry Wong, Junghoon Ki, Armen Bedroussian, and Rob Koepp. "America's Biotech and Life Science Clusters." Milken Institute. June 1, 2004. http://www.milkeninstitute.org/publications/view/231.

Dillon, Sam. "Study Finds High Rate of Imprisonment Among Dropouts." The New York Times, October 8, 2009. http://www.nytimes.com/2009/10/09/education/09dropout.html?_r=4.

Dluhy, Milan J., and Sanford L. Kravitz. "Building Coalitions in the Human Services (SAGE Human Services Guides)." In A Sage Human Services Guide, 7. Newbury Park, California.

Edwin, Amenta, and Michael P. Young. "Making an Impact: Conceptual and Methodological Implications of the Collective Goods Criterion." Edited by Marco Giugni, Doug McAdam, and Charles Tilly. In In How Social Movements Matter, 22. U of Minnesota Press, 1999.

"Explore—The Birmingham Campaign." Black Culture Connection. http://www.pbs.org/black-culture/explore/civil-rights-movement-birmingham-campaign/#.V3PMXaJmrF5.

Fischer, Greg. "Using 'Big Data' to Improve Public Health in Louisville." Citizen IBM, November 2, 2012. http://citizenibm.com/2012/11/using-big-data-to-improve-public-health-in-louisville.html.

Fixsen, D., Naoom, S., Blase, K., Friedman, R., Wallace, F. (2005). Implementation Research: A Synthesis of the Literature. Tamps, FL: University of South Florida, Louis de la Parte Florida Mental Health Institute, National Implementation Research Network.

FSG. "What Is Catalytic Philanthropy." FSG: Reimagining Social Change. November 4, 2015. https://www.fsg.org/blog/what-catalytic-philanthropy.

Furco A., 2010 "The Engaged Campus: Toward a Comprehensive Approach to Public Engagement," *British Journal of Educational Sciences*, 58(4), 375–390. DOI: 10.1080/00071005.2010.527656

"GRANTS.GOV | Find. Apply. Succeed." Search Grants. http://www.grants.gov/web/grants/search-grants.html?keywords=ECCS.

Gray, Christopher. "Are Manhattan's Right Angles Wrong?" *The New York Times*, October 23, 2005. http://www.nytimes.com/2005/10/23/realestate/are-manhattans-right-angles-wrong.html.

Gurr, Ted Robert. *Why Men Rebel*. Princeton, NJ: Published for the Center of International Studies, Princeton University, Princeton University Press, 1970

Hanleybrown, Fay. "Essential Mindset Shifts for Collective Impact." *Collective Impact Forum Blog* (blog), September 2, 2014. https://collectiveimpactforum.org/blogs/1806/essential-mindset-shifts-collective-impact.

Hart, B., and T.R. Risley, eds. "The Early Catastrophe: The 30 Million Word Gap by Age 3." In *Meaningful Differences in the Everyday Experiences of Young American Children*, 4–9. Baltimore, MD: Brookes Publishing., 2003.

Harvey, John C., Jr., James M. Loy, Gregory S. Martin, William L. Nyland, and William S. Wallace. *Retreat Is Not and Option*. Report. Mission: Readiness, Military Leaders for Kids. 1–10.

Hatry, Harry and Elaine Morley. 2008. "Guide to Performance Management for Community Literacy Coalitions" Urban Institute and National Institute for Literacy. https://lincs.ed.gov/publications/pdf/NIFLCommunityLiteracyReport.pdf

Henig, Jeff R., Carolyn J. Riehl, David M. Houston, Michael A. Rebell, and Jessica R. Wolff. *Collective Impact and the New Generation of Cross-Sector Collaborations for Education: A Nationwide Scan*. Report. The Department of Education Policy and Social Analysis(EPSA), Teachers College, Columbia University. 31. http://www.wallacefoundation.org/knowledge-center/summer-and-extended-learning-time/Documents/Collective-Impact-and-the-New-Generation-of-Cross-Sector-Collaboration-for-Education.pdf

"Home." Commit. http://www.Commit2Dallas.org/.

Hopey, Christopher E., and Joyce Harvey-Morgan. "TECHNOLOGY PLANNING FOR ADULT LITERACY." National Center on Adult Literacy, November 1995. http://literacynet.org/aztech/pg9502.pdf.

*Investing in America's Future Workforce*. Report. National Association of Workforce Boads. Washington, D.C. 1–4.

Joe. "Dr. Martin Luther King, Jr." Racisim Review: Scholarship and Actvisim Toward Racial Justice, April 4, 2016. http://www.racismreview.com/blog/2016/04/04/dr-martin-luther-king-jr/.

Katz, Bruce, and Jennifer Bradley. "The Post Hero Economy Learning to Lead Through Networks." Next City 1, no. 61 (June 10, 2013): 1. June 10, 2013. https://nextcity.org/features/view/the-post-hero-economy.

Keith, Joanne. "Building and Maintaining Community Coalitions On Behalf of Children, Youth and Families" National Network for Collaboration. Report. Department of Family and Child Ecology, Michigan State University. Http://www.uvm.edu/extension/community/nnco/collab/buildcoal1.html, 1991–1996. Part 3.

Kotlowitzaug, Alex. "The Prize." Review. August 19, 2015. http://www.nytimes.com/2015/08/23/books/review/the-prize-by-dale-russakoff.html?_r=0.

Kramer, Mark. "Catalytic Philanthropy." *Stanford Social Innovation Review*, 2009, 33. http://www.ssireview.org/images/ads/2009FA_feature_Kramer.pdf.

Kullgren, Ian K. "Cannon Gets the Connection between Reading and Crime Right." PolitiFact, February 13, 2012. http://www.politifact.com/oregon/statements/2012/feb/13/ben-cannon/canon-gets-connection-between-reading-and-crime-ri/.

LeMoyne College. "Research on Immigration Library Program Led by LeMoyne Professors Illustrates Effectiveness in Preparing Students For Kindergarten." News release, August 12, 2015. LeMoyne. http://www.lemoyne.edu/News/News-Article/ArticleId/47

Literacy Campaign. "About Us." Literacy Campaign. 2013. http://literacycampaignmc.org/about-us/.

Lochner, Lance, and Enrico Moretti. "The Effect of Education on Crime: Evidence from Prison Inmates, Arrests, and Self-Reports." *American Economic Review* 94, no. 1 (2004): 155–89.

Lohmeier, Frey B., J. Lee S, and N. Tollefson. "Measuring Collaboration Among Grant Partners." *American Journal of Evaluation* 27:383–92.

Mack, Julie. "Kalamazoo Gazette." Kalamazoo News. March 12, 2015. www.mlive.com/news/kalamazoo/index.ssf/2015/03/kalamazoo.

Manufacturing Institute. "Average High School Math and Science Scores by Selected Country." Facts About Manufacturing. http://www.themanufacturinginstitute.org/Research/Facts-About-Manufacturing/Workforce-and-Compensation/Math-and-Science/Math-and-Science.aspx.

Meyer, David S., and Debra C. Minkoff. "Conceptualizing Political Opportunity." Social Forces 84, no. 4 (2004): 1457–492. doi:10.1353/sof.2004.0082.

Mitchell, E. "Citizenship: A Guide To Good Teaching." Center For Adult English Language Acquisition. 1998. www.cal.org/caela/esl_resources/digests/civics.html.

"Ms. Joanne Arnaud Appleton." ZoomInfo. http://www.zoominfo.com/p/Joanne-Arnaud/18988329.

National Association of Workforce Boards. *The Workforce Innovation and Opportunity Act (WIOA)*. Report. National Association of Workforce Boards. http://www.nawb.org/documents/Publications/WIOA_Overview.pdf.

Office of Extramural Health, National Institutes of Health. *Top 100 NIH Cities, 2004*. Report. National Institutes of Health. 2006. http://www.ssti.org/Digest/Tables/022006t.htm.

Oosthuizen, Christa, and Johann Louw. "Developing Program Theory for Purveyor Programs." Implementation Science 8, no. 23 (2013). doi:10.1186/1748–5908–8–23.

Opp, Karl-Dieter. Theories of Political Protest and Social Movements: A Multidisciplinary Introduction, Critique, and Synthesis. New York, 2009.

Pacheco, Desirée F. et al. "The Coevolution of Institutional Entrepreneurship: A Tale of Two Theories." Journal of Management, 2010, 36. doi:10.1177/014920630936028.

Patterson, Margaret, PhD. "History." National Coalition for Literacy. http://national-coalition-literacy.org/about/history/.

Philanthropy New York. "Philanthropy's Key Contributions to Society." 1–9. August 2008. https://philanthropynewyork.org/sites/default/files/resources/Key Contributions to Society.pdf.

Piven, Frances Fox, and Richard Cloward. Poor People's Movements: Why They Succeed, How They Fail. New York: Vintage, 1977.

"P16 Plus." About P16Plus. http://www.p16plus.org/about/#sthash.cB4Fy2GW.dpuf.

Portes, A. "Social Capital: Its Origins and Applications in Modern Sociology." Knowledge and Social Capital, 1998, 43–67. doi:10.1016/b978–0–7506–7222–1.50006–4.

PRE-K-12 Education Policy Declaration, 1 §§ Building the Foundation- Early Childhood and PreK-Measuring Success (Chamber of Commerce of The United States of America).

Putnam, Robert D. Bowling Alone: The Collapse and Revival of American Community. New York: Touchstone, 2000.

Ravitch, Diane. "When Will Bill Gates Admit He Was Wrong—Again?" Diane Ravitch's Blog: A Site to Discuss Better Education for All, June 3, 2014. https://dianeravitch.net/2014/06/03/when-will-bill-gates-admit-he-was-wrong-again/.

Ridzi, Frank. "Managing Expectations When Measuring Philanthropic Impact: A Framework Based on Experience." The Foundation Review, 8th ser., 4, no. 4 (2012). June 20, 2013. doi:10.4087/FOUNDATIONREVIEW-D-12–00007.1.

Ridzi, F. (2017). Community Indicators and the Collective Goods Criterion for Impact. In M. Holden, R. Phillips,and C. Stevens. (Eds.), *Community Quality-of-Life Indicators: Best Cases VII.* (pp. 35–52). Springer.

Ridzi, Frank, and Monica R. Sylvia. "Got Coalition? A National Study of the Differences Bewteen Literacy and Non-Literacy Coalition Communities." Proceedings of National Conference on Family Literacy, Louisville, Kentucky.

Ridzi, Frank, Monica R. Sylvia, and Sunita Singh. 2014. "The Imagination Library Program: Increasing Parental Reading through Book Distribution." *Reading Psychology* 35(6):548–76. doi:10.1080/02702711.2013.790324.

Ridzi, Frank, Monica Sylvia, Xiaofen Qiao, and Jeff Craig. 2016. The Imagination Library Program and Kindergarten Readiness: Evaluating the Impact of Monthly Book Distribution. *Journal of Applied Social Science.* 1–14. DOI: 10.1177/1936724416678023 http://journals.sagepub.com/doi/pdf/10.1177/1936724416678023

Rose, Amy D. "U.S. House of Representatives Ends or Means: An Overview of the History of the Adult Education Act." Information Series, no. 346 (1987): 308.

Rupasingha, Anil, and Stephan J. Goetz. US County-Level Social Capital Data, 1990–2005. Report. The Northeast Regional Center for Rural Development, Penn State University. 2008. http://nercrd.psu.edu/Social_Capital/index.html http://aese.psu.edu/nercrd/economic-development/materials/poverty-issues/big-boxes/wal-mart-and-social-capital/social-capital.

Rupasingha, A., Goetz, S. J., & Freshwater, D. (2006). The Production of Social Capital in US Counties. Journal of Socio-Economics, 35, 83–101. doi:10.1016/j.socec.2005.11.001.

Schorr, Lisbeth B. "Reconsidering Evidence: What It Means and How We Use It." *Stanford Social Innovation Review*, January 8, 2016. http://ssir.org/articles/entry/reconsidering_evidence_what_it_means_and_how_we_use_it.

Schramm, Carl. "Law Outside the Market: The Social Utility of the Private Foundation." Harvard Journal of Law & Public Policy, 2006, 365–415.

Schramm, Carl. "What Is the Most Daring, Audacious, and Successful Grant of the Past 100 Years? A Symposium of Philanthropic Leaders." *Philanthropy Magazine*, 2011. http://www.philanthropyroundtable.org/article.asp?article=1657&paper=1&cat=139.

Senge, Peter, Hal Hamilton, and John Kania. "The Dawn of System Leadership." *Stanford Social Innovation Review*, Winter 2015. http://ssir.org/articles/entry/the_dawn_of_system_leadership.

Sherwood, Kristin. "The Spirit Catches You and You Fall Down Study Guide." Study Guides & Essay Editing. May 27, 2015. http://www.gradesaver.com/the-spirit-catches-you-and-you-fall-down.

Singh, Sunita, Monica R. Sylvia, and Frank Ridzi. 2015. "Exploring the Literacy Practices of Refugee Families Enrolled in a Book Distribution Program and an Intergenerational Family Literacy Program." *Early Childhood Education Journal* 43(7):37–45. doi:10.1007/s10643–013–0627–0.

Siporin, Max. "Ecological Systems Theory in Social Work." The Journal of Sociology & Social Welfare, 4th ser., 7, no. 4 (1980). http://scholarworks.wmich.edu/jssw/vol7/iss4/4.

Sriya, Iyer, Michael Kitson, and Bernard Toh. "Social Capital, Economic Growth and Regional Development." Regional Studies 39, no. 8 (November 2005): 1015–040. doi:DOI: 10.1080/00343400500327943.

Strauss, Valerie. "That Surprising Thing Bill Gates Said." The Washington Post, January 3, 2013. https://www.washingtonpost.com/news/answer-sheet/wp/2015/01/03/that-surprising-thing-bill-gates-said/.

Stevens, Susan Kenny. 2008. Nonprofit Lifecycles: Stage-Based Wisdom for Nonprofit Capacity. 2nd edition. MN: Stagewise Enterprises.

Strive Together. "Cradle to Career Network." Stive Together Every Child. Cradel to Career. 2015. http://www.strivetogether.org/cradle-career-network.

Stuart, Elizabeth. "China Has Almost Wiped out Urban Poverty. Now It Must Tackle Inequality." *The Guardian. Business Economics Blog*, August 19, 2015. http://www.theguardian.com/business/economics-blog/2015/aug/19/china-poverty-inequality-development-goals.

Taylor, Jared. "Demography Is Destiny." Western Voices World News, October 7, 2007. http://www.wvwnews.net/story.php?id=1064.

Terrill, Lynda. "Civics Education for Adult English Language Learners." Center For Adult English Language Acquisition. November 2000.

"The Challenge." 3rd Grade Reading Success Matters The Campaign for Grade-Level Reading Welcome Comments. http://gradelevelreading.net/.

The Manufacturing Institute, and Deloitte. "The Skills Gap in U.S. Manufacturing 2015 and Beyond." 2–29. http://www.themanufacturinginstitute.org/~/media/827DBC76533942679A15EF7067A704CD.ashx.

Toossi, Mitra. "Labor Force Projections to 2020:." MonthlyLabor Review, January 2012, 43–64. http://www.bls.gov/opub/mlr/2012/01/art3full.pdf.

Tunner, Shiloh, Kathy Merchant, John Kania, and Ellen Martin. "Understanding the Value of Backbone Organizations in Collective Impact: Part 2." Stanford Social Innovation Review, July 18, 2012. http://ssir.org/articles/entry/understanding_the_value_of_backbone_organizations_in_collective_impact_2.

U.S. Department of Education. "Promise Neighborhoods." Promise Neighborhoods. June 18, 2015. http://www2.ed.gov/programs/promiseneighborhoods/index.html.

U.S. Department of Education. "U.S. High School Graduation Rate Hits New Record High." News release, December 15, 2015. U.S. Department of Education. http://www.ed.gov/news/press-releases/us-high-school-graduation-rate-hits-new-record-high-

United States Department of Agriculture. "Obama Administration Announces Eight Additional Promise Zones to Build Community Prosperity." News release, April 28, 2015. United States Department of Agriculture. http://www.usda.gov/wps/portal/usda/usdahome?contentid=2015/04/0116.xml.

United Way. "Our History: United Way Worldwide." Our History: United Way Worldwide. http://www.unitedway.org/about/history.

Venture Capital Guide. "Venture Capital Guide." Venture Capital Guide. http://www.venture-capital-guide.com/using-angel-investors-to-fund-a-business/.

West, Darrell M. "Big Data for Education: Data Mining, Data Analytics, and Web Dashboards." Brookings, September 4, 2012. http://www.brookings.edu/research/papers/2012/09/04-education-technology-west.

Wojan, Tim, and David McGranahan. "USDA ERS—Creative Class County Codes." USDA ERS—Creative Class County Codes. Accessed June 30, 2016. http://www.ers.usda.gov/data-products/creative-class-county-codes.aspx.

Wolf-Harlow, Carole, Ph.D. Special Report: Education and Correctional Populations. Report. Bureau of Justice Statistics. April 15, 2003. http://www.bjs.gov/content/pub/pdf/ecp.pdf.

# Index

# About the Authors

**Frank Ridzi** is Vice President for Community Investment at the Central New York Community Foundation, Associate Professor of Sociology at Le Moyne College, and President of the Literacy Funders Network, an affinity group of the Council on Foundations. Frank has conducted research and written in the areas of program evaluation, public policy, and philathropy. His writings have appeared in such places as the Foundation Review, the Community Literacy Journal, the Journal of Organizational Change Management, and Review of Policy Research. Frank holds a Masters Degree in Public Administration and a Ph.D. in Sociology from Syracuse University's Maxwell School, where he has also served as Instructor of Public Administration and International Affairs. He also carries a Certificate of Advanced Study in Women's Studies. Prior to joining the Community Foundation, he served as Director for the Center of Urban and Regional Applied Research at Le Moyne College, where he still serves as Associate Professor of Sociology.

A native of the United Kingdom, **Margaret Doughty** has worked in Europe, Africa, the Middle East, and the United States. Appointed to direct the Houston READ Commission, the Mayor's Coalition for Literacy, in 1990 by Mayor Kathy Whitmire, Margaret served as executive director for twelve years before developing the national organization, Literacy Powerline, to promote a collective impact model of coalition development. Margaret managed the UN Decade of Literacy activities in the U.S. with the Right to Literacy Campaign and the Literacy Funders Network, until her retirement in 2013. In 1999 she was awarded the Order of the British Empire by HRH Queen Elizabeth II at Buckingham Palace for her contribution to the field of international literacy.

CPSIA information can be obtained
at www.ICGtesting.com
Printed in the USA
BVOW06*0520250917
495777BV00004B/6/P

PROFESSIONAL